The Artist, the Farmer, the Hunter, and the Good Guy

Diane Buzzell

ISBN 979-8-88685-643-9 (paperback)
ISBN 979-8-88943-553-2 (hardcover)
ISBN 979-8-88685-644-6 (digital)

Copyright © 2023 by Diane Buzzell

All rights reserved. No part of this publication may be reproduced, distributed, or transmitted in any form or by any means, including photocopying, recording, or other electronic or mechanical methods without the prior written permission of the publisher. For permission requests, solicit the publisher via the address below.

Christian Faith Publishing
832 Park Avenue
Meadville, PA 16335
www.christianfaithpublishing.com

Printed in the United States of America

This is dedicated to Hazel and John Buzzell, who loved us and gave us an amazing life. To my children, Jalna, Nathan, and Corey, that you may understand your heritage, why we are the people we are, how life shaped us, and to have an appreciation for what hard work can accomplish. I hope this book will give you wisdom and patience with others and these stories bring a smile as you remember us years from now and appreciate our efforts to raise you to be productive citizens and to love and serve the Lord.
To our grandchildren, someday your parents will say, "I remember when…"
Be patient and value the stories they hand down. You might learn something!
To our great-grandchildren. You pick your friends, but God gives you a family. Value where you came from.

A good man leaves an inheritance for his children's children.
—Proverbs 13:22 NKJV

Contents

Acknowledgments vii
Preface..ix
Welcome to the Farm 1
    Introducing the Buzzells...3
    Becoming an Artist..11
    The Farm 26
Family and Friends..35
    Boy Meets Girl...37
    Dad..46
    Mom..63
    Our Sister Jan..76
    Who's who?..80
    Friends Like Family..94
    A Gathering Place 109
    Let's Celebrate...114
    Farm Food..119
Farm Life 127
    Growing up..129
    School Daze 145
    Love Life 158
    Farm Boys..162
    Coulda, Shoulda, Wooda..177
    Boy Toys...184
    Lock and Load 198

- Fur Family 209
  - Fur Family 211
- Udderly Family 219
  - Udderly Family 221
  - Kind of Corny 239
- Mane-ly Family 247
  - Mane-ly Family 249
- Hold Your Horses 265
  - Hold Your Horses 267
- Never Gonna Grow Up 283
  - Never Gonna Grow Up 285
  - Next Generation 314
  - Some Random Memories of Grandma 323
  - Larry's Ad-libs 328
- Then and Now 337
  - Our Heritage 339
  - Souvenirs from Our Past 342
  - Buzzell Family Genealogy 345
  - Gerry Genealogy 355
  - Dunbar Morgan Genealogy 359
  - Leach Genealogy 364
  - Atherton Genealogy 368
  - Larry's Two Cents 374
  - Just a Penny More 377

Acknowledgments

I want to thank all the family for their stories and pictures. Thank you for trusting me to write them down for you.

Special gratitude to my husband, Larry, for his patience as I nagged for more details and while I read, reread, and read again portions to him for his corrections and additions to get it right. I love you.

To Matt Defosse for giving me the push to get started and holding me accountable.

To Kristi Seymour for sharing her encouragement and her prayers for the Holy Spirit to guide me.

And especially to Russ for the inspiration through your artwork and your encouragement in the creative process.

Last but most importantly, I thank God for placing me in this family and giving me the chance to give him the glory.

> I have not stopped giving thanks for you, remembering you in my prayers. I keep asking that the God of our Lord Jesus Christ, the glorious Father, may give you the Spirit of wisdom and revelation, so that you may know him better.
> —Ephesians 1:16–17 NKJV

Welcome to the Farm

Sunday Afternoon on the Buzzell Farm
The Family, Little Red House and Tuckers Farm
Original Painting by Russell Buzzell

Introducing the Buzzells

Every family has a story. Welcome to ours. This is actually a collection of stories of growing up on a farm in the forties, fifties, sixties, and onward and of our family heritage. It's sort of history, but it's a slice of America you won't find in history books. It deserved to be recorded, to see a glimpse of what has gone on before or maybe smile as we remember the good ole days growing up when times were a little simpler, and freedom was taken for granted. You must have seen the meme that says "I survived growing up drinking from the hose, riding a bike without a helmet…" These stories are so much more! I want my kids to say, when they hear others tell how their parents walked up hill both ways to school in a blizzard, "That's nothing! You should hear what my parents did!" I want them to admire our ingenuity and learn from our foolishness. Amazing stories. Well, maybe amazing isn't the right word. Maybe amazing we lived to tell them is better. Memories recounted at coffee time, around the dinner table, holidays, or anytime we got together. The stories have been shared over and over and we still laugh or cry or marvel at how different it was back then. And all the stories are true even though sometimes hard to believe. A common family comment begins with "Remember when?" and ends with a chuckle and "We weren't very smart!"

In the beginning, God. As these stories come to life on the pages of this book, I cannot take credit. They write themselves, and I just hold the pen. As I hope my family realizes, I love the Lord Jesus, for his sacrifice for me (and for you if you chose), to be forgiven of sin and live a life forever through eternity with Him because of

Him. Writing these stories down helped me realize how the Bible was written. The story was his story, and all those who contributed from Moses to John may have been the writers but really could take no credit. Often called authors, it was God who directed their pen. I am definitely not placing myself or these stories in the caliber of scripture, only as an explanation of how they came to be. Not in my wildest imagination did I ever think that I could be called an author, and truly, the authors are the members of the family who have related these tales, and I, as a scribe, collected and penned them all. Some members of the family might remember the stories differently, but I tried to get perspective from them all. Memories, after all, aren't always perfect. This will not be an intellectual epistle but just down home and easy like an interesting conversation. Forgive the grammar as it is meant to be the way we told them and not perfect, to include the funny and weird vernacular of our day, and I hope you don't get confused as I flip from my view to another person's point of view. Be forewarned, I am opinionated, and as I am writing this, some of those opinions will leak out of the pen as well. Bear with me, I have lived many years and see our country and life through a different lens.

My growing up years were in Holden. As third-generation American, I was strongly influenced by the Swedish roots of my family. I was blessed because by the time I was born, all the hard work had been done, and I could enjoy, not necessarily riches, but we were definitely comfortable. Dad co-owned his thriving construction business with his brother, Carl, both Navy veterans of WWII. We had a new home built on family land with a lot of help from family and probably my great-grandfather, Morfar. Uncle Carl's house and Morfar's homes flanked ours on each side. I expect my dad probably dug the cellar hole. Our cellar was stack stone walls, not poured cement, and probably my great-grandfather's brother, a stonemason, who by the way was a stonemason on the Sagamore Bridge connecting the Cape to the mainland of Massachusetts, laid those stack stone walls. While we lived there, it never leaked any water, a testament to their attention to detail. My grandfather Gigi did much of the wiring and made beautiful knotty pine kitchen cabinets. We were the only ones I knew who had a finished basement complete with fireplace, sofas, and built-in TV! Of course, the TV was twelve-inch black-and-white, and behind the wall hid a box the size of small refrigerator. There was also a kitchenette, laundry, and a bar. Although this doesn't sound like luxury for today, in time past it was pretty special although much of this was done because of the threat of nuclear war and a place to go if they dropped the atom bomb. In school we were taught to drop and hide under our desks, and many were the drills to go down in the basement of the school among the inner hallways for our protection if an unexpected attack were to happen. Our family vacationed on the Cape, eventually buying an old sea captain's Victorian to remodel and spend many weekends throughout the year and all summer long. In my junior year of high school, we moved to Ridge Road, Hardwick. The house was a fairly new build but had acreage from the original farm and a mammoth old barn, which allowed my dad to fulfill his passion for farm life and collect the animals he loved. It was the best of both worlds, but for me it didn't offer what the Buzzell family had. I can truly say money does not buy happiness, and although the Buzzell family had their struggles, I still see a support system unlike any other. Despite differences of opinions, when push comes to shove, they will help each other in whatever way they can.

For me the first story was in 1969, when I started dating Larry. We hadn't been dating for long, and I barely knew the rest of his family. He was just a hardworking farm boy who became the love of my life. Whenever I wasn't working my job as a waitress at a dairy bar, I would come to help him milk. Okay, maybe I just really wanted to see him. The farm took up so much of his time, helping to milk was a good excuse to be together. This particular day I drove up to his family farm and parked in front of the house. The house was that lovely avocado green so popular in

the 1960s and 1970s. I later learned in one of those infamous family stories that the house needed to be painted, and older brother Ralph, manager at the hardware store up town, had some discontinued paint he couldn't sell (*I think* it was probably lead-based paint, which some of you have no idea what that is, but they were phasing out of it). So he mixed it all together in a big barrel, and voilà—avocado green (although if you asked Ralph, he called it colonial green). That green was a happy accident and probably better than what it could have been, considering the variety of colors mixed into that barrel. So glad it didn't turn out pink or orange or something gross. Family and friends came and painted the old two-story federal-style farmhouse. That was just how it was done. Everyone pitched in happy to help *and* happy the color was a good color. The best thing about that house was the door; it was never locked, open to anyone and everyone.

Anyway, that day I parked by the house and headed down to the lower part of the barn where he would be milking. The barn was almost two hundred feet long, two stories high with a full cellar under the front half and another cellar under three stories in the back half. The top floor extending up two stories in the back was the haymow with the cowbarn under and the "cellar" under the cow barn where manure was scraped from skuttles that opened up behind the cows, where they stood to be milked. It was situated right along the edge of Tucker Hill Road, where Old West Brookfield Road curved around to meet Bates Street in a crazy kind of Y. I was never quite sure what the address was, but mail seemed to get there no matter what street you put on your letter, and back then they didn't have a street number. But then everyone knew the Buzzell Farm. In fact, I think everyone in North Brookfield knew the Buzzells. As I headed down the side past the front of the barn to go to the lower portion, there were several guys playing basketball at the hoop on the wall beside the tall two-story barn door. I will admit I was a little shy and chose to go down the side rather than dodge between them to go through the main door to the stairway in the midsection to the lower cow barn portion. The small area in front of the barn was so close to the intersection they were essentially playing in the road for the most part. Visibility was good, so they could easily get out of the way if a car came by, and it was probably somebody they knew anyway who would know to slow down by the farm. Heck, they would probably stop to join the game. They were having a grand time of pickup ball pushing, shoving, and taunting each other. I did notice they called each other John. It seemed odd that many guys would all be John, but hey, it's a common name.

The driveway down the side of the barn to the lower part sloped down past the old silo to a door at the lower section. As the road curved away from the barn, there was an area beyond for a trench silo filled with chopped corn for winter feed and covered with a tarp and tires to hold the tarp down. (For you youngsters and city folk, a silo is the place they kept silage. Silo, silage kind of go together. Silage is chopped corn, and in the silo, it would ferment to keep through the winter as additional feed for the cows.)

I slid the door open to the sound of the milking machines humming away. I found the guy I was looking for on the farther side of two rows of stanchions filled with cows and about twenty calves tied down the center in front of the rows of mamma cows facing their young. Getting a hug despite sweat and "farm cologne" was part of loving a farm boy, and I didn't mind. Between changing machines, carrying milk up the stairs to the milk room, and moving the cows back out to pasture, there was always time for a kiss and playful hug. Carrying milk was something we didn't think about but was a workout today's kids I swear couldn't do. Heck, most adults couldn't do either, especially twice a day, seven days a week. Each stainless steel pail filled with milk weighs about thirty-plus pounds, and each milking about four hundred pounds was carried in those pails up a flight of steep, rickety, narrow stairs to the main floor and to the front of the barn, where the milk room was. When I say narrow, to carry two pails, you had to kind of go up sideways. Those barbells in your fancy gym don't come close to the workout you get lugging pails full of milk up to dump in the cooler and then race back down the stairs in time to change a milking machine from one cow to the next. In the winter, sloshed milk made those stairs iced cream coated, slippery, and treacherous! Many were the times a wrong step slipped and bounced you down those stairs to the frozen ground at the bottom. It was an old barn, a masterpiece in its day during the 1800s, but not efficient for a modern-day milk operation. State regulations would shut the farm down when cement floors were determined more sanitary. I would like to know how the ruling class in Boston knows anything about farm systems. Our bacteria count was much lower than some others in the area, but our farm had to go under because, how do you reconfigure a two-hundred-foot, three-story barn to have cement floors?

Back to that day. As I set about to lend a hand mixing calf saver to feed the calves or putting down feed, Larry asked me, "Is anyone around up front?"

Now like I said, I didn't know his family yet, so I had no idea who was family and who wasn't, but I saw all those guys and answered, "Yup, a bunch of guys named John playing ball," which made him burst out with a laugh swinging me around in a hug. It turned out they weren't all John. They just called each other John, and if you were a friend, they called you John too. It seems the brothers liked Johnny Carson, predecessor to the progressive late-night talk show hosts of today before we knew what politically correct agendas were. The boys would often stay up together to catch his late show at 11:00 p.m. Ed McMahon would introduce the show with "Here's Johnny," and it caught on with the brothers, so to this day they call each other John or Johnny—except the one brother whose name is John. They call him Jack. Go figure.

The Main Characters

So since this is the introduction, I guess I should introduce you to the family, the main characters of the stories along the way. There's Hazel and John, otherwise known as Mom and Dad, or Pappy, and later Gramma

Ralph, Mom, Dad, Janice, Russ, and Jack

and Grampa. First of the kids is Ralph, born in 1935, the oldest, and then sister, Janice, the only girl, is about thirteen months behind Ralph in 1936. Then comes Russell in 1942. He's the artist and is kind of the one who inspired me to record these stories. He did an incredible painting of Wheeler's Surprise, a massacre that took place in this area a little over three hundred years ago. When he revealed the painting on the anniversary of the massacre at the New Braintree Library, he spent about two hours telling how he became an artist before telling all the research it took to bring the painting to life. You could hear a pin drop in that room of about two hundred people as he related his growing-up years, going to art school, and then about the painting. Even his family and long-time family friends marveled at some of his stories. Russ also had a twin, Royce, who died as an infant at only a few days old. Russ and Royce were the only ones born in a hospital. The rest were home births, which wasn't all that unusual at the time. Then there's Jack, who is really John, born in 1945. And finally, Larry is the baby of the family in 1949. Larry (not Lawrence) is his given name, and William, his middle name, was for the father of Eileen Brown, the nurse who attended at his birth. Her father was their neighbor, Billy Brown, and you might hear him mentioned in a story along the way. Larry grew up being called Larry Bill, and there are still a few who call him by that. Larry was born in January on the farm during a thaw. It was so muddy Doc O'Boyle got stuck in the dirt driveway and Pappy had to pull him out with the tractor. Larry says his coming birth warmed up the world!

Janice and Larry Bill

On the farm, when calves are born, it's a sad fact of life, but some are culled and shipped off for meat. Usually, it's the bull calves that are shipped because raising a bull is unnecessary. You only need one bull for your herd, so there had to be good reason for a bull calf to be a keeper. Russ would have been about six when Larry was born. Waking in the morning to a new little brother, he asked older brother Ralph if Larry was a keeper. Thankfully for me, he was, in fact, a keeper.

There's more family, wives and kids, cousins and friends like family, but you will meet them in the stories.

> When God created mankind, he made them in the likeness of God.
> —Genesis 5:1

Becoming an Artist

Wheeler's Surprise reveal

It was a warm summer day in August, and we were about to celebrate the completion of Russell's rendition of *Wheeler's Surprise*. As his family, we think everything he does is awesome, but we were not prepared for the reception we received. The room at the New Braintree Library was filled, as additional chairs were set up to standing room only, and respectful silence filled the room as Russ, in his quiet, unassuming manner, told his story of becoming an artist and the years of research, meticulous details, sketching, and ultimately painting this historical event. Listening to Russ giving his presentation and the rapt attention it received made me realize these stories needed to be recorded, as well as all the family stories passed around and 'round.

Russell's Presentation

Mowing hay

One of my early memories was mowing hay with Dad on a warm summer night. It had to be about 1949. I was just a young boy of about six, and brother Jack was younger than me. It was past our bedtime because it was almost dark. I'm not sure where Mom was or what she was doing, but it had to be important because this was unusual for Dad to be caring for us so late in the evening. Dad worked at a job all day as well as working our farm, and that night, cutting hay had to get done, one way or another. The moonlight was so bright it sent out clear shadows like it was daytime, and stars lit up the evening sky. Little Jack squirmed beside me as we sat on a bale, staying out from underfoot, waiting as Dad and Uncle Wendell talking quietly harnessed the horses and hitched them to mowing machines.

"Russ, come here." And he lifted me to the back of Old Nell. "Now you hold on real tight to the hames, and don't you fall off. Don't fall asleep. You understand me, boy?" I obediently nodded my head because you always did what Dad said and waited as he lifted Jack onto Tony and instructed him the same.

Dad picked up the reins, climbed onto the mowing machine, and we moved forward, Uncle Wendell and his team following behind. I could feel the ripple of strong muscles across Nell's broad back, and the hames gently rocked back and forth as we crossed the road to the hayfield, where fireflies lit up the field like a mirror of the stars in the night sky above. It was so quiet, just a soft plod of hooves, the cutter bar clicking, and the swish of hay as it lay down in swaths behind us. The horses' backs became warm and steamy with sweat, and there was a delicious smell of new mown hay. Occasionally Dad would speak to me. "You still awake, boy? Hold on tight." Slowly we made our way around and around the big field, cutting a double swath, Dad leading the way and Uncle Wendell to our right and behind us. I watched as the fireflies flitted across the sea of grass, and I gazed up in wonder at a black velvet sky. It was almost more beauty than a little boy could imagine. I'm not sure Dad would think it more than just getting a job done that needed doing, but for me it was a magical evening, and life was good.

Uncle Louie

Our farm in North Brookfield had been owned by the Adams family from the 1870s. Esther was Leon Adam's sister, married to

THE ARTIST, THE FARMER, THE HUNTER, AND THE GOOD GUY

Pop Selman. Dad and Mom moved to the farm in 1946, but they rented it from Esther and Pop until they purchased it in 1952. The Selmans lived in Cambridge but spent a lot of time, especially summers, at the farm and stayed in an apartment upstairs when they came to stay. They were sort of like family, and Esther and Pop would often take my little brother Larry shopping. Pop's brother, Louis, was a professional artist, an incredible wood carver and sculptor from the big city in New York. He suffered with depression and some alcoholism after a traumatic experience and came to live with Esther and Pop to recover and get his life back in order. He would sit at the kitchen table and draw, and I was fascinated by how he would sketch pictures.

Uncle Louie, Esther, and Pop

I really liked to draw. Brother Ralph had some books by Will James illustrated by him as well. I wanted to draw like that and tried to copy them. We also liked to watch Walt Disney's *Beaver Valley* narrated by Rex Allen on Sunday evenings. I loved watching and learning all about wildlife, and it gave me ideas of things to draw. I always wanted pencils and paper and would try to draw the things I saw. I would visit Uncle Louie daily upstairs in the apartment and show him my pictures. Children are free to express, and I expressed what I saw in my artwork. He would always compliment me and tell me I must be the best artist in my class at school, and that would make me feel really good. He was always interested in seeing what I would bring him, and he might make some little corrections and show me how to make them better, always constructive, always positive and encouraging. Uncle Louie made me believe I could be an artist. He made little sketches for me, and I just admired his talent and really looked up to him. One day I watched him sketching a cottage and the trees around it with a chisel pencil. I was amazed by the way he could just make something up like that from his imagination. I got a chisel pencil and started drawing with that "just like Uncle Louie."

He gave me a book. It was a couple inches thick, and it was tracing paper, just a big book of tracing paper pages to sketch on. One of the things he taught me was how to use tracing paper. Artists will start sketching a picture on tracing paper. It's cheaper than sketch paper, and you could easily eliminate the parts you didn't like and move the parts you do like into a new sketch. Well, I got the idea that I could take that tracing paper and put it on a picture of a buffalo in a book I liked and copy that picture. I tried to erase it and sketch it so it would look like I did it. I was so proud of myself. I brought it to Uncle Louie to show him, expecting him to be impressed with my drawing. Well, of course he knew exactly what I had done and said, "You traced that." At first, I wanted him to believe I had actually drawn this picture, but he knew I was lying to him and gave me that terrible look of disappointment. I knew he knew I lied. It hurt my feelings that I lied to him. It felt so bad that I disappointed Uncle Louis. I decided then and there I would never lie again. I will always be honest about my work. Uncle Louie didn't like tracing and wanted all my work to be *my work* and showed me how important it was to be honest.

Peer pressure

In school, I wasn't a very good student, but I was a pretty good kid, didn't cause trouble, did my best, and the teachers seemed to like me. I liked art and was getting good at drawing. I was in the fifth grade, and the teacher was a really nice guy, liked my artwork, and he would give me colored chalk to draw things on the board while he was teaching the rest of the class. It was something I enjoyed doing, and I think I was pretty good at it. The kids liked the pictures I could draw, and sometimes I would trade a picture I drew, and they would help me out with a homework assignment. It was my way to get through school. Well, one day the boys started pressuring me to draw a nude. I didn't want to do it and told them no. They kept after me and pestering me to do it. I knew it was the wrong thing to do, but they wouldn't leave me alone. I finally agreed just to get them off my back. I sat in class and drew this picture and passed it to one of the

THE ARTIST, THE FARMER, THE HUNTER, AND THE GOOD GUY

kids. It was being passed around pretty fast up and down the aisle, and the teacher noticed. He took the picture, looked at it, and didn't say a word, just putting it to one side on his desk. I felt so guilty. For the rest of the class, I was almost sick to my stomach with guilt and worry. When class ended, as we were dismissed, I tried to exit with the rest of the class, but he stopped me and called me to his desk. He knew it was me who drew the picture and was so disappointed in me. I admitted I did it, and I knew it wasn't a good excuse but told him they talked me into doing it. He just said how disappointed he was in me. I was angry with myself that I let those kids talk me into doing something that I knew wasn't right and didn't want to do in the first place. It felt so bad to disappoint my teacher, and I didn't feel good about myself either. That was the day I learned about peer pressure, and I decided I would never let anyone talk me into doing something I didn't want to do, ever again.

Starving artist

When I was a junior in high school, I thought I would like to be a forest ranger. I had an opportunity to go to a school near Boston for forestry. It was all math and geometry. I wasn't good at those subjects and gave it up after a week. I knew I could do art, so after graduation I decided to try art school. I worked doing welding at CPC engineering for $2.30 an hour to save enough for the $500 tuition to go to art school. I worked nights and got home about 4:00 a.m. I'd put wood in the furnace because that's what we did to keep the house warm and go to bed.

About 7:00 a.m. Colleen and Christy would come running in and jump on me. "Uncle Russy, you getting up?" But I would try to go back to sleep.

It wouldn't be long before Dad would call, "Are you going to sleep all morning?" So my day would begin. I would work all day on whatever needed doing on the farm and then head back to my job at CPC. I worked summers on the farm and CPC for more than seventy hours a week to pay for art school.

I applied and was accepted at Boston School of Practical Art. I commuted the first week and put on over eight hundred miles that week. I knew I couldn't keep doing that and started looking for a place to stay near the school. I saw a note on the school bulletin board for a roommate in Stoughton. I met Stanley Hawthorn, and he took me by subway to his apartment. It involved taking the subway to a surface train car to the subway and back to the train car to get there. I liked the apartment and told him it was a deal, and he brought me back to the subway to get back to my car at the school. It was my first time alone on a subway, and I had no idea how to get back. All the way I kept asking people for help, and they were real helpful, telling me which stops I needed to get off and change cars, but I was scared I would be on that subway train forever! After a while it became second nature, and one time, I even fell asleep, and the conductor had to wake me up, and I had a long walk to my car. Art school was a three-year course, and while I lived in Stoughton, I would leave at 6:00 a.m. to go to classes from nine to four. After class, it took about an hour to get to a little restaurant in Rockland, and I would have about fifteen minutes to wolf down a cheeseburger before heading to work for 6:00 until 10:00 p.m. painting cowhides for shoes, often getting home after eleven o'clock. That was the first year. The second year I worked at Brockton Public Market. The third year I worked in Waltham at Unitrode mixing chemicals. One day I dropped a big glass jug of sulfuric acid, and it broke and splashed all over me. One of the guys came in and yelled at me to get in the shower they had right there, but the acid was still eating into my foot, so I had to go to the hospital. It ruined the only pair of shoes I had, so after leaving the hospital with one shoe, I had to go to Zayres for some cheap sneakers. In my freshmen year, I met a kid from Maine with ragged clothes and no shoes. At first, I thought he was just kind of hippie-like, but then I found out he really couldn't afford clothes and shoes, just working and going to school. And boy, I knew what that was like! It was twenty cents to ride the subway, and sometimes I didn't have enough money to get to school. One time my car broke down in Stoughton. I think it was Route 128, and the tie rod let go. I could see a Chevy dealership across the way and walked over there and asked for the service manager. I explained to him I was a student, and I didn't have any money, but if he would fix my car, I would come every week and pay him. He trusted me and fixed my car, and every week I would stop in with whatever I had to pay him until it was paid off. I met some guys and sometimes I got to play basketball with them at Bridgewater State College. Summers I went home and back to work at CPC and on the farm. I helped all I could, and it was a savings to me because they didn't charge me rent. I was able to save about $50 a week for school.

Learning to focus

I learned over the years to focus on what I was drawing, to shut everything out and concentrate on my work. I worked hard to pay for my education and a place to live, and class time was all the time I had, so in class I wanted to get as much out of it as I could. It was important to focus. My friend and I were signing up for classes, and we had no idea what we were doing. We saw a class called Life Class and thought it would be drawing fruit and still life. The first day of art school we went to the Life Class. The teacher told us we were going to be drawing models, and we could focus on whatever we wanted, the whole body, the face, body part, etc. So this attractive model walked in wearing a flowing robe laced in the front. She pulled at the laces, and the robe dropped. The room went silent, and none of us could even look at each other, especially this country boy. All I could think was *Wow, this isn't the farm!* We all focused real good!

After art school

After art school I spent a day driving to Newberry Street in Boston to all the advertising agencies taking my portfolio of artwork. The agencies liked my work, and one of them knew Wayne Hanley at Audubon, editor of *Man and Nature* magazine, and referred me to him. He called Wayne right then and there and told him he should take a look at my work. I went right over, showed them my portfolio, and he gave me an assignment to paint pictures of a garter snake and a painted turtle. When I completed these, I brought them back and was hired on the spot.

Field study by Russell Buzzell

While working for Mass Audubon, I lived in Acton in a trailer for the winter. It was so cold the toilet had ice in it. I stayed there all winter, and the owner who fixed the toilet didn't do it quite right, not sealing one of the pipes off, and come spring one day, I came home, and everything in the trailer was floating. He told me I was the first guy who made it through the winter!

I liked my job, but I worked in an office, drawing maps and birds. It wasn't what I wanted to do. Although they paid me very well, it required so much inside work rather than being out in the field, where I thought I should be. I missed the country, the animals in their habitat, and just being outside in nature.

Harry and Larry with *Harry and Larry* models for *Gray's Sporting Journal* story

I went to Wayne and asked if I could work from home. To my surprise, he agreed! I moved back home and created a studio, but unfortunately, that didn't work out because there were so many distractions. I couldn't focus on my artwork. Even though the artwork itself was good, and they liked my work, I couldn't get it done quick enough. I worked for the Mass Audubon Society for three years illustrating their magazine. *Gray's Sporting Journal* came after that. I illustrated an article for Ted Williams, a nature writer who wrote an article for the *Boston Globe*. He knew my work from Mass Audubon and recommended me to Ed Gray. The first drawing I did was a pencil sketch of Alaska, and that got me the job, and I could work mostly at my own pace. That's where I drew *Harry and Larry* and *Tense Moments* (The Cat and Rattlesnake). They were created for stories in the *Journal. Gray's* had a circulation of about forty thousand, and I had an excellent relationship with them. My work was being noticed, and I was able to sell some of my work, one to a teacher in Japan!

Interesting side note, Jack Swedberg, senior wildlife photographer for Massachusetts Division of Fisheries and Wildlife, saw Dad working at the Worcester City Reservoir cutting hay with the horses and took pictures. He thought it was interesting to see horsepower being used in modern day and stopped to talk to him, only then finding out he was my father. He had a long talk with him, about his life and all the things he had done. After that Ted Williams called me to do an interview with Dad, and of course Dad talked to him like he would talk to anyone telling his various stories. Ted used the pictures Jack took for an article he wrote about him. Ted and Jack were great guys. Jack was instrumental in bringing the eagle and turkeys back to our area.

Getting started

When I paint a picture, it starts with an idea. I look for settings, lighting, and models to create the picture of the idea that comes to mind. It takes time for that idea to become a finished piece of artwork. I had the idea I wanted to do a painting of Wheeler's Surprise. Wheeler's Surprise was an Indian ambush of Captain Wheeler and his men and three Indian interpreters on their way to talk peace with the tribe's chief in New Braintree on August 2, 1675. There were subsequent raids after this ambush. Because it was so close to home, it was pertinent to our local history. Over a period of five or six years, I researched

Research samples for *Wheeler's Surprise*

and developed the concept of the painting. I went over and over it in my mind. From the first pencil study, it was about a year to the completed oil, but there was all that thought and research before I even set pencil to paper. I studied books, talked to historians, visited museums and battlefields. In the process I commissioned real Native Americans who were professional reenactors, knowledgeable about period weapons and warfare for King Phillip's War. David White is a linguistic specialist of native languages, a great person, and he gave me a lot of good information. He and his co-reenactors modeled for the Indians in the painting. They had to be dressed properly, and I needed the right lighting on the right positioning. I moved the models around to get the results I needed for the picture. Took a lot of pictures in different positions and getting the lighting right to make the scene interesting but authentic. David had good suggestions, and he was always right. It made the painting realistic.

I also had reenactors for Captain Wheeler and his men. One historian I talked to told me they didn't have side arms, but with research I learned they did in fact have side arms and the importance of placement on the body. I used a website on Wallace's Troupe of Horse Company in England that gave me valuable information on Oliver Cromwell's war in England, and Offsprey Publishing was also helpful. The early soldiers in America were English, and their clothing and weaponry would be of that period for the painting. Paul Irish, assistant to VP of Student Affairs at Holy Cross, was a reenactor and a historical authority on King Phillip's War. He went up on Buck Hill with me to model Captain Wheeler and his men.

Wheeler's Surprise

I had the idea, the research, the models, the sketches, but I needed the right setting. I drove to the Petersham State Forrest. I was looking for a magnificent white pine that would be the focal point of the setting but didn't find the one I was looking for. They all were boring. It had to be just right. It was the integral part of the design I was imagining.

THE ARTIST, THE FARMER, THE HUNTER, AND THE GOOD GUY

White pine grows just uphill from swampy areas and is native to the area. It would be authentic to the period and similar to the description given by Captain Wheeler. I got a coffee and headed to the Hubbardston State Forrest looking for the elusive white pine. I had been driving around for quite a while and then walked in the woods in Hubbardston when nature called. I had to relieve myself of that coffee. I looked for a discreet place, and as I was relieving myself looking around, there it was! That white pine to be the focal point of my painting and the setting I was looking for spread about before me.

So now the real creating can begin. There were sketches, and each one helped to develop the final composition. Then came the painting. Taking the final sketch and transferring it to the thirty-six-by-fifty-inch canvas and meticulously filling in with paint and shading took weeks, months to the completed product.

Artist proof by Russell Buzzell

DIANE BUZZELL

Wheeler's Surprise
Original by Russell Buzzell
copyright by Russell Buzzell

THE ARTIST, THE FARMER, THE HUNTER, AND THE GOOD GUY

More Artwork by Russell Buzzell

Mouse on A Christmas Tree

Larry Bill

DIANE BUZZELL

New England Winter

Tense Moments

THE ARTIST, THE FARMER, THE HUNTER, AND THE GOOD GUY

Red Devon Steers

The Crawford Farm

The Farm

The farm in North Brookfield where most of these stories take place was bought from the W. Prescott Adams estate (i.e., Esther Adams Selman). It consisted of the barn, the house, a smaller house and barn on Tucker Cross Road and about 160 acres. The number of acres is debatable.

View of house prior to 1959

The main house built in the late 1800s was a two-story structure having twelve rooms, an attic, and in the cellar, a dug well supplying the house with spring water. The front door was a double door with etched glass in the windows that opened to a front staircase. To either side of the staircase were doors leading to the left, a bedroom, and to the right, the living room. A large dining room was off the living room with a side door leading outside. Off the dining room to the left was a small room with a large grate in the floor for heat to rise from the wood furnace in the cellar and a door beyond leading to another small bedroom behind the front bedroom. Pocket doors separated the front room from the back and most likely was a grand room before they became bedrooms. In 1949 the back bedroom was Larry's birthplace. Off the back of the dining room was a large kitchen with a pantry and stairway to the cellar and a back stairway to the upstairs. A bathroom with sink, toilet, and a wringer washing machine was off the kitchen as well. I'm not sure it was a bathroom originally because it had two doors. There were two more doors in the kitchen, one leading to the shed and another out to the back field. The wall between house and two-story shed was brick, which was a curious thing. It housed Dad's welding and workshop and his harness shop. Upstairs in the shed was where Uncle Louie had his sculptures.

Going up the front staircase, a wraparound walkway to the left side of the house led to Mom and Dad's bedroom with a door leading to the attic, and to the right was the bedroom Russ, Jack, and Larry shared. There was a large room off the boys' room that was part of the apartment Esther, Pop, and Uncle Louie shared. A bedroom behind Mom and Dad's led off from that room and door leading to the back staircase with a small area for a toilet and sink (that didn't work), an upstairs kitchen, another bedroom, and small storage room. Later that became Russ's apartment, and then when Larry and I married, it became ours. There was a kerosene heat stove in the kitchen, and we would have to fill a can and lug it upstairs daily to heat the apartment.

The home was heated by a wood furnace in the cellar, and the kitchen had woodstove for additional heat as well as an electric kitchen stove. There were fir trees off the side of the house, an apple tree out front, and an elm tree about one hundred feet tall stood in the crossroad. The boys liked watching baby owls nesting there from their window. The tree came down about 1965, and Larry remembers thinking the tree was so tall it would reach the brook, but it didn't. After the farm was sold in 1974, the uninhabited house mysteriously burned down in 1975.

The barn many have said was two hundred feet long, but that was an estimated roundup. When Russ

View of barn prior to 1938

painted *The Farm* and, wanting to get the artwork perspectives correct, in his meticulous manner, calculated it was only about 187 feet. Regardless, it was an imposing structure of post and beam construction. It had two sections, and the front was earlier than the back with hand hewn beams and a peak at least 30 feet high. The front was a bank barn built into a banking for shelter for farm animals or storage underneath. The second section, added sometime later, housed an enormous hay mow upstairs and dairy barn under. Built in the 1800s, it had a cupola that was blown down in the hurricane of 1938. When the cupola came down, it cost $3,000 to fix the barn roof and took precedence over the house roof.

The little red house must have had paint on it at some point because that was what it was always called, but after years of wear and tear, there was no evidence of red paint. It was a cute little house with a porch off the front leading into the kitchen, with pantry, living room, and bathroom downstairs and two bedrooms under the eaves upstairs. It was said to originally be for hired help. Uncle Wendell and Aunt Marie with the cousins lived there and later Uncle Roland. There were other various families Dad helped, renting them a place to stay until they could afford better or moved on. In the end, it mysteriously burned while no was living there.

Little Red House

The land consisted of a large hayfield behind the house. Bordering the hayfield was Victor's side hill pasture, named for Barbara Jenning's horse Victor. We also pastured dry cows and those ready to

View of the farm house and barn from Ralph's house on Tucker Hill

freshen there. That land bordered the Tucker, Hanson, and Crawford farms. The brook ran along the side pasture, and there were two small ponds known as Big Yankee and Little Yankee, where the boys could go swimming. Big Yankee was deeper than Little Yankee.

The barn was located in the Three Corner Piece hemmed in by Old West Brookfield, Tucker Cross (also known as the dirt road), and Tucker Hill Roads. The little red house was at the corner of Tucker and Tucker Cross Roads. That was the night pasture with the brook where the cows got their water that ran through it from a culvert on Tucker Hill Road to under a bridge on Old West Brookfield.

Across from the barn along Old West Brookfield was the cornfield with the run along Bates Street and the cornfield leading to a pasture beyond. Buck Hill was on the other side of the dirt road and extended to Smith Hanson Road.

Pieces of the farm were parceled off to family before, at the time and after the sale of the farm.

Farm Genealogy

With some research from early maps and tax records, this is a little history of the land and eventual Buzzell Farm and then the little farm on Cider Mill.

1673	Land grant Matchuk Meadows seventy-seven acres cornfield
1674	Land grant John Pynchon earliest grant sawmill property (Cider Mill farm)
1717	Land grant to Samuel Barnes, the farmhouse structure on map
1718	Land grant Joseph Ayers, Buck Hill
1749	The farmhouse structure on map / little red house not on map
1830	J. Poland structure on map (house)
1830	C. Woodard—little red house

1830	H. Bannister house junction Cider Mill, Old West Brookfield, and Tucker Cross (old stone foundation remains)
1830	N. Dodge (tavern across from the end of Stagecoach / McCarthy Road)
1830	Sawmill/gristmill (Cider Mill farm land)
1870	B. W. Dean, the farm land and little red house
1870	Dean (Cider Mill farm land)
1885	Dean (the farmhouse on map)
1885	Sykes (the farm)
1898	W. Prescott Adams, the farm (house and barn on map) (also on map Tuckers, Buck Hill is Black Hill, Whitings Cider Mill at end of Cider Mill Road)
1898	Mrs. C. Smith (Cider Mill farm) C. Hubbard (Cider Mill farm) Richardson (Cider Mill farm)
1952	John and Hazel Buzzell, the farm
1967	Ralph and Mabel, Tucker Hill Road
1974	The farm sold
1974	John and Hazel Buzzell, Cider Mill farm
1979	Larry and Diane Buzzell, Cider Mill farm
1983	Janice Pixler, Stephanie Pixler, little red house
1983	Ralph and Larry Buzzell, Woodlot
2004	Nathan and Kelly Buzzell, Cider Mill farm
2021	Jonathan and Amanda's home (where the barn stood on the farm)

View of Farm from Old West Brookfield Road 1960's

Heartwarming that family is back on the farm

DIANE BUZZELL

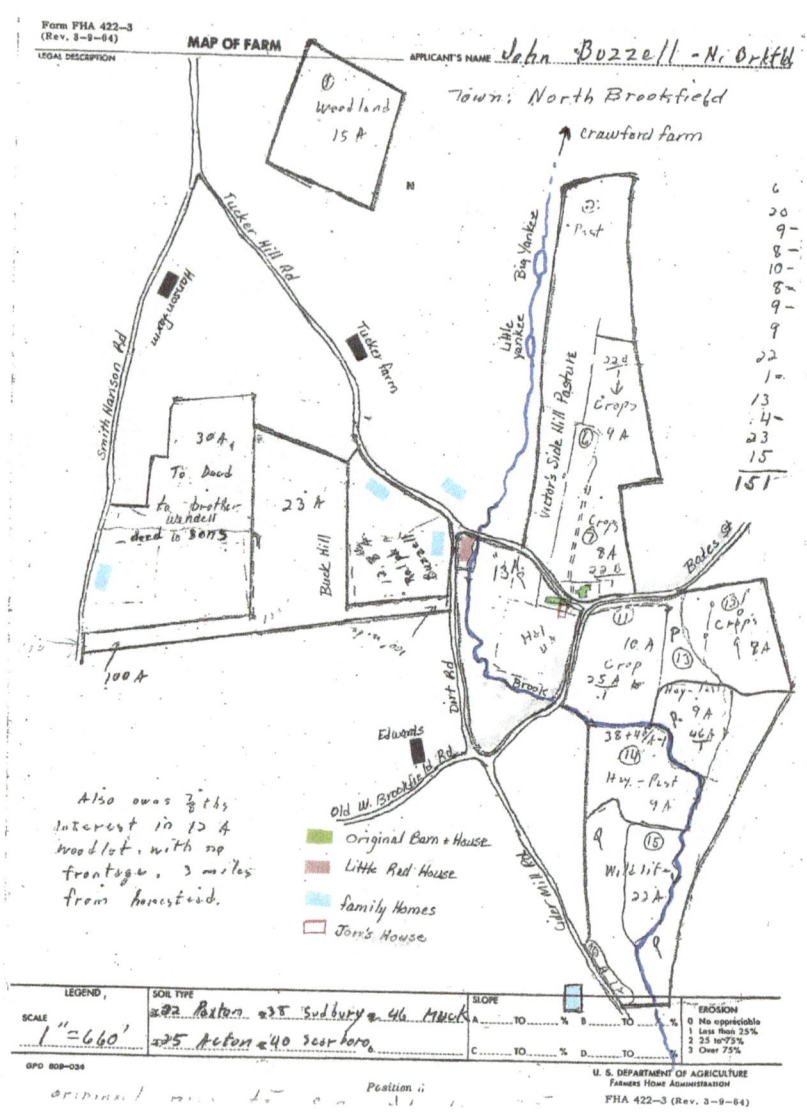

Family and Friends

Grammie and Grampie's
The Leach Farm, Hasting Road, Spencer

Boy Meets Girl

Larry and Diane: Our Story

As I consult with those whose memories are shared, I cannot help but see God's hand in all this. Long before I was born or even the family in these stories, North Brookfield was the shoe capital of the country, possibly the world. How does that apply to us? Pay attention and maybe you'll see the connection as you read. I grew up in Holden not so far from North Brookfield but also not very close. The Lindstrom family and traditions were very different than the Buzzell family but sort of the same, if that makes sense? My family is only second- and third-generation Americans, naturalized immigrants coming to make a better life, and the Buzzell family has roots in the early Puritans also coming to make a better life and connections to the Founding Fathers of this great country for opportunities we now take for granted. I remember my great-grandfather Morfar proudly exclaiming in his broken English, "I American, I speak American." Morfar built houses dotted all over Holden and surrounding towns. Larry's father's family in Maine were loggers, maybe supplying the lumber my Morfar used to build houses. My dad loved animals, and we always had a menagerie, including rabbits at Easter, many coming from the little old man in Spencer where Larry sold his rabbits. Who knows, I might have had one of his rabbits! Growing up I loved horses, and a dark Morgan stallion became my dream. In the 4H club I joined in Holden in the early sixties, one of the girls had a horse sired by Bay State Sandy (pay attention). That was a connection that meant nothing at the time but was a lead into the future. Pappy went to the Cape when he left Maine to find his fortune. The Buzzell Farm didn't leave any chance for vacation, but I grew up summers on the Cape riding in horse shows for Mr. Walker, who had a Morgan, Bay State Jeff. Pappy left the Cape, moving to Spencer hearing about a job at Klevin Shoe Factory (are you paying attention?). My dad's lifelong dream was to have a farm and moved us to Hardwick, which led me strangely to summer job at Klevin Shoe Factory (are you getting it?). There, I met a girl who had a Morgan and at the time was Larry's girlfriend. And consider my surprise when I found her family owned the pinto mare Sugar that I learned to ride on when I was a little girl. She introduced me to Mr. Buzzell, who had Bay State Sandy (hmm, Bay State?) from the same farm Bay State Jeff came from. We might have even been at the National Morgan Horse Show in Northampton at the same time. Some people would say small world. I can't believe all this is coincidence but a grand plan by the hand of God.

Diane and Bay State Jeff
Morgan National 1965

What came next is really unique. I can't say it was God's plan, but he certainly is capable of using the plans we as humans make to accomplish his plan. My family was first introduced to Larry when my dad bought a calf from Larry's dad before we started dating. Larry was intimidated by our fancy home, and my mother wasn't impressed with his dirty farm clothes. Really? Who turns up with a calf wearing a suit? But whatever. In the meantime, I was building a friendship with Larry's girlfriend. We went riding together and to horse shows, and

John, Bay State Sandy, and Select Ethan at the Morgan National

she introduced me to Larry. I remember the first time I met him we were driving by the farm, and he was outside shooting hoops. She pulled over and stopped. As she introduced us, he smiled, and the first thing I noticed was he had no teeth. Evidently, he had recently had them removed and was waiting for his denture. I didn't think much about it at the time, but I think for many that would not have been a really good first impression.

As told by Larry

My girlfriend asked me to pick up Diane from work and bring her home. She was supposed to pick her up and bring her home, but for some reason she couldn't. We argued because it was going to interfere with milking, and my day was already long enough, but I finally agreed, telling her, "Don't ask me to do it again. I don't have time for that!" I was annoyed, so I didn't do much to impress Diane, picking her up in the blue farm pickup wearing my old farm clothes. She came out of Klevins with her long blond hair and miniskirt and climbed in, and I thought to myself, "Hmmm. Maybe I could do this again." My attitude went from being so angry to not so bad. It was a pleasant ride to Hardwick, and the trip was well worth getting done late with milking.

*****

Larry was dating my new friend. I wasn't sure where their relationship was and really didn't have much interest (he was her boyfriend after all and had no teeth), but after looking back, I guess it wasn't the best. She had an interest in his older brother, Russ, and hoping for an attraction, she asked me to go on a double date to a drive-in movie with them. She instructed me that when we got there, we would go to the restroom, and when we came back to the car, she wanted to sit with Russ, which of course left me with Larry. I'm not sure why I agreed to this in the first place, but at the time I was only sixteen, and Russ was ten years older than me. Not a very good match. I think I would have been considered "jailbait." So anyway,

I sat with Larry, and as we watched the movie, we had some good conversation. Really. We talked. I was kind of impressed what a gentleman he was. As it turned out, I left my pocketbook in my friend's car and the next day had to retrieve it. When I got to her house, I told her I didn't want to do that again. He was a nice guy, and bait and switch didn't feel like the right thing to do. She took that as an opportunity to give me his class ring, his sport sweater and senior portrait, all things steady girlfriends get from their boyfriends. How awkward! I never did return those items to him. Instead, we began dating, and the rest is history.

We dated through my senior year of high school. Most of it was just hanging out on the farm together. There wasn't much time for anything but work, and we really didn't have much interest in doing anything else. He often picked me up from my job at a dairy bar after milking when my shift would end at nine. Sometimes he would come in and order something to eat while waiting, but usually he would sit out front, either taking a snooze or watching me through the windows until my shift was over to drive me home. Larry always treated me like a princess, even though his princess was usually in jeans and work shirt. For my senior class banquet, I wore a dark-purple satin minidress trimmed with fringe like a flapper dress. He thought I was so beautiful and was bragging to his brother Ralph. When he asked, "Don't you think she's beautiful?"

Ralph agreed and asked, "What's she doing with you?" Brothers can be brutally honest. Little did he know I didn't feel *that* pretty and was just grateful for a guy who didn't smoke, drink, do drugs, and for me, most important at the time, was a farmer. Later, a godly man who loved and served the Lord made my choice even better.

When I graduated, many of the girls in my class did not go to college. High school had business courses that prepared them adequately to enter the business world. Some went to school for nursing or teaching, but I wasn't one who had an interest in either of those, and I wasn't encouraged to pursue a career. My goal was to be a farmwife. It was not unusual to get engaged after high school, and many girls in my class received engagement rings as graduation gifts. Larry surprised me even before graduation day. I remember that evening in

April when he picked me up. It was just like any other evening. My day started early like his. I had barn chores with horses boarding at our family's farm and then had to be ready in time for the bus to pick us up at 7:10 a.m. After school there were barn chores and probably some workouts with the horses before either going to the dairy bar or heading to Buzzell farm. I would fit in homework whenever I could, sometimes at his farm during chores, sometimes after getting home when he dropped me off, sometimes on the bus ride to school. It was a long day, every day, no matter how you looked at it.

Looking down on the farm from the hill.
Victor's Side Hill pasture would be to the right in this picture.

That night we drove up the hill behind the house. It had rained all day, but the clouds were clearing and was becoming a beautiful night. The mist sparkled around a moon so big on the hill it almost seemed like you could reach out and touch it. His car was a '66 silver Chevrolet Impala with a bench seat, so I was able to snuggle up next to him. We were so comfortable together and even talked about our future, but this night he was nervous as he presented a ring to me, a wide gold band with a circle of silver surrounding a diamond and asking me to spend our lives together. Of course, I said yes! He bought that ring at Cormier Jewelers, and Mr. Cormier trusted him to pay for it on time a few dollars a week. We snuggled and smooched, but as I nestled into his arms and looked out over the farm and our future with the moon shining brightly over it all, I fell asleep. He loved teasing me about this, even still, but for someone with a history of sleeping anywhere and everywhere (if you didn't know, you soon will), he should talk!

We wanted just a small wedding, but you know how that goes. By the time you invite the relatives and a few close friends, it was well over one hundred. I made my dress and a dress for my sister Debbie and Larry's niece Christy, who were junior bridesmaids, and my cousin Melanie was maid of honor. Their dresses were emerald green velvet. Tim Woods was our best man, and Larry's brothers stood with us as well. And it was that same pastor who married us whose daughter had fallen asleep with Larry on prom night. (Yup, that's a story!) We wanted to be married in the fall, and every weekend there seemed to be a conflict. We finally ended up choosing the last Saturday in October, which happened to be the thirty-first. We have been teased about that ever since with jokes "Was it trick or treat?" or "What did you dress up as?" but we really gave it no thought as to what day it was, and in 1970, the thirty-first wasn't the big deal it is today. Even when a few trick-or-treaters showed up at the house after the reception, Mom had been so immersed in wedding plans she had no candy and gave them wedding cake instead. In later years, we don't celebrate our anniversary on the thirty-first because there isn't a whole lot of romance when your waitress is a witch, and restaurants are decked out with ghosts and cobwebs.

But our wedding day was perfect. It had rained all week, and the wind and rain stripped all the leaves off the trees. The church grounds were carpeted in gold. The clear warm day dawned with crystal blue skies. Larry was just as anxious that day as when he asked me to marry him. As Pastor was reciting the ceremony, Larry broke in, saying, "I do!" and Pastor patted his arm and said, "Not yet, Larry, I'll tell you when." After the service, the reception was cut a little short when Pappy showed up with the carriage and team of Dancer and Sally to drive us to the farm before we left for our honeymoon. All the guys came to take over milking for us, and Larry was admonished to "Take your bride and get going!" We went all the way to Sturbridge (about ten miles) and had just two nights away spending a day in Old Sturbridge Village and wandering Main Street. We came home to the small apartment upstairs. The kerosene heating stove in our kitchen kept it toasty warm, but to conserve fuel, we kept the bedroom door shut during the day. That winter recorded below-zero temps, which encased our bedroom windows with ice as thick as the mullions around the glass, so thick you could barely see out. The kitchen in our apartment was an adequate size, but I remember washing my waist-length hair in the sink because we didn't have a shower. If I wasn't careful and backed into the kitchen stove with my head under the faucet, I would get a pretty substantial shock!

The following year we sadly had to make the decision to sell the cows. The state had made regulations for cement floors. If we mortgaged the farm enough for a new milking parlor and improvements, we couldn't survive on what milk prices would give us to live on unless we got more cows. Pappy was getting older, and his legs were getting worse. There was far more work than we could do even with friends and family pitching in, and we couldn't expect them to continue to do that, and the farm couldn't support two families. It was just the perfect storm to drown us out. So we kept a young cow, Popcorn, for our own milk. I think just because we couldn't give up having cows. Popcorn was a big Holstein first calf heifer niece Stephanie had named, mostly black with a big white popcorn-shaped splotch on

The Hubbard Place on Cider Mill

her face. Ralph helped Larry get his first job off the farm at a hardware store in Barre. It was a whole new world for us. Mom and Dad sold the farm and bought a smaller, fifteen-acre parcel known as the old Hubbard place on Cider Mill Road just walking distance from the farm. Big enough for hay and pasture for a couple cows and his team but small enough to manage. Strangely, the person who bought the farm never lived there. The boys wanted to take some of the boards in the attic that were not nailed down and measured twenty-four inches wide and some of them twenty feet long, but Dad said they were to go with the house. Sadly, not long after, the house burned to the ground, and those beautiful boards went with it. We often went by the barn, noticing men working hard taking down the barn boards. They even waved at us when we drove by. We thought the owner was taking the barn down to sell the boards, as real barn boards and beams were in big demand at the time, until the owner accused us of taking them! Those men stole the boards in broad daylight!

So in the new chapter of our lives, Larry and I had our own small home not far from Mom and Dad. Dad was recovering from an accident with the horses at the city reservoir when Mom passed away in 1978. A heart attack followed. We were always at the farm checking or helping out, so it made sense to move there with him. We bought the farm from him. We built an addition using oak from the woodlot for a studio apartment for him, which had a kitchenette and bath, and the rest of the house became a work in progress for our family. He got a brand-new room, and we got to fix up the old house little by little. Originally built in 1790, I'm not sure what came first, the bedroom end of the house or the post and beam structure. I'm guessing the bedrooms because there was no cellar, and in the crawl space was a stone pad that originally supported a fireplace between the two rooms. There was a patched space in the floor where the fireplace would have been in the back bedroom, and layers of wallpaper covered the imprint of the mantle in the old lathe and plaster on the center wall of the front bedroom. Upstairs was a patched square in the floor in the room where the chimney would have extended up to and through the roof. There was a trap door above the living room at one point that had been replaced with a very steep staircase. Restoring the old home became a necessity as we discovered less-than-code conditions. As we tore out the kitchen, we found an electrical outlet taped together with a Band-Aid, and in the front bedroom a strange cord was plugged into the outlet and disappeared into the wall. Pulling down the old wall revealed the extension cord wired an outlet in the back bedroom and only worked if plugged into the outlet in the front bedroom. Fascinating was the corner posts that were actual tree trunks with the inside corner axed out. In the bathroom, the sink had no drain, and the tub no faucets. A short hose attached the sink faucet to fill the tub, and a basin sat in the sink that we would have to dump as it filled with water when hand washing. When we remodeled the bathroom, we discovered almost no supports in the floor under the tub. One could have submerged into the crawl space with the weight of that cast-iron tub, water, and person given the right moment. As we were remodeling one morning, Larry left for work, and I headed to the bathroom. As I took a seat, there was a small bureau against the wall, and the toilet paper roll sat on it. I was about eye level with the toilet paper, and a rather large snake came around to greet me. It was a good thing I was sitting down because I surely would have wet my pants otherwise. I exited as quickly as modesty allowed and ran for Pappy, and the two of us wrangled the snake before anyone else encountered him. It was record time sealing off the holes from the plumbing after that. Men have different priorities than women because they decided to put water access in the barn before the kitchen sink. That's when this woman refused to cook until she didn't have to wash dishes in the bathtub.

> The Lord God said,
> "It is not good for the man to be alone.
> I will make a helper suitable for him."
> —Genesis 2:18

Dad

April 4, 1910–April 27, 1988

John Henry, Dad, Pappy, Grampa was born April 4, 1910, and brought up in Sherman Mills, Maine, in the shadow of Mt. Katahdin, son of Ralph and Daisy. He was second in the family of eight with six girls, Florence, Margaret, Velma, Glynes, Barbara, Mary, and the youngest, a brother, was Wendell. He went to a one-room schoolhouse "graduating" from the sixth grade to become the bus driver picking up kids with a wagon and team. In the winter, the wagon had a covering with a small woodstove inside to keep the children warm in the below-zero temps of northern Maine winters. Kids back then were expected to pull their weight and contribute to the family. As a child, one of the jobs he had was to take his team of little oxen and tip cart down the railroad tracks, scavenging any coal left behind by the train to help heat their home and run the cookstove. Pappy related once that getting wood with his father, it was so cold he was riding the wood wagon, and his father made him get down from the load and walk in front. It was to prevent him from literally freezing to death before they got home. At just twelve years old he got a job working for the highway department driving his tip cart. Each one in the family worked hard just to survive. Life was hard. Opportunity

Back row: Florence and John
Ralph, Velma, Barbara, Baby Glynes, Daisy
Front: Margaret

THE ARTIST, THE FARMER, THE HUNTER, AND THE GOOD GUY

was minimal. The logging camps, farming, or picking potatoes were primary means of employment for young and old alike. Even into the 1970s, Maine schools would take time off to let kids go pick potatoes in the fall. The farms needed pickers, and the families needed the income. As a teen, the only sport you could say he participated in was skiing, but that was so he could get to the logging camps where he would be paid to fix and sharpen saws. Sometime in his teen years, chopping wood with a double-sided ax, he drove it into his knee cap. There were no miracle pain meds or medical treatment. It was just allowed to heal, and that injury would cause him pain for the rest of his life and resulted in having to use a cane in later years to get around.

Baby John and his father, Ralph

Life was going south

When it came time to find a wife, he finally found a girl he thought he could marry only to find out she was a cousin. In addition to being related to almost everyone in Sherman Mills, making a living was a challenge, and he decided to move someplace where he could make some money *and* find a woman. He and a friend loaded a truck with vegetables and headed south. He landed on Cape Cod, sold his vegetables, and found a job working in the cranberry bogs. He must have got some dating experience there as he advised his sons to never date twins. Pappy made the move to central Massachusetts upon hearing of a job in Spencer at Klevin Shoe Factory. While at Klevins, he worked third shift and realized with a larger pulley overhead he could work faster. He devised a replacement pulley that increased his work production and made it easier at the same time. He wasn't sure how it would be accepted, so he used it on the sly, taking it down before he left each morning until he forgot to take it to down one morning and was found out.

A working man

Although Pappy didn't have the opportunity for higher education, he was an intelligent, self-taught man. Most people don't realize how gifted you must be to be a farmer. Compared to life today, there were a variety of work skills and common sense needed to just get by. You couldn't pay a mechanic every time a machine broke down or pay a blacksmith every ten weeks to shoe your horses. You learned to do it yourself. Moms became doctor and nurse rolled into one, and farmers treated animals as best they could, only relying on a veterinarian as a last resort. You needed to interpret the weather for each season, even daily to successfully raise a crop for home and market. You didn't push a button to heat your home but planned ahead to cut and store away wood, then tend the wood furnace or stoves round the clock to keep your family warm and able to cook their food. Pappy became an expert welder able to fix or fabricate new. Pappy even installed a welder in an old potato chip truck for a mobile repair (yup, the same one sitting in our field by the stone wall today with no tires housing bricks and "stuff"). At one point he supplemented the farm working at CPC Engineering working on space capsules—yes, for NASA. One was so big after loading it on the trailer, the door wasn't high enough to move it out of the building. It was only by inches, but an inch is as good as a mile when it doesn't fit. All the college-educated engineers measured and debated how to get it out and determined the only way was to cut the door bigger and gave that instruction to Pappy. He refused because he said there was no need. They got very frustrated with him. Back to the drawing board conferring over what could be done until they finally asked for his solution. He told them, "Let the air out of the tires." The truck driver nearly fell off his seat laughing.

"I want to buy this man his supper!" And he did.

They let the air out of the tires, rolled the trailer forward out the door, and blew the tires back up. How is that for using your noggin?

Another time they were working on cylinders for underwater, and they absolutely could not leak, had to be perfect, but some were returned for leakage issues. The bosses called the crew in, Pappy being one of them. They were not happy because they could be facing all manner of retribution on the contract for their product. Pappy boldly proclaimed, "Mine don't leak." Of course, they didn't believe him and wanted proof. He explained, "Because inside each one I made I have my initials JB. That's how you can tell." And he was right, not one of his was among those that were leaking. He believed a job worth doing was a job done right. Working for CPC was kind of a culture shock for Pappy. He wasn't used to timeclocks and bosses. One day he took out his lunch and started eating, and his boss asked him what he was doing, and Pappy replied, true to form, "Eating." And the boss continued, "Why?" and the dumb question was answered, "Because I'm hungry!"

Pappy also worked on the North Brookfield Highway Department during the fifties as a mechanic. He created a sidewalk plow before any of the other towns around had one. Walt Heath was driving a plow truck one night, and it broke down. Pappy was called out to see what the problem was. After looking under the hood, he asked Walt if he had any chewing gum. When Walt replied he did, Pappy commanded him, "Chew it, boy," while he tinkered on the engine. After a few minutes, he withdrew from where he was under the hood and told Walt to "Let me have it." Walt took the gum from his mouth and handed it to Pappy. God only knows what he did with that gum, but after slamming the hood down, Walt started up the truck and was off to finish plowing. One winter a plow blade was dropped on Pappy's foot, breaking it, and he was out of work for quite a while. The family was barely scraping by financially, and it was going to be a very slim Christmas. The Highway Department showed up with a pickup load of food and gifts. The Buzzell kids had never seen so many toys at once and were incredibly blessed that year. Back then the towns took care of their own but also was a testament to Pappy's character and how well he was appreciated.

Many were the times sitting around the round oak farm table enjoying a coffee break he would advise people how to fix or improve anything mechanical from cars to tractors or heavy equipment. One fellow showed up and asked him if he could put a Buick engine in a '55 Chevy. Pappy spelled out everything from modifying the radiator to hooking up hoses. When they finished the coffee, the man left with a "Thank you, John!" Pappy wasn't a good teacher. He even said so himself. He knew what to do and kind of expected the same from you, but he would take time to tell you if you asked. Many neighboring farmers would ask Pappy if he wanted to "borrow" their equipment, often bigger and better than anything Pappy owned. It was his cue to ask, "What's wrong with it?" He could fix or make it run better, and they knew it would come back in better condition than when they brought it to him. Pappy not only fixed things, but he could take parts, put them all together, and make something new. He created three tractors from spare parts, Junior, Popeye, and Popeye II, as well as the sidewalk plow for the town. When I say he could fix anything, one time Mom bit into an apple at the orchard, and a tooth broke off her denture. She gave the two pieces to Dad, and he glued it back together with some Super Glue. When Larry got his new denture and complained the back cut into the roof of his mouth, Dad demanded, "Give them to me." Pulling out his famous used-for-everything jackknife, he proceeded to shave off the edge. Yup, he fixed them.

Many might call this hocus-pocus, but there is a method using a willow stick to find water, and Dad was quite proficient using this method helping people find the best spot to dig their wells. It entailed using a forked willow branch holding the ends and slowly walking on the property until the end dipped down. It worked like magic for him.

THE ARTIST, THE FARMER, THE HUNTER, AND THE GOOD GUY

R-E-S-P-E-C-T

Pappy loved his horses, and he had more than you can count over the years. He could handle the worst outlaws and retrain the most damaged. We were at a trail ride once, and there was someone who had a horse who didn't want to get in the trailer. They would lead him in, and he would back up before they could hitch him and then stubbornly plant his feet on the ramp. They were tying ropes behind him, treats to bribe him, begging, manhandling, but nothing was working. Pappy recognized the horse as one he once owned. Ambling over and leaning on his cane, he just commanded, "Get up in there!" That horse flew into the trailer and stayed there! His owners were amazed but so grateful they could be on their way. Pappy demanded respect, and even horses respected the sound of his voice. On the other hand, they could trust his voice. When Sandy and Diamond were in NYC, a fire truck with sirens blaring and lights flashing came from behind. Pappy just spoke "Easy," and they never moved a foot.

Regarding respect, Dad didn't mince words. He said what he meant and meant what he said, and his boys learned early on to respect him. Off the back of the farmhouse was an ell that housed a large kitchen, bathroom, pantry, and workshop shed. Refrigerator, stove, and sink and the door to the woodshed lined one wall, and beside the woodshed door was a daybed in the corner of the kitchen. A small TV was on a table on the opposite wall of the appliances with a big table that easily sat eight in the center. Across from the daybed was the woodstove against the wall that separated the pantry and stairway to the cellar from the kitchen. After the noon meal, Pappy always took a short rest on the daybed, maybe twenty minutes to be ready for the rest of the day's work. One day the boys were playing baseball in the front yard, and one of them threw a fast ball that went right over Ralph's head. It was like slow motion watching that ball as it soared toward the house and right through the window over the daybed as Pappy lay napping. Glass shattered, spraying fragments all over him, bouncing across the kitchen and rudely waking him. They knew there was hell to pay and scattered as Pappy came out the door breathing fire and carrying his bullwhip! Although spanking was an acceptable means of discipline back in the day, he seldom if ever spanked them, but they surely knew better than to push their luck that far. At the sight of the bullwhip, they knew that he meant business and headed for the hills because they knew he knew how to use it. Once when Russ and Jack were fighting out by the barn, Dad was coming up with Toby and a cart full of milk jugs. They didn't pay attention to his heed, and he snaked the bullwhip out, wrapping it around their legs and tripping them. They learned when Pappy said "Stop," you stopped, and no fight was worth it after that.

Quoting from Russ, "Dad never abused us. He was good to us, but he expected us to listen and do as we were told. I don't remember him ever hitting us, but when he was angry with us, it was because we deserved it."

Acting the part

Pappy could have gone to Hollywood because of his driving skills. A producer asked if he could handle a six-horse hitch and, in true Pappy fashion, responded, "Of course I can!" He was best known for his Morgan team of Sandy and Diamond. They were part of a four-horse hitch with Sandy's offspring, Sonesta and Wonder, pulling a stage coach in the movie Hawaii with Julie

Photo by Robert Lilysrom
Telegram staff

Andrews and Carol O'Connor. He argued with the director, getting very angry that no sane coach driver would ever gallop into town. It wasn't safe or true to life, but they wanted it for effect, so he didn't win that argument. Fortunately, there was a Whitman to head up the horses when they came to a stop. That's Hollywood! After coming into town, he had to drink a "yard" of ale from a glass thirty inches tall. And it was real ale! They took so many retakes he was getting tipsy! He did say that Julie Andrews was a lovely, gracious lady, and every time I see the *Sound of Music* or *Mary Poppins*, I wonder if she ever thinks of John Buzzell.

There was also a children's show, *Howdy Doody with Buffalo Bob*, that Pappy was on. They announced his name wrong, and he wasn't terribly happy about that. He gave a hayride for the cast of the *Merv Griffin Show*, and Merv was another very gracious person who didn't seem to take his celebrity too seriously.

Life is a parade

Pappy drove in parades for different companies, Worcester County Bank, Spags, and others. He drove in Northampton, Worcester, Springfield, and New York City as well as local town celebrations. In Northampton he would drive people in the coach from the Northampton Inn to the fairgrounds where the National Morgan Horse Show took place as well as the Tri-county Fair. Larry rode shotgun with him and once received a $20 tip. He handed it to his father, and Pappy told him, "He didn't give it to me, boy. You keep it." It was a fortune, especially for a kid at that time. When he drove for Spags, somehow they didn't pay him. When Mr. Spag found out, he drove from Shrewsbury right to the farm sporting his signature white cowboy hat, driving his Cadillac. He stomped up into the hayfield where Pappy was raking, with a check and a huge box of fruit, cheeses, and bread, thanking him personally and apologizing for the delay. For you young ones, Spags was sort of discount store before there were discount stores, actually more like Amazon because you could get anything and everything there from toys to plumbing supplies to garden plants and much more, and the prices couldn't be beat. The store was cramped and always crowded with bargain hunters. Everyone went to Spags! Mr. Spag didn't offer health insurance to his employees. At that time insurance wasn't mandatory, but he often paid their medical bills out of his own pocket. It was cheaper than paying insurance, and I think his goodwill won over his employees as well. Health care was actually affordable, and in a catastrophic event, people joined in to help out, and providers worked to minimize payments. Side note, my aunt worked for Spag's for a while.

Back in time

Pappy also worked at Old Sturbridge Village with Sandy and Diamond when it was more like an actual village and less like a museum. Larry would often go with him, playing in the dirt or fishing in the mill pond. Many thought he was part of the village, but he was just there playing and keeping out of trouble. He liked hanging about the blacksmith shop where Pappy's good friend Bert Shaw worked. Bert liked to make horseshoe nail rings and give them to the kids that came through. When management found out he was giving them away, they told Bert he couldn't do that because then nobody would buy them in the store. They chewed him out, but he stood up to them. His boss told him he needed to listen to his superiors, but Bert retaliated with, "I have no superiors and damn few equals!" The same could be said about Pappy. Pappy's days of driving his team at the village came to an end when he tied the reins to the brake and went into the store, which in the old days would have been appropriate, but a kid climbed up and loosed the reins, and Sandy and Diamond started off. No one got hurt, but the village fired him for leaving his post. Of course, the kid never should have done that, and in the old days, kids would have known better or maybe at least known what they were doing, but times were changing, and that was understandably a risk the village couldn't take.

Buzzell family continued a working relationship with the village with Uncle Ken and grandsons Nate and Corey working there through the years. Ken drove like Pappy did, and Nathan raised and trained the team Eddie and Henry.

Ken and his team

Eddie and Henry with Nate

Corey and Nathan at OSV

THE ARTIST, THE FARMER, THE HUNTER, AND THE GOOD GUY

Guns for General Washington

His last big event was a reenactment of the Knox Trail. During the Revolution, General Knox brought ammunition from Fort Ticonderoga, New York, to Boston, where General Washington was desperate for munitions in 1776. The 1976 re-enactment were teams of horse in January with sleds dragging canon from northern New York down and across the state of Massachusetts along the Knox Trail (much of Route 9) coming right through the Brookfields and Spencer on to Dorchester Heights. Pappy devised hidden wheels on the sled runners so they would "slide" on bare, plowed roads. It was quite an undertaking in the cold, so he wore his signature bearskin robe and came east with General Knox riding with him all the way into Boston. Reenacting wasn't new to him. He was also instrumental in the reenactment of the Siege on Foster Hill in West Brookfield. Larry remembers his dad driving a wagon of people meeting Indians at the top of the hill and racing for the fort. The Indians' plan to burn down the fort was foiled by the divine intervention of a sudden rainstorm putting out the fire before it began.

Back to the future

Pappy worked his horses for the City of Worcester, keeping the hay mowed around the reservoirs. He trailered Tom and Jill, his team of bay Belgians, and worked every day with them hitched to an old-style horse-drawn mowing machine. Horses were less polluting than tractors near the water. They were a good, steady team, but when the cutter bar hit a low-hung bees nest, they were frantic with biting bees and got to thrashing about. The mowing machine has a long pole that goes between the two horses and connects to a neck yoke where traces connect front to back to the whiffle tree. As the swarm of bees attacked them, the horses reacted to get away, and Tom bucked up, getting his back leg over the pole and breaking it. What was left of the pole went down jabbing into the ground. As the horses bolted forward, it acted as a catapult, throwing Dad into the air over the horses. Why he wasn't killed is a miracle, but he was terribly banged up with broken ribs and bleeding profusely from the blood thinner meds he was taking. Any other team would have bolted, but he managed to get up and get Tom and Jill back to the truck. By the time they got him to the hospital, he was in shock and went into cardiac arrest, but being the die-hard Yankee he was, he pulled through. For a while, Russ took over while he recuperated, and Russ had a similar experience hitting a bees nest. He had gotten off the rig and was unclogging the cutter bar when the bees started swarming, and the horses took off to get away. Fortunately, he was behind the rig or he would have been seriously injured from the cutter bar. The horses only went to the water's edge and stopped, but he said it was pretty amazing to watch the machinery go so fast as they ran off. He caught up to them, and they completed the day's work. Then, we lost Mom after forty-six years of married life together. Weeks later Dad suffered a heart attack, and he retired from working for the city. After that Uncle Ken took over the job from Russ.

Tom and Jill circa 1978
Photo by Jack Swedberg

Uber Sam

As Pappy got older, his eyesight started failing, as happens to us older folk. He was bound and determined to keep driving, but when we brought him to the registry, he failed the exam, and they would not renew his license. He thought he would drive anyway and told our town cops he would just drive around town, but they had to tell they couldn't let him do even that. So Pappy decided to rig an old riding lawn mower to drive. His vision was so bad he asked his friend Chaney to help him fix it. Chaney was working on the mower when Larry drove up the driveway passing by them within a few feet, and Pappy asked him who it was. Chaney in shock answered, "John, that's your son!" Chaney realized he had no business even driving the mower on the road and told him that the mower wasn't anything he could fix, too far gone. That didn't stop Pappy. After that he resorted to hitching up Sam, a dark seal-brown pony we had to a little four-wheel buggy and drove him all over. Thank God for Sam because he was street-smart and nothing upset him, so we knew he was as safe as he could be with him. Sam knew the way home and all the stops along the way. Friends along his route would come out with carrots or a pail of water and chat while Sam rested a bit, and then they would be on their way again. At home Pappy would employ one of the kids to unhitch Sam and put up the harness and wagon.

The man, the myth, the legend

Dad passed away on April 27, 1988. He chose to die like he lived, on his terms. His declining health caused him to be repeatedly hospitalized. On one trip, the EMTs were preparing to load him in the ambulance. Pappy wanted his bright-red down jacket on. The EMT tried to explain to Pappy that he couldn't wear his jacket in the ambulance, but they would keep him nice and warm. Pappy literally took the matter into his own hands. He reached up and grabbed the EMT by the collar of his shirt and told him in no uncertain terms, "I want my jacket on."

Helplessly the EMT looked up at the accompanying officer for guidance, and he was told, "I guess I would let John wear his jacket."

At the hospital in his frustration over his health, he asked Aunt Mabel, visiting him before her shift as a nurse, "When is this going to get better?" She answered him honestly, telling him it wasn't going to get better. He responded with "Well, then I might as well die." And he did. That night. His funeral was a special tribute to him as Uncle Ken drove his team hitched to a flatbed wagon that Jack painted up special for the occasion to carry his casket to the cemetery. It was a beautiful procession as we all walked behind.

Pastor Dave said at his funeral, "I can just imagine John driving a chariot of white horses showing God *how it's done!*"

April 1988

The angel answered me, "These are the four spirits of heaven, going out from standing in the presence of the Lord of the whole world. The one with the black horses is going toward the north country, the one with the white horses toward the west, and the one with the dappled horses toward the south. When the powerful horses went out, they were straining to go throughout the earth. And he said, "Go throughout the earth!" So, they went throughout the earth.

—Zechariah 6:5–7

THE ARTIST, THE FARMER, THE HUNTER, AND THE GOOD GUY

Baby John and Florence

Eight-year-old John

Dad

John and his sisters

They couldn't afford a pony   Eighteen-year-old John

John, 1929   John, 1980s

Mom

June 27, 1910–October 18, 1978

Hazel and Roland

Hazel, Mom, Gramma. As I started writing about Mom, I realized how little I knew about her. As her daughter-in-law, she was such a blessing to me, loving and accepting me into the family without hesitation. I observed her devotion to her children and grandchildren, and she was the model of patience but held high standards and expectations. She passed away only eight years after I became a Buzzell, but there are sweet memories of her I will cherish forever. To this day I think of her and try to be the mother-in-law to my children's spouses she was to me.

Hazel Arlene Leach was born on the family farm in Westmoreland, New Hampshire, on July 27, 1910. She was the daughter of Arthur and Bertha (Atherton) Leach with an older brother, Roland, and younger sister, Dorothy. The family moved to Spencer, probably because of Atherton family living there. Mom went to Wire Village schoolhouse, growing up at the Leach Farm on Hastings Road. I didn't get to meet them, but what I heard from the brothers were the Leach and Atherton families were really good people, hardworking, kind, and honest, and Mom was just like them. In 1938 Grampa Leach lost most of his herd to tuberculosis when the government was testing for it. The government gave him $25 per cow disposed of for testing positive. It wasn't nearly enough to recover his milk business, especially after the hard times of the depression and stock market crash.

Sidenote about the Leach family farm in Westmoreland. There was a large brush fire on the farm. On the tracks that went through the farm, a train hauling tanker cars with kerosene was stopped because of the fire. To prevent an explosion, they shot holes in the tanker to release the kerosene. The kerosene soaked into the ground, polluting the well, poisoning Hazel's aunt.

Ladies and gentlemen

There was a time when women were ladies and men were gentlemen. Mom was always a lady, not as in a high society way, but in character. As I look at what is happening in our society, we have fallen short of teaching our youth the value of character. Seldom did she raise her voice, but when she did, it was well worth paying attention. When John and Hazel were courting and yes, that was a real thing, Hazel expected to be treated like a lady. Story has it that the first time John went to kiss her, she made it clear in no uncertain terms as she took hold of his hands to prevent their wandering, told him, "You may kiss me, but you may not touch me." She had boundaries. and she intended to guard those boundaries as ladies should. Boundaries can also be respect in the way you speak to someone using proper language, and

John and Hazel

THE ARTIST, THE FARMER, THE HUNTER, AND THE GOOD GUY

there were boundaries you didn't cross when speaking to a lady, elders, children, or those in authority, like teachers, policemen, and employers. Today the *f* word is a normal part of language, but it wasn't always that way. Your character is showing when you include that in your vocabulary. It was true then as it is now. Men were considered scoundrels if they were to lay a hand on a woman or child, and society treated them as such. Brothers were taught never to hit your sister or any girl *no matter what*, and that translated into mature relationships that women were to be respected and protected. As women today strive for equality, I think that equality has caused the loss of respect for women in today's culture. Now she is just one of the boys.

John, Hazel, and Dana

John and Hazel were married November 18, 1931, and went on to celebrate forty-six years together. It was a small wedding, just four people. Dana Andrews was the best man, and after the pastor told John he could kiss his bride, Dana said "I'm the best man. I get the next one!" and surprised Hazel by spinning her around and planting on a quick congratulations kiss. They started out married life living in a little portion of a farmhouse, and John milked the cows to help pay the rent. Mom loved her children equally, different but equally. She read a lot to the kids, having a collection of Golden books for that purpose. She loved fall and picnics in the orchard and baking pies.

As told by Russ

If we are good, it is because of Mom. She never really hugged us or told us she loved us but we just knew how much we were loved. She was always there for us. She was the most caring person. Mom always made sure we were well fed, and we always had clean clothes. She had meals at five o'clock, but if for some reason we weren't at the table, she would make sure we had something to eat. She always had time to listen to us, and if we were ready to listen, she had wise advice. We had complete freedom, but we knew what she expected of us, and we loved and respected her enough to live up to those expectations. On the other hand, we didn't have much time to be bad.

Politically speaking

Hazel had strong political views. She was very conservative, but she was very respectful even if she wouldn't vote for someone. She was very upset when Kennedy won but grew to love him. It wasn't uncommon to talk politics around the table, but there was never any hatred, just an exchange of ideas to make our country better. However, I remember watching a politician on TV, and she quietly uttered her opinion and then slapping a hand over her mouth apologized for being disrespectful.

Woman of her word

Mom didn't make biscuits for good reason. Pappy had Chaney and Charlie at the house helping with something. It was suppertime, and Pappy made the usual last-minute invitation to them to "come to supper." There was plenty of food, but the biscuits were a little hard. The men had been drinking a little and started making fun and tossing the biscuits back and forth around the kitchen. After they left, she adamantly told Dad she would never make biscuits again. And she never did.

High expectation (as told by Russ)

I was not a good student. I didn't care. I got my report card, and there were several F's. I didn't think too much about it and gave it to Mom. I was going out to the barn to do chores, and she followed me right out there. She was sooo upset and yelling at me. She told me she was so disappointed in me and knew I could do better. I *had* to do better, or I would never amount to anything! I was really surprised she would be that upset, but I guessed I better pay attention and at least try to do better! She made me realize how important education was to her, how important I was to her!

THE ARTIST, THE FARMER, THE HUNTER, AND THE GOOD GUY

I hate Lauton

Haying is a *wait, wait, hurry up* process. You wait for it to grow, wait for just the right weather, and then hurry to get it cut, raked, and baled before rain would come to spoil it. It typically took two to three days to cut, cure, rake, and bale. Rained-on hay would mold and lose nutrients, so it would be worthless as feed, and with the cost of equipment, fuel, and manpower, you did everything possible to make it come out right. One night they were getting hay. It had probably been a long day of raking and baling in the hot sun, and as often was the practice, neighboring friends and farmers were helping to bring in the hay before bad weather rolled in, or maybe just because there was more hay to rake and bale the next day. Leaving it in the field would only put off the inevitable, and if you had the help, "Let's get her done, boys" was the mantra, and all hands were on deck. We often co-opted with other farm families when many hands were needed, and like the old saying, many hands make light work. When it came to haying, many hands were a Godsend, and it was with them one night, we were able to get in 1,100 bales! (Calculate 1,100 times 60 pounds!) The tractor pulled the baling machine that would pick up raked hay, compacting it into bales and pushing them out the back, landing ten to twenty feet apart depending on how thick the hay had grown. Kids were assigned to roll bales together in a pile. Creating piles made it easier to pick up as the truck wound around the field. The older and stronger walked from pile to pile, meeting the flatbed truck at each pile to throw the bales up to another strong one stacking in the back of the truck. Stacking was an important skill. Bales are three to four feet long, about eighteen-inch square weighing in from sixty to eighty pounds, and needed to be placed together like a big 3D puzzle. Of course, they weren't all perfect to fit and had to be stacked in a way to keep them from falling off the truck on the way back to the barn from wherever the field might be. If not packed right, it could collapse and roll of the truck, and no one was happy about restacking the truck. When nearby it was a treat to sprawl ten to twelve feet up high on top of the load, holding it all together for the ride back to the barn. No seat belts there!

Larry was just a little guy of about four, maybe younger, and keeping company with the big guys, his job was mainly to stay out from underfoot. I guess he wasn't doing such a great job at that because long about dark, Loten tossed him into the cab of the truck. Loten (to Larry who couldn't say Loten, it was Lauton) had just missed him tossing a bale. Keeping an eye out for the little moving target was stressful and slowing down the job. It was late and hot. Everyone was probably tired, hungry, and tempers being tested just a little. Larry didn't like it one bit, insulted he was relegated to the cab particularly being tossed through the open truck window, but youth in that day didn't argue with their elders, and he just sat pouting quietly until he got back to the house.

Mom and Larry

Back at the house he stomped into the kitchen on the way to his room to lick his wounded pride, making the angry statement to Mom, "I hate Lauton!" but she was having none of that.

"You come right back here and sit down!" she commanded urgently but calmly. Grudgingly Larry returned, plopping in a chair as she started her questions. "Now tell me why you don't like Loten."

So hoping to gain support to prop up his grievance, he answered, "He threw me in the window of the truck."

"And why did he do that?"

"Because I was in the way, and he threw a bale and almost hit me!"

"So you don't like him because he doesn't want you to get hurt?" She looked him in the eye and continued, "So you are angry because Loten was watching out for you?" She waited, but he couldn't answer. "So you are mad at Loten because he cares about you?" She didn't expect an answer. How do you argue with Mom's logic? Such a wise mother. We should all be so wise.

THE ARTIST, THE FARMER, THE HUNTER, AND THE GOOD GUY

Running away (as told by Larry)

I loved going places with my dad. Pappy would always stop somewhere to get some kind of treat, and I particularly like root beer and Hostess snowballs [still does]. One day when I saw Dad taking off, I was so disappointed he hadn't sought me out to take me with. Heartbroken, I ran into the house to ask Mom where he was going. Mom didn't give me the answer I wanted to hear, and now I was angry. Indignantly I announced, "I'm running away." Mom didn't seem too concerned.

She said, "Well, you will probably get hungry, so let me fix you a sandwich." And proceeded to make a couple peanut butter sandwiches, wrap them up, and put them in brown paper bag for me. I took my bag, marching out the back door up to the top of the hill behind the house. It was quite a walk for me because I was still a little guy, and when I got to the top of the hill, looked around, and decided I didn't have anywhere else to go. So I sat down, looked out over the farm, and ate my sandwiches. I guess home wasn't such a bad place after all. Mom knew a sandwich would help and was all I would need to change my mind.

School truants

Mom also had an interesting way of dealing with us playing sick to avoid going to school. If we tried to pretend we were sick or wanted to sleep late, she would tell us that was okay, but we couldn't get out of bed all day. We had to stay in bed all day! So we had to really be sick because staying in bed for little boys was worse than going to school. As we got older, we tried to get out of going to school by insisting we didn't feel good. She would give us that look and say, "You just milked fifty cows and now you're telling me you don't feel good enough for school?" Darn! Her wisdom had no bounds.

"Oh shit!" (as told by Larry)

When I was about eight years old, I came in the back of the house into the kitchen and saw Dad driving off through the window. I asked Mom, "Where is Dad going?" and she answered, "Uptown."

I was beyond disappointed because he always took me wherever he went. How could he leave me? I expressed my disappointment with, "Oh shit!" It was a very bad choice of words, and timing was even worse because Mom was holding a broom. She came after me with that broom and drove me under the daybed. "I'll have none of that language in this house, young man!" I have to say I knew better, but Mom made sure I'd think twice before I said it again.

The insurance salesman

Mom was more devoted to her children and grandchildren than anyone I ever knew. Her loyalty, support, and most likely prayers were a lifeline every child needs, even grown-up kids. Everyone needs insurance, at least that's what we have been trained to believe. Hard to think, but we had no insurance when Larry and I were first married, and when we did get insurance, it didn't cover much. We paid about $1,100 to birth our babies in the hospital and paid monthly installments in time for the next one to be born. Life insurance was little more than a savings plan, but insurance salesmen would give their spiel of how we couldn't live without it. This particular guy could see that the family was living little more than hand-to-mouth, and when he realized Larry was the last boy on the farm, he wasn't very complimentary on what he considered his work ethic and critically accused him, "If you cared more, you could be a better farmer." By this time the farm and equipment were old, and although running, there were new, bigger, and better that would have made a huge difference in the workload but way beyond their means. Boston had also regulated impossible demands. Costs to update were prohibitive. Larry worked his butt off putting in easily eighty hours every week, seven days a week with little time off, and it wasn't cushy work either. Besides the milking, there was planting and harvesting, repairs and maintenance, and what many don't think of was heating that big farmhouse with wood. It took about twenty cords of wood to keep the wood furnace in the cellar going and a smaller box stove in the kitchen too. Cutting and hauling from the woodlot, splitting, and then stacking it in the cellar after throwing it down was a full-time job in itself. Thankfully family and friends often helped out, but then there was keeping those fires going day and night. Many were the times after collapsing on the couch after late-night chores Pappy would admonish him to, "Keep the fires going, boy." Anyway, this night Mom was furious with that salesman and none too happy with Pappy after this criticism. Coming to Larry's defense after the salesman left, she admonished Pappy, "How could you sit there and let him say those things about your son! He cares more and works harder than any boy I know!"

Chivalry is not dead

Mom and Dad never displayed a huge amount of public affection, especially in later years. Dad was pretty much crippled up with arthritis. Didn't walk well even with a cane, but he drove her to do her grocery shopping and waited patiently in the car for her. One day at the IGA, Mom came out with her cart, and loading the bags into the car, she accidently bumped the car next to them. The young man in the car became irate even as she apologized. Much younger than her, he was totally disrespectful, getting out of his car and making a terrible scene. "Get in the car, Hazel," John demanded. Calling the man over to his window, he beckoned him to come closer as the man spewed forth vulgarities. As the man bent over at his window, cursing and swinging at him, Dad grabbed the neck of his shirt, pulling him inside, and rolled up the window. As the man struggled to remove his head from the window, Dad smacked him a few times and let him know that his behavior was unacceptable. I think he even started his ignition to drive home his message. He did however roll down the window before taking off, mainly due to Mom's adamant persuasion. As Mom told me this story, I was just imaging the scene. I can't imagine what a judge would say if this young whippersnapper pressed charges, but nothing ever came of it. And how could he admit he was bested by a crippled old man protecting his wife to anyone. The most impressive act of chivalry I can think of.

The right path

Mom wasn't terribly outspoken about her faith, but getting to know her, I observed the quiet relationship she had with God. She loved Jesus, and her favorite song was "What a Friend We Have in Jesus." I have Larry's church cradle roll, and I'm guessing she did her best to steer her kids in the right direction. Larry remembers going to church with her every Sunday. Reverend Packard was getting ready for retirement, and church attendance was waning, but Mom continued faithfully attending, bringing her children with her. Pastor Packard came to the house one day carrying his antique 1901 bolt-action single-shot .22 rifle. He asked Mom, hoping she didn't mind, if he could give it to Larry, saying, "I don't know anyone else I would rather give this to." Think of it! A pastor giving a twelve-year-old boy a rifle! Times sure have changed.

A Diane memory

My parents sent me to Sunday school, and later I was baptized and confirmed. It was pretty meaningless at the time. I didn't understand what I was doing or what it all meant. My mother told me all good people went to heaven, and I just guessed that all good people did these things and should do what I was told. Mom Buzzell didn't drive, and I became her ride to church. It took time, but eventually I learned there's a lot more to heaven and faith than just being a good person. I learned that not all people go to heaven. Good, bad, or anywhere in between can go to hell. Yup. I was on the path to hell. That realization came the summer of '78. Some people have a great salvation story with an awesome prayer, but when I pondered the question *How do I get to heaven and not go hell?* I just knelt on the floor with my children as they played with their blocks and toys around me and prayed to Jesus. I told him I didn't know what to say or if I was saying the right thing or doing it the right way, but I wanted to live forever with him, and I couldn't do it on my own. From that day on Jesus has walked beside me, leading me, guiding me in his ways. It has been a journey, and although there had been many who planted seeds, I thank God especially for putting Mom in my path. Although I drove her to church, it was Mom who brought me to the Lord. It was only three months later the Lord took Mom home to be with him. That night we woke for no reason and lay in the darkness listening. Suddenly, the phone rang, breaking the silence. It was Dad telling Larry Mom was gone. He didn't understand and asked, "What do you mean? Where did she go?" The shocking truth was she had died. It was an unexpected, devastating heart attack, and the funeral is still just a blur. As we walked into the calling hours, Larry had some last words to say to his mom, and looking at the body lying in the coffin, he realized it was no longer her but just an empty shell, not his mother. Her spirit had moved on to heaven. Little Stephanie seemed so calm. Larry told her it was okay to cry, but her response was, "Why? She's with Jesus." We had no doubt she was in heaven but missed her so terribly, and heaven seemed so far away. Looking back, she must have suspected her time was near. She did a few things unusual for her, like asking her sons to watch out for Stephanie if anything happened to her and eating a much larger meal than usual for her that night. She told Stephanie she was tired and needed a rest. Uncle Wendell believed she knew, but none of us had any reason to believe there was anything wrong. That first Sunday after the funeral, I walked into church and stood staring numbly at that long pew where I would have to sit by myself. Thankfully, Uncle Wendell saw me as I stood in the aisle hesitating and quickly came to sit with me. It felt really lonely without her, but it is such a comfort knowing we will meet again someday. If you haven't accepted the gift of salvation Jesus offers, don't wait. Do it now because you don't know when it will be too late. We all have sinned and need Jesus to get us to heaven, or the alternative is separation from him and your loved ones for your future. Keep it simple. Believe in him and have faith in his work on the cross to forgive your sins, and he will do the rest. Let the Holy Spirit work through you to grow you in faith, and Jesus will be right there walking with you all the way.

> She speaks with wisdom, and faithful instruction is on her tongue. She watches over the affairs of her household and does not eat the bread of idleness. Her children arise and call her blessed; her husband also, and he praises her: "Many women do noble things, but you surpass them all."
>
> —Proverbs 31: 26–29

Mom

Dorothy, Roland, and Hazel

Visiting Colorado

Mom, Dad, and Larry Bill

Mom and Janice

Gramma, Tiny, Joe, and Jim

Gramma loved the little ones

Gramma and Jalna

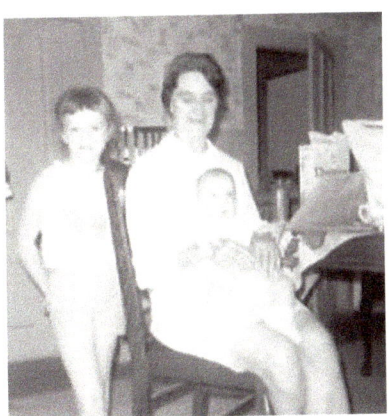
Gramma with Jim and Christy

Our Sister Jan

November 4, 1936–August 11, 2013

Janice was a wonderful sister, daughter, mother, friend. Generous and thoughtful, funny, intelligent, and a great storyteller, which seems to be a family trait. At the time of this writing, she has passed and is dearly missed. She was smart, graduating near the top of her class with good grades all through school. Although she didn't ride horses on the farm   much, she was a good rider. As a little girl, she liked paper dolls and loved to read. She was the only girl in the family of boys. When Mom was expecting the fifth and final child, Jan prayed with Mom for a sister, but they got Larry, so I guess God wanted her to be the rose among all those thorns. She was beautiful. So beautiful she was once mistaken for Elizabeth Taylor in an airport. She loved her family, her girls, and her grandchildren.

At twenty, she married Robert Pixler with a wedding at John Ingalls place. It was a small wedding, just the family. Her new husband, Red, as he was best known, had been in the Marines with brother Ralph. His family was from Colorado, and he took her home to Denver until their marriage ended, and she came back to Massachusetts to live near her family several years later.

She was opinionated politically, a Kennedy Democrat, which is almost Republican these days. One story at a party, Ralph sharply warned Larry before Jan got there to *not* talk politics, and we all knew how tough that would be for Larry. Later when someone asked, "Who you going to vote for?"

Ralph didn't hesitate a second and piped up, "Bush." Larry gave him the hairy eyeball, and Ralph quickly changed the subject before much debate got going.

Larry later said to Ralph, "You told me not to talk politics, and there you go right off the bat blurting it out."

And Ralph responded, "I know. I don't know what I was thinking!"

Yes, she was opinionated, but aren't we all? It's a free country, for now anyway. But despite her political views, Larry said of her that Jan always made you feel welcome, even if you were Republican.

Jan was well-known for her tag sales. For years she lived on Route 9 in Brookfield, which was the perfect place to sell her wares. She would go to out-of-the-way tag sales and flea markets and find things at

Christy and Jan

dirt-cheap deals, bring them home, clean them up, and resell. Pretty little dresses for girls and toys every boy would want. It was the bargain basement of Brookfield, and she had regulars who came to check her "new" merchandise regularly. She made extra spending money that way and always had something perfect for everyone. She was the epitome of the personal shopper.

History isn't always pretty. This is difficult to write, but I am sure she would want her story to be told, to be remembered, to give others hope. We all have faults and weaknesses, and Jan would be the first to admit her struggle with alcoholism. There were the dark days with heartbreaking memories, but with the help of AA and the grace of God, Jan overcame the demon in the bottle. It was not easy. It took great strength.

Jan with Collen, Jake, and Brandon

In the early days of recovery, I remember getting a call from her. She had been doing so well for quite some time, so this was unexpected to hear her say, "I need a ride to detox." We picked her up, and she slurred, "I don't know what I was thinking. It was just a little nip I found under the sink. I didn't think it could hurt, but as soon as it went down, I knew I was in trouble." I believe that was the last time she drank, and for over thirty years she sponsored others in AA and was outspoken on how to help those in the battle. Her sense of humor kicked in as she regained her driver's license, calling the family and singing, "I'm on the road again." When Jan was diagnosed with her cancer, the family came to her appointment for the proposed treatment. When I say family, we

Stepahnie and Jan

THE ARTIST, THE FARMER, THE HUNTER, AND THE GOOD GUY

filled the room and surprised the doctor as we crowded in, standing room only all around her. The news wasn't good, and she told me later after making the choice not to seek treatment that she wasn't giving up. She just wanted quality time with her family rather than a long, drawn-out wasting away. She didn't want to be remembered that way. We didn't anticipate how quickly the cancer would take her, and maybe she didn't either, expecting some months of life at least, but it was only thirty days before she went home to Jesus.

Siblings

Every life has its dark and cheerful hours. Happiness comes from choosing which to remember.
—an Amish Proverb

Who's who?

Family

When I joined the family there were so many who would come and go it was hard to know who they were and how we were related, who belonged to whom. So this chapter gives you a little insight on that fact. When I say a little, I mean just a beginning. I am still discovering more family through the memories, how we are connected and met more family through the writing of this book.

Brothers and sisters

    Ralph married Mabel (Tucker).
    They have Joseph and James. Joseph and Tina have Catharine. Jim and Christine have Sam and Carley.

THE ARTIST, THE FARMER, THE HUNTER, AND THE GOOD GUY

Pictured here with Mabel, Aunt Mabel, Joe, Ralph and Jim.

Janice and Red's (Robert) girls are Christy, Colleen, and Stephanie. Colleen has Jake and Brandon. Christy and Stephanie have the cutest dogs.

Janice, Christy, Colleen, and Stephanie

Russ is a great brother and an awesome uncle to all his nephews and nieces.

Jack and Sheila's girls are Renee and Michelle. It's hard to count all the kids Renee has had because she gives them up at the end of every school year. (She's a kindergarten teacher). Chelly and Dave have Thomas, Andrew, and Marie.

Larry and Diane have Jalna, Nathan, and Corey. Jalna and Arthur Talbot have John, Mike, Lynnea, and Logan. Nathan and Kelly have Brooke. Corey and Jess have Seth, Deacon, and Gavin.

THE ARTIST, THE FARMER, THE HUNTER, AND THE GOOD GUY

Visiting Grampie and Grammie Leach (as told by Larry)

I always liked visiting Grampa and Grammie Leach. They were soft-spoken, down-to-earth people. I never heard them raise their voices. Dad would sit and visit Grampie in the living room, bringing him a small flask of whiskey that he would slide discreetly into his jacket pocket. Mom would sit in the kitchen to visit with Grammie. Sometimes I would take a nap on Grammie's bed. It was a small farmhouse with a beautiful garden surrounded by a perfect stone wall out back. I would sit on the stone wall and chew on rhubarb picked from Grammie's garden. The house was always dark with the shades down so it wouldn't hurt Grammie's eyes. There was a huge map on the wall over the couch, and I would stand on the couch, leaning over the back to look at it. There were animals in each state, bears in Maine, elk in Montana, bison in Wyoming, and fish in Florida, etc., and I was fascinated by it, drawing my finger over it, pointing where we were on the map. Grampie one day took it off the wall, rolled it up, and gave it to me, and I still have it today. There was always tall glasses of fresh orange juice and pink and white coconut-covered marshmallow cookies, and after, Grammie would let me play the old victrola. It was tall with a cabinet on the bottom holding a stack of records each a quarter inch thick. Above the cabinet held the horn the sound came out of, and on top was the turntable with a hinged cover. I would wind up the crank handle, and squeaky tunes would sound out of the big horn. There were funny old-fashioned comedy songs, and my favorite was "Don't stop me! Don't stop me! My wife is sick! She ate too many cucumbers. You going to get the doctor? No, I'm going to get more cucumbers!"

Down in the barn was a basketball hoop, actually a five-gallon can with the bottom cut out nailed to the wall. Originally the can had a bottom, and you would have to climb a ladder to get the ball out when you made a hoop. Somewhere along the way someone thought to cut the bottom out to make it easier to play. It was probably about the time they exchanged the peach basket for a net in regulation play.

I think I was only eight or nine, but I remember Grammie being sick and Mom going over to take care of her sometimes with Aunt Marie. I don't remember their funerals. When Grampie and Grammie passed away, the Leach farm was sold. Uncle Roland was Mom's brother and lived with Grammie and Grampie Leach. He came to live in the little red house when they passed. That would have been in the early sixties, and he lived there until he passed on February 7, 1970. He was a hard worker, a quiet man, and stayed to himself most of the time. Mom also had a younger sister, Dorothy (1914–1963), or Aunt Dot as we knew her. She was married to Donny (or Earl) Lavigne and had three children, Donny, Beverly, and Sonny. Like other relatives who didn't live nearby, we didn't see much of them and sadly have lost track of them.

Just a sad sidenote: Back in the fifties, Arthur Leach's cow fell through the ice and was later found behind where Charlie's Diner is today.

Maine roots
A Diane memory

When we sold the cows and before Larry went to work at his new job, we took a trip to Maine with Mom and Dad. Dad didn't want to be there to see the cows leave, and a trip to Maine was a good diversion. It was early spring, and heading north meant we would see snow when we got there. There was no snow in Massachusetts, and crocus and spring flowers were popping out all over, but in Maine the snowbanks were so high it was like going through a tunnel, higher than we could see over. We went to visit various families in Sherman Mills. Every place we went was unannounced, but we were welcomed, and they just set more places at the table for us. We visited with Aunt Barb and Uncle Elisha, and they had a little home over a little country store next to a river. I remember their floors were spotless, so shiny, and she made prayer cake for us. They had a bathroom but encouraged us to use the outhouse off the kitchen. There was a short wooden walkway, and the view through the two holer was the river about twenty feet below. Never would that pass today! Aunt Barb was a minister of a small church, and the service was really different than anything I had been to. They sang choruses and were definitely in the spirit. It was before I had become a Christian, and it was probably one of those seeds planted that would take root as I attended church with Mom. We saw the old school Pappy went to and the old homestead. It was like walking back in time. Elisha complained about some kids egging a car, and when we asked if they called the police, he shook his head, saying, "We don't have any police." They handled all that stuff themselves and only called the state police if there was something really bad.

Dad is third from the right in the back row.
Taken in front of the school house. There's
probably sisters and cousins in this too!

Larry remembers visiting Maine as a child, and all the families had a bunch of kids. Six kids were a small family. The kids were all well-mannered, and everyone seemed content although they had next to nothing. No toys and TV or fancy clothes and shoes. When their parents said it was time for bed, they didn't talk back, just went to bed. Breakfast was early and substantial with smell of homemade bread waking you in the morning, and everyone pitched in to get chores done.

Gramma Buzzell Rockwell (as told by Larry)

I didn't know Gramma Buzzell well because we didn't go to Maine often. That was such a long trip to northern Maine, but I do remember her coming to stay with us sometimes. Grampa Buzzell was quite a bit older than her and passed away before I ever met him. Gramma had remarried by the time I knew her. Grampa Rockwell was quiet and low-key, which was a rather odd match for Gramma. Even at her age she had a strong, outspoken personality. You didn't mess with her, but I was fascinated by her down east Maine accent. I remember asking her one day where my dad was, and she responded, "Don the rud apiece." and not really knowing what she meant. Once when she was visiting, she had an argument with Esther. She had been doing a spoon dance (using spoons to make rhythm) in the kitchen and making a little too much noise. Esther came downstairs and asked if they could hold the noise down a bit. Her request, knowing Esther, was probably just a little demanding, and that didn't set well with Gramma. She got mad and told Esther to get her "arse" upstairs. Gramma waited at the bottom of the stairs armed with a broom to slap her if she came back down. Also heard tell how back in the day in northern Maine, the menfolk would go off to the logging camps, while the women left at home were at the mercy of some lowlife who would take advantage of the unprotected women. She met them at the door with a shotgun. Like I said, you didn't mess with Gramma.

These stories may seem a little harsh, but Daisy Dunbar became a wife and mother at the tender age of sixteen. If I have it right, she was on her own when Ralph Erastus Buzzell, thirteen years her senior took pity on her and married her to give her a home. She raised eight

THE ARTIST, THE FARMER, THE HUNTER, AND THE GOOD GUY

children at a time and place when there were no maternity wards, supermarkets, or running water. It was this strong personality that gave her the strength to persevere. She was a great cook, and chances are she killed and gutted her own chicken for supper and raised and put up vegetables to feed her family. She most likely gathered her eggs and milked the cow, as well as made substantial meals for her family on a woodstove, not to mention keep her brood warm in the cold northern Maine winters while her husband was off to the logging camps. She kept an immaculate home with a broom and scrub brush and probably washed her clothes with homemade soap on a washboard. I'm willing to bet she knew how to use the shotgun and could use it more than intimidate when it came to protecting her family. I admire her abilities and fortitude, and she obviously passed on that *can-do* attitude to her children. She was always kind to her grandchildren, and when she visited Massachusetts, she got along well with all the family. Sadly, as she got older, she suffered from dementia, and her last days were in a rest home, where she acted like a little child hiding candy in her blankets and under her pillow.

Buzzell cousins

There are lots of cousins, but the closest cousins were probably close because they lived in the little red house on the farm. There was Uncle Wendell, Dad's brother, and Aunt Marie, then Wanda, Bobbie, Susan, Mike, and June. Larry spent a lot of time at the little red house playing with the cousins. He remembers well all the kids in that little house, and at suppertime, he would get ready to leave, and Aunt Marie would say, "Where are you going? Sit down." There was always room for one more. Then when he did leave, they would see those white sneakers running up Tucker Hill Road heading for home

Bob, Mike Susan, Wendell, Marie, June, and Wanda

till he disappeared by the barn. And etched in his memory is the pancake contest with Uncle Wendell, wolfing down pancakes to see who could eat the most the fastest. Uncle won 21 to 19. Larry had his fill of pancakes, and to this day he doesn't want another. Cousin Bob was a couple years younger. They played whiffle ball behind the little red house, camped on Buck Hill, and had hot dogs over campfires. They played army and would "take Buck Hill," running from rock to rock, hiding from imaginary enemies. It was with Bob that Larry found the legendary white rock, and they were sure it was from outer space. (That white rock was moved to grace our front yard, preserving it for posterity.) At one point Bobbie and Larry thought it would be fun to fire rocks at each other. Bob was on a slope behind the little red house and Larry on the hill by the barn. It was a good distance, and neither one should have been able to fire off a rock that far, but Larry did, hitting Bob in the head. Larry felt really bad, but hello? What do you expect when you throw rocks at each other? When we all grew up and became parents, it was déjà vu watching our kids together.

Greens

Roy Green grew up with the boys, practically lived at the farm, and was best friends with Ralph. He helped on the farm like he was one of us. He was great at running the tractors and especially the bulldozer, packing the corn silage. He also ran the loader when we yearly spent the day cleaning the manure out from under the barn. All the farmers around would come with their tractors and manure spreaders sometimes five, six, or more, and we would spend the day cleaning out and spreading the manure on the fields as fertilizer. Pappy would be kept busy welding because inevitably there would be a rock that would break a spreader and need repair. In the hurricane of '54, Roy's mom lived in the house on East Brookfield Road, and there was a brook that runs between the house and the road. It was like a raging river and washed out the driveway. His mom couldn't get across for any food, and he stood at the edge and threw loaves of bread and tuna so she would have something to eat. Larry remembers being amazed that he could throw a loaf of bread that far! Roy married Cindy, whose father was Ben Pierce. Ben was a cousin of Pappy's, so now Roy was officially family.

Browns

Pat Heath Brown was our cousin. Velma, dad's sister, and Walt Heath were her parents. Russ remembers Pat living with them for a couple years and loved her like a sister. She was always a big help to Mom, and she and Janice were really close, like sisters. They got an apartment in Worcester together and worked at Brown Shoe after graduating school. It is where Janice got shoes for Larry he remembers so well. When Dave Brown was dating her and wanted to marry her, Russ felt like the protective brother. He warned Dave, "You better be good to her." And Dave was very good to her. They had three children, Stephen, Douglas, and Jennifer.

Gerald was Pat's brother. Gerald served in the military and found a German girl, Maria, married and brought her home with him. They had two daughters, Wendy and Kimberly, and a son, Donald. Mom spent many hours with Maria, helping her learn what she needed to become a US citizen.

The Ghize cousins

Aunt Glynes

More family who often visited were Aunt Glynes, Dad's sister, Uncle Jimmy with cousins Donna and Little Jimmy. It was always fun having them, and they enjoyed the freedom the farm offered. Jimmy was a hot ticket and close to Russ. Donna loved picking blueberries and being with her cousins.

They lived in Shrewsbury and were quite traumatized by the tornado of '53 that went through. Donna would hide under the table fearful of coming out whenever there was a thunderstorm. It was understandable considering there was only the cellar hole remaining of the house next to theirs. Little Jimmy walking the street after the destruction came home telling his mom he found a $20 bill on the sidewalk. Aunt Glynes asked him what he did with it, and he replied, "It wasn't mine. I left it there." Some would say that was foolish, but I think he showed good character. Uncle Jimmy owned a car dealership, and both kids got new cars to drive when they got their license. We suspect he was helpful to Dad getting him good deals on cars. I believe the '66 Chevy where Larry proposed to me was from the Ghize dealership. Aunt Glynes was always kind to Mom, taking her shopping whenever she came to visit.

Ingalls

John Ingalls is a cousin of Dad's. His mother was Dad's father's sister, Laura Buzzell Ingalls He served our country as a sniper during WWII in Germany. After he got out of the Army, he was a big help to Dad on the farm during the late forties. He met Ruth, his wife, at the Wilson Farm. Ruth was a victim of childhood polio, a kind and caring person. Both were well liked and enjoyed hosting get-togethers at their home on the lake. Cookouts and boat rides were great memories. Their son was Douglas.

John and Ruth Ingalls

Lanes

Uncle Ken was really our cousin. His mom was Dad's sister, Florence. He and his wife, Aunt Lorrane, moved to Massachusetts with Lori Ann and Ronica about 1978. The other daughters were

THE ARTIST, THE FARMER, THE HUNTER, AND THE GOOD GUY

married and living in Maine, Nancy, Kandes, and Darlene. Ken was an expert woodsman, teamster, and hard worker. Toward the end of his life, he was at a country fair with his team of horses for a pulling event. He suffered a terrible heart attack. The girls called us to tell us they would be removing life support and to let the rest of

the family know. We were shocked and saddened but not for long. The next morning, he woke up wanting coffee and something to eat. As the day progressed, he insisted that he get out of bed against the nurses' wishes. Ken became known as the miracle man recovering with only a small percentage of his heart left and continued to work his team. Those are the tough genes this family is made of.

Darlene, Dennis, Lori Ann, Nancy, Kandes, and Ronica

Tuckers

Tuckers lived up the street on Tucker Hill Road. The family was a staple in town, even the church was known as the Tucker Church, having ancestors who helped found and build it. The kids worked their farm just like the Buzzell boys did, working beside their dad, milking cows by hand, getting hay, and driving tractors. When their barn burned, the Buzzells did what farmers do, helped one another out. The Tucker cows moved to the Buzzell barn, and they milked side by side until they could rebuild. Eventually, it was only natural that a Tucker would one day become a Buzzell, and that was Ralph and Mabel. Joe Tucker, the father, worked at the asbestos factory in town and suffered with asbestosis. One year when he was sick, the Buzzells and Whitmans got the winter wood supply for them, cutting and splitting all they would need to stay warm all winter, and they did it all in one day! It was a regular assembly line with some hauling out wood, some limbing, some on the saw cutting chunks, and others splitting and piling until it was all supplied for the winter. Just being neighborly.

Mabel, Joe, Margaret, George, and Rose
Catharine not pictured

THE ARTIST, THE FARMER, THE HUNTER, AND THE GOOD GUY

If you're here, you're family!

Front: Mark and Richie
Row 1: Jennifer, Renee holding Pam, Ronica holding Jeffrey, Michelle, Grampa and Jake, Jalna, Sue, and Tim, Stephanie
Row 2: Bob, Bette, Becky, Colleen, Christy, Janice, Marie, Larry with Nate
Row 3: Jim, Mabel, Joe, Rich, Mike, Sheila, Wendell, Dave, Pat, Diane
Row 4: Lori and?(peeking from behind) Ralph, Lorrane, Ken, June

Friends Like Family

As you read this chapter, it is meant to help sort out the references to different characters as you read the stories as well as some memories of them. There are so many more than just those listed here that were more than just friends.

Farmers are the most independent people in the world. It is kind of hard to describe relationships in a farm community. They live their lives doing life independent of rules, time clocks, and bosses. There are good friends, but then there is community where even if you aren't close friends, you have respect and a commonality. You may all farm differently, and that's okay. You do it your way. A tractor breaks down and you show up to bale their hay, and they do the same for you. It's much like most families, where you love each other just because you are supposed to, but you are realistic to abilities and personalities. We really couldn't survive without helping each other out. People who weren't farmers didn't understand what farm life is like and would sometimes make complaints out of ignorance. We have been asked why that cow is so noisy calling to her baby in the barn the first few days after she freshens. We let the cow out to pasture with the other cows, but she would stand near the gate and make a terrible racket bellowing. It's called separation anxiety. They get over it like any other mom, just got to give them a little time. Others weren't happy about the smell or cow manure in the road, or even worse the bovine traffic jams as the cows had the right of way to cross the road to pasture. One time we got a complaint at three in the morning because a cow was bellowing and could we please make it be quiet. Larry stumbled down in the dark through the pasture, and the cow was in the midst of calving. Any woman will tell you that you don't shut up when you're giving birth! Moving to the country has perks they hadn't considered. But one neighbor was so forgiving when the cows got out and trampled through their garden with the response to our apology, "That's okay, it happens sometimes." God bless them for understanding!

There were several farms that bordered the old farm. Edwards and Billy Brown's were down Old West Brookfield Road. Tuckers was off to the northwest edge of the property up Tucker Hill Road, and Crawford's bordered to the north the big field behind the house. And Richardson's down Bates Street.

Billy Brown (as told by Larry)

The brook was kind of the line between us and Billy Brown, but we had one cow that crossed that line quite often, grazing on alfalfa on the back side of his hill. He also had a field of really good strawberries and a road side stand where he sold his homemade ice cream. People came from all over for his ice cream. He was good to us kids in that he never minded us fishing in his pond or tramping through his fields. The pond had some pretty serious snapping turtles. We went fishing there one day and had a string of horn pout in the water. We went home for some sandwiches and came back to finish fishing, and when we pulled out the string, all that was left were the heads of our fish. Another time we had spent a hot afternoon rounding up his cows when they got out. Let's say Billy was a little frugal because he rewarded us with an eight-ounce bottle of Coke we had to split between us. Later that night we were sleeping out and decided we needed a late-night snack. Raiding his strawberry patch, we sat in the moonlight eating our fill of strawberries.

A buck for the buckaroo

Billy was a good neighbor and often helped us out. He was there whenever we needed him. He hired Russ to herd his cows to the barn every day at three o'clock. Russ would ride his pony Ned with Lady the dog following to bring in the cows. It got so the cows would see him coming and head for the barn so he didn't have to do much, and Billy rewarded him with an ice cream cone from his stand. It was a pretty good deal especially because Mrs. Brown would meet Russ once a week at the door to give him a silver dollar.

Mrs. Brown needed help once when she fell, and Ralph and Russ went over to help. She insisted on paying them although they really didn't want anything. She gave them each a quarter, which may not sound like much, but that was back when a quarter would pay for more than a gallon of gas, and a cup of coffee was a dime. Billy had an older man as a hired hand, Oscar, and he loved seeing Russ come and would spend some time to pat Ned and Lady. Billy had a big team of black horses he worked his farm with, and his daughter Eileen would ride them, galloping up the road. They were kind of hot, in other words, spirited. Sadly, there was a terrible accident when the horses spooked, running over Oscar and killing him.

Edwards and Colteys

Edward's, formally the Coltey farm, was our visible neighbor across the night pasture. Before Coltey's, Uncle Wendell owned the farm. Larry was friends with Ronnie Coltey, rode the bus to school, played FFA ball, and went fishing with him. Ronnie would say that Larry had it made with the school bus because he could see it coming a mile away while he had to be out at the corner waiting for it.

I'm a dummy (as told by Larry)

Ronnie came to me with a baseball card and wanted to trade this one card for my three shopping bags of cards. I laughed and thought he was crazy. Why would he think one card would be worth dozens in exchange? It was an original Babe Ruth card probably worth thousands today. I was a dummy.

The Edwards bought the Coltey farm in the sixties. Maxi was one of the cattle dealers that came around. If we had a cow or calf to sell, we would call Maxi, and he would give us a price and would haul them off. He served all the farmers, and sometimes, he would stop by when he was in the area just to see if we had anything to sell. This afternoon while he was waiting for Dad to come out, he was making small talk and told me, "There sure are couple of good-looking tomatoes next door."

I guess I was a little naive because I had no idea what he was talking about. I was thinking in my thick head maybe he was referring to their garden with tomatoes and said, "Hannah always has a great garden, and I bet her tomatoes are good-looking," but he was talking about Ellen and Janet. Yup, I was a dummy.

Good Neighbors

Ellen used to say she loved to hear me calling the cows. Early in the morning after putting their feed down, I would call the cows to the barn for milking. Standing in the doorway, I would yell, "Cumboss! Cumboss! Cumboss!" And in the early morning mist, it would echo through the valley. Sounded almost musical. Closest I ever got to singing. When I joined chorus at school, the teacher asked if I could just move my lips.

Ellen and Janet had two brothers, George and Richard. Their father was George as well. Not sure where they were, but Hannah, Mrs. Edwards, asked if we could help unload a trailer truck load of hay. It was no job for just Hannah, who was just a little bit of a woman, although tough and strong, and Richard, so, of course we were willing to help out. There was a hay conveyor we used to move hay, and we had it rigged from the bumper of the truck up to the loft. Russ was on the truck, tossing bales to me to put on the conveyor, and Richard and Hannah were in the loft, taking the bales off and stacking. We were moving right along when Hannah yelled to us to take a break. They invited us to have pizza. Enjoying the meal and conversation, Mr. Edwards was telling a story about seeing the ugliest woman in his life when his sister-in-law just happened to open the door and walked in. He quickly added, "I take that back." The timing was perfect. Of course, it was all in jest, but she didn't know what he was saying or what we were laughing at but was betting it was about her!

George Crawford

What a tangled web we weave. Lilian Crawford was George's mother and lived with George. Lilian was Joe Tucker's sister. So George would be Joe Tucker's nephew, and Ralph married Mabel, Joe's daughter, who would be Lilian's niece and George's cousin, making Ralph a nephew by marriage.

As told by Larry

I was searching the side hill for a new calf. I saw it hiding under a juniper so I jumped on it, and to my surprise, another calf jumped up and took off running. I left the first calf and took after the running calf, chasing it through brush and junipers about a mile until we got to Crawford's farm, where it stopped at a barbwire fence. I tackled it, and we rolled down a banking into a ditch near the road. Just then George Crawford came by with his pickup and stopped. Called to me to throw him in the back, and he gave us a ride home. We were both beat by then. There was no more fight in the calf, and I was so glad I didn't have to lug him all the way back home. Thank God for George!

On the border between Crawford's and Hanson's in the 1940s, rosebushes were planted along the fence line to keep the cows in, like they did in Europe. It worked wonderfully, but today those rosebushes without supervision have spread like weeds invading pasture and woodlands all over the surrounding land.

Hansons

Myrtle Hanson lived next door to Joe Tucker, and her property overlooked our farm. She was George and Stanley Hanson's mother, and Mrs. Bus was her mother, living with Myrtle. Tucker Hill Road bordered the backside of the Hanson Farm on Smith Hanson Road, so family was nearby. Mrytle was a good neighbor, but she had a strong personality and didn't mince words. Myrtle chased Larry and Ralph with a broom once when the cows escaped and trampled her gladiolas. Another time, going by the farm, her car broke down. She marched into the barn where Larry was working and told him her car wasn't running and was parked outside. Larry asked her if he could give her a ride home, and she replied to his ignorance with, "Of course I want a ride. I'm not walking up that hill."

Dad and George Hanson were really good friends. The boys grew up with Davey Hanson, and at the time of this writing, Davey is the only milking farm left in town. Davey might want to thank Pappy for his mom and dad getting married. When George was dating Rose, he would come home late, night after night. One night he was so sleepy, he went into the ditch on the way home. Pappy got the tractor and hauled him out, telling him, "Dammit, George, marry that girl before it kills you!" Larry ran into Davey, and he said he still remembers his father telling them a story way back when (about fifty years ago) how Larry was dating that blonde, and she was wearing a purple minidress for a dinner dance. George isn't speechless often, but I guess he was that night.

There was an understanding between Dad and George. "John, why don't you borrow my rake?" which meant his rake needed fixing, and there was no one else who could fix it better than Dad. It was just a standing joke, when George would come in the house, all the boys would run out the back door in case George wanted them to help him with something. He would race to the door calling after them, "I see you!" Always a good for a laugh. George was also selectman in town for about twelve years. George said you make enemies in politics because no matter what, there's going to be someone who isn't going to agree with your decision, and eventually you will tick off everyone in town at one point or another. I think he spoke from experience. Larry also remembers George as selectman, asking him if we were going to homeschool.

Larry told him, "I suppose you don't like the idea. No one else seems to think we should do it."

And George responded, "Are you kidding? I think the whole town should do it. Would save us a boatload of money!"

When George tore his old barn down, the bats that had a home there had no place to go. The next thing we knew the bats had invaded our attic. We called an exterminator, and he told us the best thing we could do is wait until dusk and watch them exit, and then after dark when they had all flown out, nail flashing over the places they were going in and out. Well, there was unfinished walls around the windows upstairs, and bats were like flying rats. They can squeeze their bodies through cracks, and they had found some tiny cracks around those windows. Larry went up on a ladder nailing flashing while the bats swarmed around him. We sealed off the attic so they couldn't come downstairs until we knew they would all be gone. A week later we went up to find a few dead bats who had been locked inside. As he was searching the floor on his hands and knees for dead bats, Larry looked up to find one sitting upright perched on a table. He didn't expect to come eyeball to eyeball with a bat, so he was so startled by it he jumped back until he realized it was dead.

Hussey

Jean and Julian Hussey with their family, Keith, Susie, and Little Jean, were close family friends. Jean was a precision machinist and made a lot parts for Dad when he needed replacements for whatever he was working on. They also collaborated on a rugged two-wheel horse cart with motorcycle tires. They went on all the trail rides with the horses. Mandell and Sandell were offspring of Sandy, and where Sandy essentially was a Buzzell family member, it made the Husseys extended family. If they weren't at the farm, Buzzells were often at theirs.

As told by Larry

I was at the Hussey home, and Little Jean and I were the only ones at home. She got a phone call from her boyfriend, and he wanted to see her. Without any other way, she got the bright idea to saddle up Mandell and Sandell, and we took off. I was scared to death, but she told me not to worry, that Sandell would follow Mandell anywhere. We galloped down Main Street of Belchertown to where we found her boyfriend. We rested the horses while they chatted, and then with a goodbye kiss we were off for home again.

The Lazariks

The Lazarik family was one of the families who rented the little red house. There was Patsy, Pepper, Pumpkin, and Pat. Pat liked fishing and would take Larry to Doane's Pond to fish. Pat's mom introduced Larry to pumpernickel bread, making sandwiches with Spam and ketchup for them to snack on while fishing. Pat was good friends with Jack, and they often went fishing together. One time at the Quabbin, they were with Louie out in a boat, and it started taking on water. They were bailing and rowing as fast as they could to get back to shore. None of them were great swimmers and probably didn't have life jackets, so they were putting great effort to get back to land. Jack remembers as they came close to shore, Pat jumped from the boat and in his words, "Pat wanted to get back on land so bad I swear he ran on top of the water!" Pat was there the day Larry lost control of their old jalopy coming down the hill and leaped from the ground right up into the dump truck to avoid being hit. Pumpkin and Larry tried dating but never made it past the friend zone.

Sonny O'Day

Sonny would get state jobs working his big bulldozer. One day the track on his bulldozer broke. Besides the cost to fix it, every hour he couldn't work cost him as well. Pappy took his welder rigged potato chip truck right to the job and welded it all back together for him in no time. Sonny wanted to pay him, but Pappy refused any payment, thanking him for all Sonny had done for him over the years. A few weeks later, Larry remembers sitting with Pappy in the kitchen hearing a loud rumble, and lo and behold, there was Sonny unloading his bulldozer. He proceeded to remove several big boulders from the hayfield behind the house. They were in the way, and haying around them was time-consuming, awkward, and took up space where hay should be. When he completed the work, Pappy wanted to pay him, and he said, "You don't owe me nothing, John." It would have been expensive to move those rocks if he hired Sonny, but this is how friends paid it forward. Pappy always told the boys whatever you do for someone will come back to you, and this is one prime example.

Frank Partridge

Frank was quite a character. Little in stature with thick eyeglasses, he always had a pipe in his mouth. He was good with horses and helped out at the farm, just being neighborly. He volunteered to harrow the cornfield across the street from the house, and he set out going round and round but never set the harrow down. Pappy never laughed so hard. Had to be done all over again. He helped Larry a lot with gardening, giving him advice on how and what to plant. He helped us out when we got married, giving us a living room set, tables and chairs, and other sundry household items to get us started. He drove a little pony on the trail rides to Vermont. That pony could be a nasty little thing, but he handled her. Irene and her son, Rick, came on the trail ride with us one year, and when Frank realized her age and she was the mother of Rick, he commented, "By god, you kept well." Irene was so tickled by it she laughed and asked if she was a pickle. When Pappy sold the farm, Pappy bought the farm on Cider Mill, where Frank was renting, so he moved into the little red house. The little red house was a perfect place for him with a barn for his pony and Mumsy his cow. He lived out his days passing away in the little red house.

Phyllis Smith (as told by Russ)

I can't remember a time when Phyllis wasn't at the farm. She was always a friend, like a sister to me. She always wanted to help out. She loved the horses, especially Diamond, and we rode on a lot of trail rides. She had a really great family. Her father ran the pharmacy uptown.

We got a new Case tractor. It had a narrow front end with no power steering, and it would shimmy something awful going down the road. If you hit a bump, it would almost rip the steering wheel out of your hands. It had a hand clutch and a foot clutch, which took some getting used to. Phyllis liked to try everything and wanted to drive that tractor really bad. She talked me into showing her how to drive it, so I did. I got her up on the tractor, and we started off. She was having a terrible time steering it and drove it right into the side of the barn. Course we weren't going fast, but it bent the steering rod. She felt awful. I was afraid Dad would be mad at Phyllis, so I told him I did it partly because it was my fault for letting her drive. Well, Phyllis spoke right up and owned it. She took the blame and insisted it was all her fault. She's a good person. Dad didn't say much and was able to fix the tractor. Her dad did come and want to pay for the damage, but Dad said it wasn't necessary. That wasn't the only time the steering rod was bent. It turned out to be a poor design, and Phyllis was only one of many to bend it.

Phyllis and Dad with Lady

One day Phyllis came to the farm driving a 1938 Buick Roadster with wooden spoke wheels. Dad looked it all over and really liked it. We all got a ride in it. Her father got it somewhere, and from what I guess, she had to really beg to get him to let her take to the farm. Really cool car.

She loved the farm and the family, and she loved to try everything and was always getting me to try new things. She was a lot of fun, but more than that, she cared about people. She took a collection when Rip had his accident, and she just decided to do it on her own. She was just a good person.

John Treadwell

Pappy met John when he worked for John's father, who ran a large chicken farm. He worked there with Billy Bissell and Channey Wamback. Their friendships were created and built while working together tending chickens. John was a big man with a big personality, bigger than life with big opinions. He was a little rough around the edges but a hard worker and solid character. He had oxen and well-known at pulling contests like Spencer Fair, Eastern States, and other country fairs at the time. Larry remembers at one fair where he was pulling his oxen. His team took a long hard pull, and then he let them stop. As he stood there, John asked the judges to let him know when time was running out and just patiently waited beside his team as the crowd watched, wondering what he was doing. As his time ran down, the judge warned him, and he said to his team, "Let's go, boys." The team leaned hard into their yoke and pulled to an impressive win. Those seconds he gave them were the rest they needed to finish the job. Big John was one of Pappy's best friends, so much a friend that when Pappy was at the bank applying for a loan, John came in, and as the bank explained to Pappy, he would need a cosigner. Big John spoke right up and volunteered to co-sign, saying, "I'll co-sign for Buzzell any day."

Chaney Wambach

Chaney was another friend who would drop everything to help out and often at the farm. Working at Treadwell's, he had a little run-in with a rooster. They were sorting roosters to keep, and this one lost out when he bit Chaney, ending up as a reject. Chaney was an expert mechanic and good with cows. He lost his thumb with a cordwood saw but was the best hand milker, faster than anyone even Dad, even without his thumb. Chaney tried all four branches of the military to serve in WWII, but because of his thumb, or rather lack of thumb, he wasn't accepted. He treated kids like people, talked to them like what they had to say was important. When the family toaster bit the dust, Chaney gave them an old toaster he had. This one had also seen better days because Pappy got a shock from it, and his angry reaction was to throw it under the big oak kitchen table. Of course, who shows up but Chaney, and Ralph, just a kiddo at the time, alerted Chaney with, "Hey, Chaney, your toaster is under the table!" No hard feelings, just a good laugh.

THE ARTIST, THE FARMER, THE HUNTER, AND THE GOOD GUY

Whitmans

Loten and Blanche, Ralph, Kent, Forrest (Boydie), and Gloria made up the Whitman family. There were so many times the Whitmans helped us out, and we helped them. So many good times with them as well. They had horses and were part of the Western Riders, having gymkhanas at their farm. Blanche used to make wreaths to sell at Christmas, and Larry remembers helping her go out and collect bags of princess pine for her to make the wreaths. Ralph was one of the judges when Larry won a trophy on a trail ride. Larry asked Pappy if he thought he got it because Ralph was a friend, but he assured him, "Boy, you know Ralph. If he didn't think you deserved it, you wouldn't have got it." Ralph announced that Larry was courteous when passing and helpful to other riders, and that was why he won. During Hurricane Carol of 1954, the water was up to our barn. It washed out upper Tucker Hill Road and Bates Street. We had to go down Tucker Hill Road by the barn to the dirt road to West Brookfield Road to leave the farm. We never saw Canadian geese around here at that time, but during the storm, a Canadian goose got disoriented. We had a wild game supper with Canadian goose, raccoon, bear, pheasant, and venison, probably other game too. It was a fantastic meal. Always really good food at Whitman's farm.

Whitman Family

The man in the window

The family had been out to a movie and came back after dark. As they drove in the driveway, there was clearly a man in the upstairs window. They were all a little startled by the image, but Dad said it was probably someone from Maine. They had an open-door policy, so anyone who came could go in and make themselves at home, but to reassure Mom, Dad went in to see who it was. He went through the entire house, and it wasn't family from Maine or a friend waiting for them to return. No one was there. Dad couldn't find anyone. It has been suggested whoever it was might have left through the back door, but we will never know who the man in the window was.

Illegal aliens?

It was in the early 1960s. Pappy was in the field behind the house when he saw something really unusual. It went straight up from Tucker's valley and zipped off in lightning speed. He was so alarmed by it he disconnected the rake from the tractor and quickly drove down into the valley looking for more evidence of what on earth it could have been. As he got to the dirt road, Uncle Roland, who lived in the little red house at the time, was standing in the road staring off at the sky.

"Did you see that?" he asked Pappy.

"I saw it! What was it?"

There was no explanation, and there was equally no explanation when Tucker's cows showed up later coming down the road, not from their pasture, dazed and completely milked out. It was the strangest phenomenon, and no one knows how the cows got out or how they came from that direction or who milked them. At a gathering around the campfire, conversation came up about UFOs, and Uncle Walt told Mom, "We don't have anything to worry about because aliens only take the smart ones!" referring to Velma and John. He was cracking a joke about his wife and brother-in-law but not very complimentary to Mom!

Mr. Hubbard

When we moved to the little farm on Cider Mill, there were several strange, let's call them, visits. A variety of people had experiences that couldn't be explained. We called our visitor Mr. Hubbard because back in 1949, Mr. Hubbard had lived in the house, and legend has it he committed suicide with a shotgun behind the barn. Now years later, Larry had come home one night and parked in front of the barn. As he was walking from the car, he got the chills and eeriest feeling someone was watching him. He looked around, and not seeing anyone, he hurried to the house. Only a few nights later, a friend, Mike, told him he had thought he heard someone out by the barn, but no one was there and described those same chills and the feeling someone was watching him. Then Lori swore she saw who she thought was Larry go around the side of the barn. As she followed him around the barn. She got chills and the eeriest feeling like someone was there, but no one was.

Another night Roy was in the kitchen facing the living room door, having coffee with Larry, and asked, "What's Diane up to?" When he answered I was shopping, Roy was puzzled and asked, "Well then, who was that in the living room?" No one!

Our children often ended up in our bed when "the voices" would wake them. I asked little Nathan, about four years old at the time, if he heard the voices, and he said, "Yes, but I tell them to be quiet, and I go back to sleep." Not so with his sister. I wasn't sure if they really heard voices until late one night, I heard the voices. I thought it was the kids playing in bed and went to admonish them to go to sleep, but they were sound asleep.

Our neighbor Richard stayed with Pappy one time when we went away, and all night he heard "them" going up and down the stairs by our bedroom. After that he slept in the recliner in Pappy's room and told us not to ask him to stay in the house again. There were several other instances that were unexplainable, like a cast-iron lamp flying across the room and appearance of a glowing form. At first it was kind of a joke, but now we started taking it more seriously. While renovating we found a baby shoe in the two different walls. I thought they must have been lost in there by mistake, but I learned that in early times, they would put a shoe in the wall to fend off spirits. Guess we should have put those shoes back, but I did one thing better. I walked around the house, praying over it, asking God to take away the spirits and seal them from returning. He did. We never heard from them again. Another early history tradition is that lilacs were planted where someone died. There is a lilac bush to this day out front, and there was another by the little red house too.

Family and friends like family, 1991

A Gathering Place

Working the farm with four boys in the family, the dinner table was a very important place. It was where the family gathered morning, noon, and night. It was a place of fellowship, instruction, a place to draft out plans for the day and assign tasks. Mornings, a small tabletop television from its perch opposite Pappy's seat would be on to inform us of the news of the nation but more importantly—the weather. When WBZ meteorologist Don Kent came on, talk was silenced for the forecast, and Pappy would either agree or reformulate his predictions. We needed the weather predictions for harrowing, planting, and even more importantly when to cut the hay. We needed three days of hot, dry weather to cut and cure the hay to make it palatable. Rained-on hay could mold or at least wash out valuable nutrients that would feed the livestock through the following year. Moldy hay could even make the livestock sick. Much of work was planned around the weather, so Don Kent was an important celebrity on the farm, loved for good weather predictions, and cursed when he was wrong. Seeing a black cloud meant working as fast as we could to beat the rain and get the hay under cover, sometimes driving the truck onto the barn floor as the wind picked up and the first drops of rain would pelt us. It was almost gratifying to race the weather and win.

Every morning there would be a large double boiler with oatmeal to start the day with coffee or cocoa and toast. I'm not sure about the others, but Larry could often polish off half a loaf of bread with breakfast. After chores was a second breakfast, eggs (Ralph's chickens made sure they were fresh) and bacon, ham or Spam, and more coffee or cocoa, sometimes pancakes. Noontime was a dinner. Not a lunch. A lunch was just a snack. By noon they had already put in six to eight hours, and there was still the rest of the day's work to follow. So almost always it was potatoes and meat and plenty of it. Supper was also a large meal, and Mom had it ready at 5:00! You were on time or you missed the meal. She would fix you something later but it wouldn't be supper. Meals were simple, filling, and bountiful. Seconds and thirds meant there were seldom leftovers. There were favorite meals. Mashed potatoes with corn and ground beef was a favorite, sort of like shepherd's pie, but this was a little different in that it was all mixed together. And chicken pot pie!

Mom, Marie, Larry, Wanda, Russ, Jack, Bobbie

Russ always said Mom's chicken pie was the best. When she planned to make this dish, she would simply tell Ralph, "I need a chicken," and he would go out to the henhouse and slaughter it fresh, which we all believe made the difference. As much as we liked her apple pie, it was the scraps of dough she would roll out with cinnamon and sugar that was the treat we all craved. Wednesday was always some kind of Italian dish, but most loved was American chop suey with huge chunks of tomatoes and ground beef. Cream dried beef was also often on the menu piled on top of mounds of mashed potatoes. One of our favorite desserts Mom made was angel food cake with strawberries and whipped cream. While we were still using the forty-quart milk cans to store our milk for delivery, the cream would come to the top, and we

Ralph, Mabel, Hazel, Charlene and Ralph Whitman

could scoop off fresh cream for her to whip, and it was so good. Nothing like it today.

On Saturday night it was a given that Pappy would have mixed up a big pot of baked beans, a special Maine recipe with old-fashioned molasses and salt pork kept in the cellar in a crock of brine. Those beans slow baked all day and seemed to feed an army as friends and relatives knew the standing invitation to come and join in. People came and went as they ate in shifts around the big family table, and some brought their signature dish, like Lorrane's biscuits or Marie's mac and cheese to go with real frankfurters, the kind with skins. There would also be cookies, cakes and blueberry or apple pies, strawberry shortcake, or a carved-up watermelon in season. It wasn't Saturday if you didn't have beans. Sundays always had a big meal, roasts and all the fixings.

A Diane memory

If you were at the farm at mealtime, you were expected to come and eat. I don't know how Mom managed to feed all the people who came and went at mealtime on the farm or how she planned her shopping, but she did an amazing job of it. If you left the table hungry, it was your own fault. Years later after Mom had passed, I remember putting a small chicken in the oven and running to a friend's house for an errand and getting a call from Larry, "Dad wants to know if we have enough for company?" I explained it was just a small chicken, thinking he would understand that meant "no," but getting home they were all invited, and I had to improvise. I added more potatoes in the pot to make mashed potatoes, stripped every shred of meat off that pitiful little chicken, and made a white sauce to mix it in with peas and a pan of biscuits, the whole time praying over the meal. If Jesus could feed the five thousand with a few fish and some loaves, I guess he could multiply the chicken and potatoes for my little crowd. Felt just like Mom for a day!

DIANE BUZZELL

Good to the last drop

    Maxwell House coffee was a staple. Everything went with coffee. Any time of day or night the kettle was on, ready to brew a cup of hospitality. In a workday that started by 5:00 a.m. and lasted sometimes into well after dark, a coffee break and some good conversation was always welcome. It was a way to refresh and get a second wind or to stop and ponder problems and solutions. Coffee was a cure-all for almost anything that went wrong because everything looked better after a cup of coffee. On the center of the table was a lazy Susan that boasted a spoon jar, sugar bowl, salt and pepper shakers, a small pitcher of raw milk fresh from the cooler, cookie jar, and napkins. Around the lazy Susan were coffee cups, actually restaurant-style white earthenware mugs, and almost as soon as they were washed and dried, they would be back in service. Pappy always sat in the seat near the stove, and his coffee cup would be tipped upside down on a napkin waiting for him. At this table, relationships were saturated with the cup of coffee. Advice was given and usually, taken to heart. Instructions on just about anything could be had from fixing a carburetor to where to get a good cow to how to patch up your pants. You talked politics and remained friends, mourned a loss together, celebrated good fortune, or admitted failure. It was all good around that table and a cup of coffee.

    Sometimes the coffee cups would run short, and you were expected to pitch in and cleaned one if you needed a cup. If cups were in the sink, it was often a habit with the boys to pass the cups to each other by tossing them from the sink to where ever they were seated. You had to watch out for flying cups, and God help you if you were sitting in the line of fire. As the guys came in from chores one day, they were sitting down and talking to one another, as Larry went to the sink and grabbed some cups to start tossing them across the kitchen. He tossed one to Russ. Unfortunately, Russ wasn't paying attention, and the cup bounced off the middle of his chest with an audible thunk and onto the table, almost taking Russ down. Getting hit with one of those cups was like a baseball rocketing at you.

Farm families probably deserved food subsidies more than anyone else but didn't apply maybe because of pride and most likely believed they could take care of themselves. In those days it wasn't a check or debit card to pick out what you wanted at the grocery store. You went to the welfare office, and they gave you a box of food. Friends willingly shared any extra they didn't use. There were cans of powdered milk and eggs, bags of rice and beans, flour and oatmeal, blocks of orange cheddar cheese—not Velveeta. Real cheese! Cans of chicken and pork and real butter. The food wasn't packaged so pretty, but it was sooo good. But like today, many who really need it don't apply. To my knowledge, they never applied for the food, but surplus from friends would sometimes show up and was greatly appreciated.

Let's Celebrate

Holidays were celebrated, but there was little time off. Animals still needed to be fed and cleaned out, milking still needed to be done, and depending on the season, just about anything could interfere with holiday time. Easter, Mother's Day, or Memorial Day could mean cows calving and planting to do. Father's Day, Fourth of July, and Labor Day, there could be hay to get in or corn to chop. Thanksgiving, Christmas, or New Year, the cold was likely freezing something up or causing other problems. Larry liked to celebrate Christmas by giving the cows an extra scoop of grain and silage just because. At Christmas we got candy, especially ribbon candy, tangerines, and grapes in our stockings. At Easter we got a basket with a chocolate bunny, jelly beans, and the big colored sugar eggs. We would hide the eggs for each other and try to find them. On birthdays Mom was always sure to make our favorite cake.

Thanksgiving

One Thanksgiving there was a terrible snowstorm, unusual for any year. Aunt Mabel had offered to cook the turkey. The roads were so bad they had to haul the turkey down Tucker Hill Road on sled, dragging it on foot, trudging through the snow. At Thanksgiving and Christmas, Dad would carve up the turkey, and everyone gathered around the big dining room table to eat their fill. As always, Mom's cooking was simple but ample with mounds of mashed potatoes, squash, cranberry sauce, gravy, and an assortment of pies.

Christmas was in the bags

Mom made Christmas special for the whole family. She loved Christmas and fussed over getting just the right presents for each one. The money came from grain bags they saved. The bags made of burlap was what the grain we fed the stock came in. We got 10 cents a bag for good condition, 5 cents for fair, and 2 cents for poor. Rats would chew holes in the bags, and that would make them worthless. Dad would turn them in at the Burlap Company in Worcester, and what he received would determine the Christmas budget each year. The boys remember Dad giving Mom $40 and telling her that was all she could spend on Christmas. She made sure whatever she spent on one, she would spend equally on the others. She would give them the Montgomery Ward or Sears catalog and tell them to circle what they wanted for $5, and she would order it. One year Mom ordered from Sears, and the order didn't come, and it was getting nearer day by day to Christmas. She was fussing that she would never order from Sears again, being so worried that she wouldn't have any presents for the kids. But on Christmas Eve the Sears truck pulled into the driveway with the order. Other families got more Christmas presents. Even the "poor" families they knew, the kids got more than them, but they never seemed to mind. Every year was about the same. One toy, some piece of clothing and a stocking of fruit and candy. During the war, Ralph remembers getting cardboard farm animals because the war effort was taking all the rubber.

Larry, Mom, and Russ, 1967

When Mom did shop, it was always in Ware, but she had to rely on Dad to take her because she didn't drive. She liked the town of Ware at Christmas because it was always decorated so pretty.

As told by Russ

Christmas was always a good day. Mom loved Christmas, and she would get all us kids to come and sit together to sing Christmas carols. We weren't such good singers and didn't really want to sing, but Mom didn't like it if you didn't sing. We had a cardboard fireplace and, of course, the Christmas tree. Janice would hand out all the gifts. One year I got a basketball, and Jack got a gun. We were up at two in the morning playing ball in that barn where Ralph set up a hoop for us. Every year Mom would give us the Sears or Montgomery Ward catalog and tell us we could pick out one thing as our big gift for about $5. One year I wanted an Alamo set that was $5.95. That's what I got that year for Christmas and loved that set. I played with it all the time. Years later I was at work, and on the break table was a catalog of old antiques, and in there was the same Alamo set I got as a kid. It was valued at $750!

One year, I was probably about six or eight, I had heard that the animals would talk on Christmas Eve. After we finished milking and had supper, I went to the barn to listen. I waited and waited and waited to hear the animals talk. I got so tired I finally gave up.

Another year Jack went snooping in a closet in the little room we called the furnace room. The furnace room was really just where the grate where the heat rose from the wood furnace in the cellar, and in the winter, it was the warmest place in the house, so we hauled the big galvanized tub in there for baths. Nobody really used that closet, and Mom kept blankets and things we didn't often use there. Well, that closet was where Jack found a pile of presents tucked away under a blanket. "That was when I stopped believing in Santa Claus" (quote from Russ).

As told by Larry

One year Russ and Jack and I were sneaking down the stairs about four in the morning to check out the presents in the living room. One of us let out a huge fart. We all stopped and looked at each other and started laughing. One of us said, "Well, if that doesn't wake Dad, nothing will." And we stopped being so quiet and tromped down the stairs.

Another year Russ had done a beautiful painting of a deer in the woods. It hung on the living room wall. Ralph was admiring it and said to Mom, "I have to ask Russ what he wants to get for this painting. I would love to buy it from him."

Mom answered him, "Don't worry about buying it. He's giving it to you for Christmas." Oops! Mom didn't really mean to let the cat out of the bag but too late now.

A Charlie Brown Christmas

It was getting close to Christmas, and Mabel sent Ralph for a tree. She wasn't very explicit about what kind of tree she wanted other than she didn't want anything too big. When Ralph arrived home, the tree didn't quite meet her standard. It was small, sadly forlorn, and very much like the tree Charlie Brown picked out. When he asked her what kind of tree she wanted, her reply was "Not this tree!" Like Charlie Brown, Ralph was determined that his sad little tree wasn't so bad and proceeded to mount it on his barn roof, lights and all!

Clambakes

We had late summer clambakes. Visitors from Maine came and slept in the barn. They bedded down there complete with outhouse behind the stairs going to the loft. There were fifty to sixty people who would come, family and friends, and it became a regular event. We had bean hole beans cooked all night in a hole in the ground. Dad would dig a large hole and build a fire in the hole. As it burned down and the coals were glowing hot, he would put a large kettle of beans in there and cover it up. The hot coals would cook the beans all night, and they had a taste different from other beans, sooo good. We also had cornmeal fed clams steamed with lots of butter, hot dogs, and hamburgers, home grown sweet corn, and biscuits. There was so much homemade food to feed everyone who came. We had a campfire in the run to the night pasture with chairs to sit around it. The kids would play hide-and-seek. There were so many places to hide in that big barn. One unfortunate seeker wasn't familiar with the barn cellar where the manure was. It looked like it was solid ground, and he went charging across, sunk in up to his neck. We had to haul him out and hose him down. Mom gave him some of our clothes. We didn't hide in the cellar after that. Someone would bring a projector, and we would watch home movies in the barn. The good time would extend late into the night. Of course, there were hayrides piling onto the big hay wagon and sing-along to a guitar someone would play. The clambakes became so popular that friends were inviting friends. It became so big it was unmanageable, so it was decided to stop having them.

Front row: Janice, Gloria, Russ, Joyce, Chick Hevy, Ralph, Thayne and Wayne, Lorrane, Ken, Mom, Dad, Jack, Harold Lane behind Dad

Farm Food

There was a time when cooks used what they had to measure. A cup might not be eight ounces. It could be great-grandmother's old teacup with a broken handle handed down and what worked with the way they cooked, so these are all approximate amounts. Don't be afraid to experiment. Please understand Pappy never measured anything.

Pappy's Beans

In a large pot, soak about a pound of beans overnight. (If you got them bulk like Pappy, you might want to look them over and cull out any pebbles or rotten beans.)

Next morning *early*, in a large bean pot, add:

> half box of brown sugar
> two large spoonful of molasses
> one medium-size whole onion
> good-size chunk of meaty salt pork about the size of your palm (bacon will do in a pinch or even a stick of butter)
> spoonful of dry mustard (or two spoonful of jar mustard)

Drain off beans from soaking and add to bean pot, should be about three quarters full of beans (navy or yellow eye preferred).

Add boiling water to cover beans.

Start at 400 degrees until water boils and reduce heat to 325 and bake all day. Check often to add water as needed.

One of my favorite memories was of Pappy on Saturday morning sitting at the head of the table ordering anyone within range, instructions for getting the beans ready. Even the grandchildren would be scrambling to get the ingredients and follow his directions. My job was to put the beans to soak the night before, and that included sorting and rinsing them, looking for any debris like leaves or small pebbles that may have migrated into the twenty-five-pound sack of beans during processing. Brown sugar came in one-pound boxes, and he would break about half a chunk off in the plastic wrapper. He had molasses in a five-gallon pail. I filled a jar to make measuring it out a little less messy.

Canadian War Cake

(This recipe handed down from Great-Grandmother Daisy Buzzell Rockwell)

- 2 c. coffee (or water or combination)
- 2/3 c. lard (shortening/butter)
- 2 c. brown sugar
- 1 c. raisins
- 1/4 tsp. salt
- 1/2 tsp. nutmeg
- 2 tsp. cinnamon
- 1 tsp. gr. cloves
- 1 c. chopped nuts
- 4 c. flour sifted with 1 tsp. baking powder
- 2 tsp. baking soda mixed with 1/3 c. cold coffee (or water if you don't have enough coffee)

Boil sugar, coffee/water, shortening, raisins, salt, and spices for five minutes. Let cool. Add to flour mixture. Add baking soda mixture. Mix thoroughly and should be quite stiff. Add nuts. Spread into a greased and floured 13x9 cake pan. Bake at preheated 350 degrees for thirty to thirty-five minutes or until knife comes out clean. When cool, dust with powdered sugar optional. Keeps well.

THE ARTIST, THE FARMER, THE HUNTER, AND THE GOOD GUY

Aunt Barb's Prayer Cake

> 1 egg
> 2 rounded tbsp. cold shortening
> 1 c. sugar
> 1 c. milk
> 1/2 tsp. salt
> 3 tsp. baking powder
> 1 tbsp. vanilla
> 2 c. flour

Beat egg. Add sugar, salt, and vanilla. Beat in shortening. Add baking powder and flour. Pour in greased 13x9 pan. Bake at 350 degrees. Pray for twenty-five to thirty minutes that it comes out all right!

Aunt Barb taught me this recipe on my first visit to Maine in 1971.

Chicken Pie

> Kill a chicken, defeather, skin, and gut.
> Boil until meat falls of the bones.
> Make pie crust with 2 cups flour, and salt sifted together.
> Cut in 2 tablespoon lard until crumbly.

Add just enough water to form ball. Refrigerate until ready to make pie.

Strain broth to make gravy. Heat in pan to boiling mixing in flour until smooth and thickens.

Salt and pepper to taste.

Blanche potatoes and cut in bite-size pieces.

Line pan with meat, potatoes, and miscellaneous available vegetables. Pour gravy over.

Roll out pie crust. Place over pie crimping edges and bake about forty minutes at 350 degrees till crust is golden.

Pappy's Fudge

> 1/2 box brown sugar (about 2 c.)
> 1 c. white sugar
> about 1 c. peanut butter
> 1/2 c. cream (canned milk will do)
> 2 big spoonfuls of marshmallow fluff
> couple handfuls chopped walnuts optional

Combine sugars and milk in saucepan. Over medium high heat, bring to boil for about four minutes until a small spoonful dropped in cold water will ball up. Remove from heat and quickly stir in peanut butter and marshmallow. Spread in large pan and cool. Cut in squares. Share and enjoy.

Icebox Cookie Dessert
(Larry's favorite dessert made by sister Jan)

> Famous Chocolate Wafers, about 3/4 of the box (We called them Icebox cookies)
> Bananas (about 4) sliced thin
> *Real* whipped cream (1 pt. cream, 1 T. powdered sugar, 1 tsp. vanilla beaten till thick)

Layer in a loaf pan lined with foil. Freeze until solid several hours. Slice and serve.

Molasses Cookies

> 1 c. molasses
> 1/2 c. sugar
> 1 large egg
> 1/2 c. shortening (lard)
> 1 c. warm water
> 4 tsp. cream of tartar
> 2 tsp. baking soda

1 tsp. gr. cloves
1 tsp. cinnamon
1 tsp. nutmeg
3 c. flour more or less

Cream sugar and shortening. Add molasses and egg. Mix well. Dissolve cream of tartar and soda in warm water and stir into mixture. Add spices to flour. Gradually add flour until good handling consistency. Drop by spoonful or roll and cut. Place on cookie sheet and bake at 350 degrees. Makes thirty to forty cookies.

American Chop Suey

Box of macaroni cooked until tender.
Can of stewed tomatoes.
One pound hamburg broken in small chunks and browned.
Mix together. Sprinkle generously with parmesan cheese.

Cowhand Casserole
(It's not what they called it, but it needed a name; otherwise known as Shepherd Pie Buzzell style)

Boil pot of potatoes.
Mash with milk and butter till smooth.
Brown hamburg.
Add to mashed potatoes and stir in corn.
You like corn? Add more corn. You like more meat? Add it.
The more you make, the more you can feed.

Ralph's Favorite Sandwich

>Mayonnaise
>Grape jelly

Apply each generously to a slice of soft white bread and put together.
Don't knock it till you try it!

There were lots of other favorites. Kielbasa boiled dinner and chicken stew covered with biscuits spilling out over the pot, and creamed dried beef in creamy white sauce over toast. Favorite treats were the cinnamon rolls of leftover pie dough almost more sought after than the pie and peach upside down cake or angel food cake with fresh strawberries topped with lots of real fresh whipped cream. The whipped cream made the difference on almost any dessert.
Good food, Good meat, Good God, Let's eat!

Farm Life

Cutting Ice

GROWING UP

First homes

The family started out in Spencer near the Leach Farm but moved to Molasses Hill Road in Brookfield. There, the farm had a fifty-foot bank barn and some outbuildings, a chicken coop among them. A bank barn was built into the side of a banking with the open side facing the south meant for shelter and storage.

Molasses Hill, 1942

Its area is all grown up now, but at the time, a favorite pastime for Ralph, just a little guy then, was watching across the valley as the train chugged along, and this began his lifelong fascination with trains. He one day told little sister Janice that the train was going to come up the hill and run right over them, and she, in true little girl fashion, got hysterical, crying in fear of being run over. Dad was not happy about that, and Ralph was expecting a lickin' for upsetting her, but that lickin' didn't happen. While they lived on Molasses Hill, the Hurricane of '38 swept through. Ralph remembers Dad crawling across the road on his hand and knees to get to the house and seeing the henhouse disintegrate and

The Wilson Farm, 2020

whisking the chickens away in the wind. Most of the chickens came back after the storm, but there wasn't a henhouse to come back to. While living in Brookfield, Pappy had a friendly little heifer out to pasture in what is now Nanatomqua Mobile Home Park. One night someone slit her throat and slaughtered her in the field, leaving the carcass. The police assured Pappy they would find out who did it, and sure enough, the guy had a few too many drinks in the bar and started bragging about it soon after. Unfortunately, Pappy was not compensated for the loss of his heifer. When WWII broke out, they sold the farm at Molasses Hill and moved to the little brown house on what is now Route 9 across from the old Brookfield Motors. Pappy had been rejected by the military for service probably for his bad knee or maybe his asthma but was employed for military defense manufacturing at Worcester Press Steel. Of course, they had to have a cow, and Pappy hitched the cow to the bumper of the car and drove down Route 9 leading her to their new home. After Brookfield they moved to the Wilson Farm on Wilson Street, Spencer. On the Wilson farm, the kitchen curtains caught on fire from a candle in a pumpkin. Mom was desperately trying to put it out but wasn't having much luck. God provided a man who just happened to be going by, saw it, and stopped to help and put the fire out. He had just bought a fire extinguisher. Coincidence? I don't think so. It was a God incident! Ralph remembers they went to watch the Halloween parade in the center of Spencer, but Russ was little and so scared by it they had to take him home. He doesn't know why but Russ remembers Jack sitting in the high chair eating breakfast, the radio playing, and Ralph and Jan getting ready for school. Kind of funny the little things we remember as kids. From the Wilson Farm, they moved to the farm in North Brookfield in 1946. Just a few years later, Larry was born there, the only one to be born on the farm. He was a bottle baby and loved his bottle. He was walking and talking and hadn't given up his bottle. Some even made fun of him wondering how long he was going to carry that thing around with him. But as with all children, time makes all the difference. One day he bit the end of the nipple off, and it sprayed him in the face. He was disgusted, ranting, "Dam bot broke." But it was the end of his love affair with his bottle.

THE ARTIST, THE FARMER, THE HUNTER, AND THE GOOD GUY

Thou shalt not steal (as told by Russ)

I was in the second grade, and I would go into the newsroom and look at all the books. I never had any money. I wanted a deluxe *Lone Ranger* storybook so bad. I looked at it and wanted it so bad I just decided to take it and walked out of the store with it. I walked home, and when I got home, Dad and Mom were waiting for me. It was a small town, and everyone knew each other, so when I walked into the house, I knew they knew what I had done. I could see how disappointed they were in me. It was just an awful look. Dad took me back up town and made me bring the book back. I was ashamed of myself and decided I would never steal again. After that, I felt awful because whenever I went in the newsroom, the people in the store would watch me. They didn't trust me, and of course, why should they. But that made me feel even worse that someone couldn't trust me.

Star (as told by Russ)

When were little, Dad would sometimes lay down with us at bedtime, and we would beg him to tell us a story before going to sleep. Our favorite story was about his little ox, Star, who pulled his tip cart. Dad and his sister Florence were coming home with Star in the oxcart. They were suddenly caught in a bad blizzard storm. It was terribly cold with the wind blowing freezing snow pellets into their faces as the temperature dropped. They finally had to climb down in the back of the wagon and huddled together under a blanket to try to stay warm and just let Star go. Star made his way home trudging through the snow, bringing them right to their door. If it wasn't for Star, they would probably have frozen to death.

Benefits

There are benefits to having older brothers and sister. With big sister working in Worcester, Larry got many a pair of shoes from Brown's Shoe, where she worked with cousin Pat. When Ralph returned from the Marines, he surprised Larry with a real baseball, not to mention a glove. Dates often included little brother Larry Bill to go get ice cream or treats. Older siblings set the example to look up to, how to work, and treat one another.

Boys shared rooms and beds. Growing up in an old farmhouse, there wasn't heat in the bedrooms, so sharing a bed with the big buffalo skin blanket covering them in the winter was for warmth and survival, especially when they broke the window in their room. Pappy gave them a challenge meant as a discipline and learning lesson by telling them it was their room, and they had to fix the window. When they woke in the morning and through the broken window a blanket of snow had blown in to cover them, the message and lesson was made ultimately clear. Thankfully that heavy buffalo robe protected them, so they never noticed the cold, and they learned how to fix that window pretty quick. In that big house, it could also be a little scary, but sleeping with a brother who kept hatchets and guns under his pillow made us feel safe. Not sure what we needed that protection for, except maybe the imaginings in our minds.

The Jewish cattle dealer's son (as told by Larry)

Jeffrey Aframe was one of my best friends growing up. We were together all the time, and he lived on South Main around the corner from Bates Street. Jeffrey had the best birthday parties with all his family there celebrating, and I was completely awed at his Bar Mitzvah. Friends, family, food, and an amazing number of gifts. I didn't understand what it was all about at the time, but I sure admired his family. His father was cattle dealer and often picked up cows from us for resale or slaughter. Sometimes I would get to ride with them as they picked up cattle from various farms. Riding in the big cattle truck, Jeffrey could keep up a steady stream of conversation. One time he looked at me and said, "Why am I the only one talking?" and his father quickly interjected, "He's quiet so he can learn something. You can't learn if you are talking all the time." A wise father.

We had a long morning, and it was time for lunch, but I hadn't brought a lunch. Jeffrey's father generously offered me a sandwich, and I was hungry until I found out what it was. Cow's tongue. I guess I wasn't really that hungry because I politely turned that down.

Sometimes we would spend time at the slaughterhouse. While Mr. Aframe did his paperwork or networked with other dealers, we had time to kill. There were machines in the break room with root beer and cupcakes, but we would take them out to the main part of the building, where they did the butchering, to sit on benches along the wall. (I know, kind of morbid.) One day one of the butchers, he looked like a pirate with his kerchief wrapped around his head, came walking by. He leaned down in front of us, smiled a toothy grin, and with his knife ran it along his arm, shaving the hair off. That scared the wits out of us, and we ran like the dickens to find Mr. Aframe. I'm sure he was just messing with us, but it was very effective.

Because Jeffery lived closer to town, I would spend the afternoon on Halloween with him. We could go all over town together as the sun set, filling two shopping bags with candy treats until long after dark. When we got back to his house, we dumped it all on the floor and traded candy with each other while eating way more than we should have. He was a great friend.

A really rude awakening

Pappy was planting corn in the big field behind the house, and Ralph was harrowing with the Popeye tractor. In the tractor bucket lined with hay, Russ and Jack were napping. They were about six and three years old. As they came near the apple tree, a limb caught the lever of the bucket, tipping Russ and Jack out onto the ground. It happened so quick Ralph didn't have time to stop. Russ was on the ground and remembers seeing the front wheel coming at him, running right over his head! Fortunately, the ground had just been harrowed, so the dirt was broken and fluffed up, and his face was pushed into the soft overturned soil. Still, it was the weight of the tractor going over! Ralph was able to stop as Russ saw the back wheel of the tractor coming at him and frantically rolled out of the way. Ralph had run over Jack's back as well, but he got up running to the house, yelling to Mom that Ralph killed Russ. Pappy saw the whole thing happen and figured Jack couldn't be hurting too bad, but Russ was rolling on the ground. He suffered a big headache, but if that was all, I guess he was blessed, and God was watching out for him. How does anyone live through that!

Out! At the ball game

Russ isn't the only one Ralph came near to killing. Baseball is the all-American pastime. All the brothers played. In one practice, Ralph was tossing up balls and hitting them for the boys to catch in the outfield. He talked Larry into pitching a ball to him. Larry was hesitant and resisted with "You'll kill me." With fourteen years between them, it had to be a bit intimidating to pitch to big brother Ralph, but Ralph assured him he was going to hit a high fly ball, and he would be fine. Larry wound up and put one over the plate. *Crack!* Unfortunately, the high ball was a line drive smack into Larry's forehead, knocking him out cold. Ralph thought he did kill him! Mom came screaming, doing her best to revive him. All Larry remembers is Mom's fuzzy face over his as she worked to wake him up.

Make-up games

The boys liked sports and unfortunately, or maybe fortunately, it was a time when they didn't have the access to organized sports, but that didn't stop them. They found time and resources to play and hone skills. Real balls and bats were a premium, so they used what they had available. A favorite pastime was firing off pitches at the telephone pole using stones and small rocks. If you could hit the pole with a stone, obviously a ball would go over home plate. They made up a game, if you hit the pole, it was a strike, and a miss was a ball. They would try to get three strikes rather than four balls. They kept count and who was the best pitcher by the outs. (This pitching experience came in real handy when came to facing a bull.)

They had to take advantage of minutes between chores for batting practice with whatever was at hand. No helmets or protective gear. In a moment of downtime, as Russ and Larry were picking rocks out of the field and waiting for Pappy to come back with the tractor, they challenged each other who could hit a rock the farthest. They found some hefty sticks and chose from the rocks they were picking to toss in the air and hit across the field. They were hitting pretty well and lobbing them a good distance until one particular hard hit, and the bat slipped out of Russell's hands in midswing, flinging around at Larry, hitting him in the chest. It knocked the wind out him and bruised his ribs, but he was not seriously injured. By then, Pappy was back with the tractor and time to get back to work, so that was all there was for batting practice that afternoon.

A great playroom

The front bedroom wasn't used for much, mostly storage, but give little boys a chance, and it was the perfect place for imaginary forts and hideaways. Because it wasn't used and it was out of the way, no one took notice of the project they began. Over a couple weeks they hauled in sand, dirt, and stones, tree branches for trees, and the Wild West spread out across the large room with mountains, valleys, and dessert. What fun they had with their set of cowboys and Indians complete with horses. There were all kinds of shoot-'em-ups at the OK Corral. It became a whole room of Wild West fantasy. They even brought in their own BB guns and took aim shooting outlaws and bandits off the mountain sides. It all went well until Mom happened to go in one day maybe to find something or store something away. Surprised to say the least, she couldn't believe she didn't know they had done this, but it was the perfect setup. They just came in the front door and didn't track through the house. It wasn't really done in secret. They just thought it was a good idea to do and did it. Mom thought it would be a good idea to take it all back outside where it belonged. She didn't get mad, boys will be boys, but she did make them clean it all up, every last grain of sand.

Finders keepers (as told by Larry)

Tony and I spent a lot of time at the brook. It wound through our farm and was a constant source of fun and exploration. It was different all year long. In spring the water would rise with the spring rains and melting snow and ice. Summer, there would be fishing until the heat would dry it out, and it would be little more than pools connected by slow-running water. By fall, it would come back to flowing again, and winter, it would ice over. It was the best amusement park ever. Summers it was a great place to get wet and cool off while rummaging through the cool waters looking for whatever we could find, and the bridge was a great place to get out of the sun and cool off in the shade. There was the high bridge on Old West Brookfield Road to sit under, and over by the little red house, there was a culvert under Tucker Hill Road we would crawl into barely big enough to squirm into. We would follow the length of the brook and the things we would find! Snakes and frogs, salamanders and turtles, and beer! Tony was in the culvert, and I asked him, "Find anything good?" and he said "Yeah, A six-pack!" Someone thought it would be a good place to store some bottles kept cool in the pool under culvert. Not sure if they were left behind by some fishermen or maybe someone who didn't want Mom and Dad to know about them, but finders keepers. They were ours now! But then that didn't work out so well. We secretly went up to the barn and drank our fill, only to get really sick. (Cousin Sue, when hearing this story, responded in amazement, "Larry, I can't believe it! I never thought you did anything bad!")

Give me a brake

Larry was a runner from the time he could walk. His long legs stretched out long strides even when he was walking. In high school he was known as Spidey and on the track team well-known for his speed, even managing to make some records in high school. He owes some of his success to working on the farm. First of all, he worked harder than most adults do at full-time employment, *and* he went to high school at the same time. Carrying milk and running up and down those barn stairs in boots prepped his muscles and lungs. The amount he worked on the farm and worked out with the team used up every spare calorie and kept him at a trim 145 pounds for his five-eleven build. But there's another reason why he ran so well. As a kid, most of his friends and brothers had bikes. He didn't. Didn't really want one either, but of course, when his friends would go for bike rides, he had to run and soon realized he was a little more tired than the rest of the group. The family never had much money, but his mom found a bike for him for next to nothing. Of course, it wasn't new. Shiny new bikes would have fenders, lights, a horn, and big fat tires. This one had almost no shine, no fenders, and probably little tread, but the tires were up, so it was a go. Now to learn how to ride it. He was about nine years old, and training wheels were not an option partly because of the size of the bike but most importantly his ego. What boy could live down training wheels! So brother Jack encouraged him the best way to learn to ride was just to get on and ride. Proceeding to push him down the hill of Old West Brookfield Road and letting go after a few feet, sent him on his way. He stayed up, but by the time he reached the bottom of the hill, he was out of control and ran into the railings on the bridge. Brakes? What brakes? So after that experience and the fact that the bike was totaled and Larry pretty banged up as well, he went back to putting one foot in front of the other.

If Mom only knew

Kids are kids. Actually, we are all human, and by the time we are adults, we have had plenty of practice pushing each other's buttons, and no family would be normal if there weren't a few skirmishes along the way. Usually, it was over something stupid, and most of the time differences were settled among themselves because you really didn't want Mom or Dad to settle it for you.

Teenage boys can get rough, and who knows what started this one, but they were successful at keeping it under the radar. It was an old farm and short on amenities. No tub or shower and just a tiny bathroom sink. Well, let's just say the big kitchen sink was more convenient. Think of three teenage boys getting ready for school in the morning with only *one* sink, not to mention only one toilet for everybody (and they complain today if there is only one bathroom and no master). They were in the kitchen after chores, finishing the second breakfast, and Russ was cleaning up at the sink. They were probably arguing over who was supposed to do something they didn't do regarding chores or maybe who gets to use the sink first, but Jack didn't like what Russ said, so he threw a cup of cocoa in his face. Russ, who was usually pretty mild mannered, responded fast and furious with a right hook that laid Jack out cold on the floor, blood oozing from his nose. That was when they heard Mom coming down the stairs. Quick! Larry and Pat, a visiting friend, dragged Jack into the pantry, while Russ started cleaning up the blood and cocoa, ready to distract Mom from the two guys frantically trying to revive sleeping beauty! As Mom took in the disarray, she curiously asked, "What is all the blood from?"

Russ, smooth as silk, explained, "I cut myself shaving." You had to love Mom because she believed him.

The Star Theater

The Star Theater, which now houses a sandwich shop and other businesses, started out as a church, believe it or not, when the church across the street divided over slavery in the 1860s. That was bad enough, but it is sad we no longer have a theater in our community. The films were wholesome for the most part with actors you could look up to and lessons kids could learn from and a good influence on us. Buses actually came from surrounding towns bringing patrons for the shows. Prices began at 25 cents and went to 50 cents. As a little boy, Mom and Dad brought Larry to see a John Wayne western. It was so exciting, and he wanted one of the orange slushies so badly Dad treated him to one. It was a tall cold drink, and he slurped it down way too fast and ended up throwing it up all over Mom and Dad. They had to bring him home, and they all missed the rest of the movie. Ralph used to go to the Star Theater to watch the cowboys and then go home and practice what the cowboys did, leaping

THE ARTIST, THE FARMER, THE HUNTER, AND THE GOOD GUY

over his horse's rump to mount, riding hanging off the side of his galloping horse, as well as other probably just as dangerous stunts. One day he told Janice he was going to be Superman and jumped off the barn roof using a grain bag to fly. He learned a grain bag does not work like a red cape, and he dropped like the sack he was wearing. He only did that once! The theater had Christmas programs for the schoolkids, and they would march from school to the theater to watch Christmas cartoons. Presents and treats would be handed out for a fun afternoon. As kids got older, they thought they could take advantage of the one person running the whole theater by starting "fights" to distract him. When he came to break up the fight, others would run and grab some candy. That didn't last long because the chief started sitting in the back as a monitor. The boys used to walk the couple miles up Bates Street and through Windemuth fields to get there for a show, and after we would run between streetlights in the dark to get home. As teenagers it was a go-to place for dates and meeting up with friends.

Town hall

The town hall was used for a lot of things. It is long forgotten how at one time it was used to premier Broadway plays by George Cohan, who spent summers in North Brookfield, calling our town his adopted home. The grand hall upstairs was the place for dances and town celebrations as well as basketball games. Russ played in the town hall coached by Paul Ekland. The boys played their own game at the farm hoop on the barn, but when Russ came to play on a team, he had no idea how to execute plays in a real game. Coach could see he could shoot and told him to just go in the corner and stay there and we'll get you the ball. His shot made him a valuable player!

Makeup game

Ralph and the Whitmans would drive around town looking for anyone who would like to play ball, filling the back of their pickup truck. Ralph, Kent, Boydie, and Ralph W. would pitch and field, while the younger kids would hit and run. They had a name for each kid. Larry was Harmon Killebrew, his all-time favorite player for the Minnesota Twins. When Larry got up to hit, they would yell "Back up!" or "Go deep" in the outfield because Larry could hit pretty well. They were essentially one big team, so when they got three outs, that would be the end of the inning and the start of a new inning. They would try to get as many runs as they could in each inning. As another way to create a way to play, Ralph bought Larry a rubber ball and taught him to throw it at the wall, and if he caught it, it was an out, and if he missed, it was a base run. Each time he missed it, the runner would advance, and three outs would end an inning until the game ended. He played like it was a real game with two teams. He would throw the ball hard, and it would bounce back hard, so he had to really work to catch it. He created games playing basketball all by himself playing both teams. There weren't always many kids around and so making up ways to play was his way of making fun.

It ain't over (as told by Larry)

Joe Tucker was our neighbor and Mabel's dad. She asked me once to help him get in hay. She was driving the tractor, and we were piling hay. As we went around the field, I was trying really hard to do my best to get as many of the bales as possible to save Joe's energy, but I have to say, I would come around the other side of the truck, and he would already have it done. Even at his age and his health, he could best me. He was a man to look up to.

Joe Tucker

As Joe got older, I got to know him better. We shared a common interest in baseball. He would often cut out the box scores and tape them to a post card and leave them in the mailbox for me to find. Sometimes we would watch games together. His daughter Rose was having a party one of those times. When I showed up and saw the party going on, I suggested I could come back another time, but Joe said, "You see those two chairs? Those are for us. Sit down!" We watched the game with all those kids partying around us, and they never once crossed in front of the TV. Joe was a Baltimore Oriole fan, and we took him to see the Orioles play against the Red Sox in Boston. The Sox were winning, and we were all cheering, and we kept apologizing to Joe that it was Red Sox territory. Joe just replied several times with a calm "It's not over." In the last inning, Boog Powell was up with two men on and hit a home run, and the Orioles won 4–3. So Joe apologizing to us said, "I told you it wasn't over." Joe and I became good friends despite our age difference, and I regret not getting to know him sooner. As he became bedridden, I made a point to go sit by his bed to visit and talk baseball or watch the games together.

Ask what you can do for your country…

Corporal Ralph

Ralph was fourteen years older than Larry when he left school in his junior year and went off to join the Marines at seventeen to serve his country, so Larry was only about three at the time. He served in Korea in the demilitarized zone, as well as Europe and the Pacific. He was stationed at Paris Island, North Carolina, and Camp Lejeune, and Camp Pendleton. In boot camp, Ralph was going down a cliff and drove a stick that punctured through his legging and into his leg. The corpsman told him to be a man and keep marching, but it got infected, resulting in blood poisoning and two days in the hospital. While on leave in California, he drove a '47 Chevy out to third base at Anaheim, which was an open ball field where semi pro games were played. The third baseman tried to get them to leave, telling them police were coming, but they wouldn't leave, and they got arrested, spending the night in the Santa Anna jail. They were servicemen having a little too much fun after a little too much to drink and dried out overnight before going back to base. End of story. There are probably many other tales to tell, but he often recalls those times as "Those are the days I don't remember." And says that as he gets older, he has CRS (can't remember stuff). Ralph said he didn't care to promote to more than corporal because he didn't have a plan to stay in the service. He could have been more. In fact, they offered him $600 and promotion to sergeant if he reenlisted.

By the time Ralph came home from the service, to Larry, his older brother was little more than a vague memory. So much so that when he saw him coming across the front yard to come into the house, Larry didn't recognize him and told his mother, "There's a strange man here."

Mom had to tell him, "That's your brother!"

After military life, there were some adjustments. The boys were still sharing rooms, and Larry remembers his older brother coming home after an evening of some celebration hearing his older brother singing "From the Halls of Montezuma" quite enthusiastically as he tried to climb the stairs to their rooms. Celebrating had strongly influenced his ability to put one foot in front of the other, and those stairs seemed to be quite a challenge! He could be heard encouraging his imaginary cohorts to try again, "Come on, boys, let's take this hill one more time!" And military life also affected his vocabulary a little bit. While Mom was on the phone with Pastor Packard, she was asked what color uniform he wore. She called to Ralph asking for the answer to this question, and to her dismay, he yelled back, "Cowshit green!" I'm sure she was a little mortified, not to mention disappointed in her son's description within hearing of the pastor.

Janice with the Red and Ralph

THE ARTIST, THE FARMER, THE HUNTER, AND THE GOOD GUY

How we roll
Conversation between Ralph and Larry

"We were coming home from California, me and Red, to Red's father's ranch in Colorado. We were on the highway up in the mountains when we ran out of gas."

"How did you get home?" asked Larry.

"We just coasted down the mountain just about all the way to Denver. Course back then we didn't have power steering or brakes, and we just put it in neutral. Couldn't do that today. You'd go over cliff."

While they were at the ranch, of course they took the horses out for a ride. Red's father thought Ralph from Massachusetts had to be a greenhorn (cowboy term for inexperienced). I mean, who really rides horses in Massachusetts? He saddled up a horse for Ralph and led him out for him to mount. Ralph grabbed the saddle horn and swung up like the old cowhand he was. It so totally surprised *and impressed* Mr. Pixler and created a new respect for Ralph.

Can you hear me now

Jack had been working at Norton Company and, rather than be drafted, chose to enlist in the Marines like his brother Ralph. It was the era of the Vietnam War, and it was either enlist and serve where

you chose or get drafted and go where they sent you. He was a really good shot, and they wanted him to be a sniper, but Jack thought radio operator would be a better choice. He was fortunate to have never been deployed to Vietnam, but a few times that seemed evident, and it upset Mom terribly whenever she would get that news. Either way he was ready to serve our country when many others headed to Canada.

Served in the country

Larry had a really high draft number and was the last boy on the farm. They had instituted regulations to prevent families from losing all a family's boys at war and the need to keep the family farm running. When he went to the draft board, he was told draft numbers went up to 365, and his was 325, so by the time his number would have come up, the draft would have already ended. He served at home on the farm. I don't know how the farm would have survived without him.

School Daze

School days were different. I mean, it was the usual for us but not like today. Girls wore dresses every day. Girls were made to kneel, and their skirts had to hit the floor or they were sent home. Boys wore trousers and button-down shirts, and haircuts were trimmed clean and short. No jeans or T-shirts! We had school shoes. Sneakers were for gym. We prayed every morning, recited or listened to scripture, sang a hymn, the National Anthem, and said the Pledge of Allegiance. No one was offended. Lunches were 25 cents, and a carton of milk was 3 cents. The lunches were nutritious, simple foods, and there were no choices. You ate what was served or brought your own lunch. The teacher sat at the table with her class and made sure everyone used their manners and cleaned their plates. After lunch was recess, and we would be outside getting fresh air every day even on the coldest days, and the teachers were outside with us. Pouring rain was the exception. We were expected to behave and dreaded if our parents were told we had done something wrong because we got double punishment. Getting whacked on the knuckles with a ruler was an acceptable discipline. From the farm there was a bus, but it was much faster to walk cutting through fields and down back roads. We could beat the bus home the three miles to home and often chose to walk.

Ralph and Janice attended first and second grade at Brookfield Elementary School on Maple Street. Living on Route 9 at the time, it would have been just a short walk across the street through a field to the school, but the police wouldn't let them cross Route 9 there. They had to go up to the Gables and cross there to walk down Maple Street to the school. From Brookfield, they moved back to Spencer to live at the Wilson Farm on Wilson Street. They started school at the Main Street School but for only three days before Mom and Dad talked to the school and switched them to the Pleasant Street School, attending fourth and fifth grade walking about a mile to get there. The big brick building had two doors, one for girls and one for boys.

Saved by the cattle dealer (as told by Ralph)

Janice and I were about eight and nine when we moved to Spencer from Brookfield. In Brookfield we just had to cross the street and a small field to get to the school, but in Spencer we had to walk about a mile to the brick schoolhouse on Pleasant Street from the farm on Wilson Street. I was walking alone this day, and I don't know why Janice wasn't with me, but it was a good thing, a really good thing! As I got to the intersection, a big dog of Shepherd mix came flying across the street. I was too young to get away and no place to really go, and he grabbed me by the leg and latched on. Ripped my trousers and my knee. I struggled to get away, but that dog had no intention of letting that happen. As he was chewing on my leg and I was trying to get away, we both tumbled off the street and down an embankment toward a stream at the bottom. I thought I was a goner because as we were rolling over and over down the hill, kicking and screaming, that dog biting and chewing all the while on my leg. At that moment, a cattle dealer in a truck coming up the road saw what was happening. He stopped his truck and ran after us down the hill, beating off the dog with his cattle cane. He asked me my name and said he knew my father, gave me a ride home, and explained to Mom and Dad what had happened. Dad was none too happy and went right to the house where the dog owner lived and said in no uncertain terms, "If that dog ever bites one of my children again, I will not go to the police. I will be coming here!" There was probably more said, but the man got the message because we never saw the dog again.

THE ARTIST, THE FARMER, THE HUNTER, AND THE GOOD GUY

4-4-4

Russ went to North Brookfield Elementary four years at the old school on School Street next to the Fire Department, first through fourth grades. Then he went four years in the fifth through eighth grades at the old high school, which became the elementary school on Grove Street, and four years at the new high school. The new high school was built in 1958. His class was the only class to go four years in the old elementary school, four years in the "new" old elementary school, and four years in the new high school, all three schools in North Brookfield.

The dog ate it

Russ liked almost everything Mom made. Almost. He didn't like deviled ham sandwiches. She made them for his school lunch. At school, children had to leave their lunches in the coatroom near the entry. There was a dog who often would sneak in and steal lunches. Russ left his lunch by the door for the dog. At lunchtime of course it was gone, so he was allowed to call home for a lunch "because the dog ate it." Dad came and took him for a hamburger. I don't think that happened too often before he was found out.

A good sport

George Hanson was our neighbor and Russ's FFA basketball coach (Future Farmers of America). Their team, made up of just North Brookfield farm boys, was okay for this area. In fact, they actually beat the high school's varsity team, but when they played a hotshot team from the city, it wasn't pretty. The team was beating them up pretty bad and making fun of them, and Coach stopped the game. He called their coach, the team, and the refs and told them, "Everyone knows how good you are at basketball, but there is no reason to make our team look that bad. This isn't fun for either team, so let's just have fun playing ball or you can just go home." After that the city team stopped toying with them and played a good game, and everyone went home a sportsman thanks to Coach Hanson.

DIANE BUZZELL

Keeping company

North Brookfield had a unique setting for the school district. The elementary school was situated next to the Fire Department on School Street across from Grove Street. On the corner of Grove was the asbestos factory where the Police Department is now and opposite corner was the rubber/shoe shop. Along Grove Street sandwiched between the high school and the asbestos factory was a little Methodist Church. Growing up in these schools meant asbestos snow on the windows and sills, and the aroma of rubber from the rubber shop permeated the buildings even when the windows were closed. When the windows were open, sometimes it was necessary to sweep the asbestos off the desks. (I often wonder why the population of the town isn't dead of asbestos-induced cancer.) Across from the high school, later elementary school was Central Street and John's Barber Shop, where many of the boys had their hair cut.

Larry only attended the first grade in the old elementary school. When it closed in 1956, he started second in the old high school building, which became the elementary school. Fourth-grade teacher Mrs. Berry read the Bible to her students every morning, and reciting the pledge and singing the National Anthem was routine. Recess was a walk to the common, where sandbox, swing and slides, baseball diamond, and basketball hoops waited for the children to run off their energy. There were two variety stores where they would sometimes sneak cross the street to get candy when the teachers weren't looking. At Christmastime the children were marched down to the Star Theater next to the library on Main Street, where each child received a Christmas present and treats of popcorn and candy.

Although they had atom bomb drills to drop and hide under our desks (like that would really help), it was a peaceful scene like out of a Norman Rockwell painting. It was peaceful probably because they were expected to behave, and discipline was issued pretty strongly. One time Larry got into an altercation over a girl, a girl he had no interest in, but the other young man was spurned because she liked Larry. Larry defended himself, but both boys were brought before Principal Miss O'Coin. She made them both lay their hands on the desk as she executed several smacks with a wooden ruler over their knuckles for fighting. Larry was offended that he received the same discipline when he was the one attacked and only defended himself. After this, he determined he would *never* fight over a girl again. Miss O'Coin was also a stickler for decorum. Somebody passed gas in class, and she proceeded to open every window and allow the winter breezes to clear the air. Larry recalled sitting there freezing as she suggested next time whoever did that would excuse himself to the restroom. Miss O'Coin was strict, but she made a difference in a lot of young lives. Hearing stories about her, I had an image in my mind that was completely destroyed when I met her the first time in church sometime after Larry and I were married. She was long retired, a petite woman, and when she learned I was Larry's wife, she gushed about what a good boy he was and how she had known he would grow to be a fine young man. That was after Larry asked if she needed him to help her up the church steps, and her tart response was, "Of course I do." We need more Miss O'Coins in our schools today.

My one and only A (as told by Larry)

The brook in the night pasture was a great place to play and explore. For the most part, it wasn't too deep although there were a few pools. The water ran clear and cold, and the cows drank at it daily before the beavers were allowed to take over and pollute it. There were trout for fishing, and suckers ran in the springtime. We had to watch out for the snapping turtles, and some of them got pretty big. As kids, we had fun catching mostly frogs and snakes, but there were rainbow and box turtles and some salamanders too. I was lucky to have this habitat, and it helped me get my first and only A in science class. The assignment was to bring in the largest reptile, and I managed to capture a garter snake that was about three feet long and an inch and a half around. Carrying it to school in a big box, I impressed the teacher and my class and then benefited by being allowed to leave class to release it in the swamp behind the school with the mandate, "Not near the school!"

Freshman initiation (as told by Russ)

I remember the first day of high school, and they had all of us freshman up on stage, and we were supposed to go to the microphone and say something. I was so shy and didn't know what to say. When I got up to the microphone, Phyllis was sitting right there in front. She was a couple years older than me and my good friend, always at the farm riding horses or doing chores together. She could see I was nervous and kind of whispered to me, "Tell them you like tight sweaters." I was so nervous I didn't think about what I was saying and blurted it out. Well, that was not a good thing to say. Gol' dang Phyllis, getting me into trouble.

As told by Larry

There was a tradition of freshman initiation at the high school. I got two senior girls as my mentors. Initiation was pretty harmless, carrying books and standing in line for them at lunch, but there was also at least one daring challenge. Mine was to fill a bag of apples at the orchard after hours in the dark. They took me down the orchard road and sent me in. I was in the middle of filling my bag when a police car with a spotlight came driving by. I took off running right into a barbed wire fence, slicing my forehead open. I dove down on the ground as the girls took off, leaving me to fend for myself. I felt like I was in Nazi Germany, lying flat on the ground in the grass, bleeding as the spotlight swept across the orchard. Finally, the police drove off, and I crawled to the edge of the road and waited for the girls to come back and get me.

Late again (as told by Larry)

As each of us boys came of age, we started doing chores beginning with feeding the calves before we took on the responsibility of milking the cows on our own. At about eleven years old, we had to get up at about 4:30 a.m., when Pappy would yell up to us. Oatmeal with fresh cream, toast, and cocoa would be waiting to help drive the sleep away. Generally, six toasts accompanied the oatmeal. As with most boys, we were always hungry, but we weren't the only ones who were hungry. Down at the barn we had, give or take, about twenty calves waiting impatiently to be fed, bawling their welcome. We used little paint pails to mix their milk and pass it out. Newborns would have to wait for their mothers to be milked because right after a calf was born, the milk would be colostrum loaded with the calories and antibodies a new calf would need. After about three to four days, the colostrum would transform to milk, and we would start them on Calf Saver, a powdered milk meant for calves so the cow's milk would go in the tank to be sold. We started off newborns with bottles but moved them to pail as soon as we could teach them. Teaching them to drink from a pail could be a challenge but made it much easier feeding in the long run. You would dip your fingers in the milk, and then they would naturally suck on your fingers as you lowered your hand into the pail. They would suck in milk and come up for air and sometimes butt the pail and get it all over you, but it didn't take long before they would learn that milk was in the pail, and they would strain on their collars when they saw you coming ready to drink it down. It took about an hour to feed them all and clean the pails if everything went right. Afternoon chores there was more time for cleaning out manure from the calves and putting down fresh bedding. After morning chores, it was back to the house to clean up for school and probably more breakfast. The oatmeal was cooked and kept in a double boiler so it would be still warm if we wanted more before the bus came. I was very particular about cleaning up because farm kids would be teased and bullied for smelling like the cows, and I couldn't stand that, so I made sure I was clean. We had chore clothes and boots and school clothes and shoes, and I never interchanged them.

From feeding the calves, we graduated to milking. Of course, we had been helping with milking, learning how to do it, and what habits each cow had. We knew the process and, by the time we were fifteen or sixteen, could step in and do it ourselves. There was often someone around to help out, but it was our responsibility to get up, eat, and get chores done in time to get to school on time. Every morning was a little different. Rainy days the cows were wet and muddy and needed more cleaning. In the winter things would be frozen and iced over. Springtime we would have cows freshening (giving birth) and new calves to add to the routine. Cows were creatures of habit, and when they were freshening in the spring or drying off in the winter, it disrupted their routine and ours. I was late for school so often. I did my best, but sometimes it just couldn't be helped. One morning I was rushing, as was my usual morning routine. Milking had an order, and as you milked three to four cows, and they finished their feed, you would open their stanchion and let them out. Well, in my rush, I opened stanchions one after another for three cows and then released the next cow, but the milking machine was still on. She backed out popping off the vacuum hose and ran out the door. She still had the strap around her belly and the machine swinging back and forth as the teat cups released one at a time. She started running and bucking, panicked by the machine banging her legs, belly, and udder, as I raced after her, helpless to stop what was happening. She crossed the field kicking and bucking, leaving a trail of pieces of the milking machine. I followed, picking up pieces along the way, but I also had two cows in the barn with machines on and others waiting, so I resolutely left her to kick off what was left of the machine so I could finish milking those who were left in the barn with the two remaining machines. When I finally finished milking, I searched the field for the machine, strap, and any pieces I could find, bringing them back to the milk room to clean before I could head into the house and clean myself up.

Needless to say, I was extremely late getting to school, and when I came into the school building, Mrs. Murphy, the assistant principal, was waiting for me. She grabbed me by the ear and dragged me into the principal's office. She was beet red with anger because although this was only one of many times tardy, this time was hours late. Mr. Frizzell looked at us as we walked in and asked what was the problem. "He's late again!" came Mrs. Murphy's tart reply.

I hung my head as Mr. Frizzell turned to me and asked, "Why are you late, Larry?"

Looking him in the eye, I responded with a sigh, "I let a cow out with the machine on." Well, Mr. Frizzell burst out laughing. He had been a farmer, so I knew he was imagining a cow running frantically around the field with a machine on and probably wondering how I could manage to make that mistake!

Mrs. Murphy, totally exasperated, spit out, "Well, what are we going to do with him?"

Mr. Frizzell, still chuckling, told her, "Let him go to class. He has already put in a longer workday than we will."

The assassination (as told by Larry)

We had been in gym class. After gym, everyone took showers before going back to class. It was expected, even the girls. We hadn't heard any announcements and were heading to our next class. Walking to class as usual, we were talking, and one of the guys was cracking jokes. Ray burst out laughing. A teacher came out of his classroom, grabbed Ray by his shirt, and forced him up against the lockers and angrily told him, "This is no time for laughing. President Kennedy has been shot!" It was the first we had heard. If the teacher's assault wasn't shocking enough, we were speechless by the news. When we were allowed to go to our room, it was complete silence. We all just sat quietly waiting to hear what was happening. It was like a moment of silence that went on and on and on. And the terrible news was he had died. It was the same year we were told we couldn't pray in school. North Brookfield was the last school in all of Massachusetts to end prayer, but we continued, gathering at the flagpole. Our country needed it more than ever.

Spidey

In high school sports, Larry's nickname was Spidey because his skinny, lanky frame was all legs and arms. In one of his classes, they were measuring calories. Larry's calorie intake was something like six thousand per day, and the teacher didn't want to believe this skinny kid ate that much. Larry has always judged a meal by quantity, not quality although as he "matures," he realizes he fills up quicker than he used to.

No "I" in team (as told by Larry)

I started out playing for a junior high team and remember a game against West Brookfield. I was a guard and guarding their guard. He had the ball, and I was running around him and somehow got the ball. You know how fast that happens, but I had run around him so many times I didn't know where I was. There was no one at the other basket, so I figured that must be ours and ran down and laid it in just beautiful. Problem was, it was their basket. The crowd was quiet. The refs weren't sure what to do, and when I realized what I had done, I felt awful. George Vassel was my coach, and he was awesome. He took me aside and said, "That's okay, Larry. Bob Cousy did the same thing," which made me feel a lot better. (Bob Cousy played for the Boston Celtics.)

I played sports as a North Brookfield High School Indian. I was on JV and varsity basketball, FFA basketball, and captain of the track and field team. I had great teammates. I was late to almost every basketball practice because of the chores I had to do before getting there. Every practice I did three laps before I could practice with the team for arriving late. I would walk in the door, and Coach would put up his pointer finger, and circling it meant three laps. Andy Leach was the captain of the basketball team, and in a team meeting, the team decided I shouldn't have to do the laps. He went to Coach Boyd on my behalf. I appreciated that, but Coach told him I was part of the team and had to follow team rules, and being late meant laps. I loved the sport, so I did the laps. I wasn't a great player but loved the game. In one game I got elbowed in the nose, and it was bleeding like crazy. Coach sent me to the locker room. Captain Andy was with me and was doing his best to help stop the bleeding, and frustrated, I said, "If we only had something to stop the flow."

Captain Andy asked me, "Do you have a quarter?"

I was baffled. A quarter? What would you do with a quarter? And it hit me! It was an away game, and we were in the girls locker room.

I think Andy liked me. One of our drills was for foul shots. Two guys were paired, and however many shots you missed would determine the number of laps you would have to do. It was meant to cheer each other on because neither one wanted to do laps. Andy often picked me because I was good at foul shots, not much else, but foul shots I could do. We would often get done and be showered by the time the others finished.

It was near the end of game. We were at seventy-eight points, and we all wanted to hit eighty. Coach set up a play for me. I was a second stringer, so the other team wouldn't be expecting me, but I could shoot from the corner. The play was going just as planned. I was passed the ball and put it up and round the rim and out. I couldn't help myself. It slipped out. "Oh shit!" Whistles blew! Coach yelled at me to sit down. Not only had I failed to make the eighty points, I failed my team, my school, and my family. Still not a proud moment. I got a technical, which was severe, similar to today's games. But in that day if you said the *F* word, it meant expulsion from the game, and you would be benched for the next two games. Unfortunately, what I see happening today, that word can be said, and technical may result, giving the other team points, but that's about all. No shame, no discipline.

My parents rarely came to my games. One game in Belchertown, Dad came to my game with Jean Hussey. I was second string, and Coach played me and another player, Tim, every other game. It was not my game to play. Tim knew Dad was in the stands and offered to go to Coach and switch with me. I told him not to mess with Coach, so I sat the bench, and Dad never got to see me play.

A marked man

A farmer playing sports had a lot of challenges. I worked hard, and farm work gave me a lot of opportunities for injury. On the farm, you learned to shake it off and keep going. One time before practice I was racing through milking, trying to get done so I wouldn't be late. I had my back to the cow next me as I was putting the machine on the cow next to her. I guess I startled her, or maybe she was just annoyed with being jostled about as I pushed between them, but she hauled off and planted a hoof in the middle of my back and knocked me flying. I didn't have time to cry about it and kept working to get milking done. Later, after practice I was in the showers with the team, and they started laughing at me. "What's so funny?" and the answer was "You have a perfect black-and-blue hoofprint on your back!"

Track Star

Track was easier because meets and practice were right after school, and I could do chores after. And I was running all the time. Running up the stairs with milk, running after cows, running in practice. I was a natural. I had the school record of fourteen minutes seven seconds for 2.7 miles at school for two years. We raced Holy Name, and they had an awesome runner. Coach Bullard instructed me to stay right behind him all the way. It would worry him and tire him out and "then turn it on" at the school drive and run past him. Well, I stayed right behind him all the way, and at the school drive, I finished right behind him. He was good! But he also made me run my best. We sat in the locker room after showers and had a great talk before the rest of the runners came in.

We were supposed to compete with Tantasqua, but it was cancelled, so Coach said we would have a practice instead. I was starving as always and went down to the pizza house and bought a small pizza. I ate it on the way back, and when I drove into the school parking lot, there was the Tantasqua bus. Somehow there was a miscommunication, and they showed up. I burped pizza all the cross-country way. Worst meet of my life!

The shortcut

We were running cross-country against Southbridge, and I was way out ahead of everyone. I came to a place on the trail, and the marker pointed up the hill. I headed up the hill, but someone had purposely changed the marker. And I was offtrack. I heard the other runners laughing and realized they were on the trail below me. I was kind of angry figuring out what they had done. I just plowed down the hill through the underbrush and briars, getting all cut up in the

THE ARTIST, THE FARMER, THE HUNTER, AND THE GOOD GUY

process. I ended up winning, but Coach asked me what happened when he saw me. He was concerned about leaving the trail, but I assured him I had run farther than the others and they lost fair and square even though I had to take that shortcut.

Pray about it

At the time, 1967, prayer in school was being challenged in the courts. We were the last school in the state to stop school prayer, even meeting around the flagpole before school to pray. The team wanted prayer before we started our meet. When the team asked Coach to pray, he said, "I can't, but Buzzell can." So we prayed before our meets.

Athlete of the Year

Back: L. Jablonski, L. Buzzell, M. Boulette
Front: R. Earle, J. Judycki, R. Hanson

Dale was senior class president. He was an awesome kid and a bright student. He was a friend to everyone, and he was a superb athlete. His last words were, "I'm going to go get a pizza. I'll be right back. I'll take my meds when I get home." His car was split in half on Route 148 when he went into a seizure. It devastated us. We wore black patches on our uniforms in his memory. He would have been Athlete of the Year. He deserved it. But he wasn't there. I received Athlete of the Year. I wanted to give the trophy to his mother. Coach and my teachers told me Dale would want me to have it. After all these years, I still wish I had given it to his mother.

LOVE LIFE

Did you know the number 7 is a biblical number meaning completeness? Starting with the seven days of creation, the number 7 is used over seven hundred times in the Bible. Just a fun fact thought I would throw in.

First love (as told by Larry)

Number 7 has always been my lucky number. I was born on January 7, and when I was seven, I won an ice cream cone with the number 7, and I gave it to Holly so I could push her on the swing. It was a special memory for me but not so much for Holly I guess because all grown-up, she doesn't remember.

*****

This story can almost be repeated verbatim by our children having been told so many times partly because his affinity for the number 7 but also because it was about Holly. At seven years old, she was his first love, whether she knew it or not. As they grew up, Larry was attracted to her and made an attempt to make a move on a hayride one time in the dark, suggesting they share a kiss as they passed between the light poles, but she responded kindly, "Let's not and say we did." It was a disappointment, but they were and still are good friends. He remembers coming upon Holly somewhat desperate on the side of the road with her car out of gas. It was a little Volkswagen, and his friend Ray who was with him said all it needed was to switch to the auxiliary tank. Problem solved and Holly was beyond thank-

THE ARTIST, THE FARMER, THE HUNTER, AND THE GOOD GUY

ful! She was and is always a kind and sweet person and our good friend. Larry was beyond upset when someone was mean to Holly.

As told by Larry

While in high school, I didn't date much. I just didn't have time. I grew up with Pumpkin, a close neighbor. We were good friends, so I asked her out on a date, but when we kissed good night, we both burst out laughing. She said it was like kissing her brother, and I agreed. Sometimes friends are too much like family!

I dated the principal's daughter, Becky. I had put about four hundred bales up that afternoon, milked fifty cows, and I was exhausted. I picked her up, and as we were driving, I knew I was so tired I couldn't get through the date, so I turned to go down by the farm heading for the dirt road. I told her, "I'm tired. I have to stop. Just give me a few minutes." She anxiously hugged the passenger door while I put my head back and closed my eyes. After about twenty minutes, she woke me up.

"You weren't kidding. You really were tired."

I think she thought I was going to attack her, but I just needed a nap! We went out to eat at a little restaurant in Spencer, and she was stirring her soda with her straw, and a piece of ice flipped out and down her blouse. Always the gentleman, I asked her, "Can I help you with that?" and she gave me the look and said, "No!" Of course, I was only trying to be helpful.

Friday the thirteenth

Then came a big date with the pastor's daughter, Pam. I got my chores done early, and I had been looking forward to this one for days. I was so excited. When I came into the house, Jack was standing near the phone in the corner of the dining room, and I went up behind him to playfully punch him like we often did, but as he heard me, he turned, and in his hand was a twelve-inch bowie knife. I was already in full motion, and the knife sliced my three fingers, opening the meat on one finger to the bone. My date became a date with Doc

O'Boyle and his comment was, "I brought you into the world, and now I'm patching you up." After healing, I remember when he pulled out the stitches. All went well till it came to the last one. He warned me this one was probably going to hurt, and as he pulled it out, it felt like he ripped it all wide open again. Thank God he left that one for the last! To this day when my hands get cold, that finger aches awful. And I will never forget the date because it was Friday the thirteenth.

But! I did get to date Pam again. I even took her to the junior prom. Back then we decorated the gym and had a DJ playing all the latest hits. The girls dressed in beautiful gowns, and guys wore their best suits. I think I must have borrowed mine because I didn't have a suit. After the dance we left the school in a line of cars, heading to a party at one of the kids' homes. As we were coming down South Main Street, I knew there would probably be drinking at the party, and I looked at Pam asked her if she really wanted to go. She responded "I hate parties!" so I made a quick detour down Bates Street to the farm, leaving the line of cars. I'm sure there was some comments, "There goes Buzz!" We drove up on the hill behind the house, and we talked and laughed, but as usual, I was tired and needed a nap. I dozed off, expecting it to be a quick nap, but Pam fell asleep too. It was really late when we both woke up, and I had to bring her home. I told Pam we would just tell him we fell asleep, but she said, "He will never believe you." What a dreaded ride that was, and when we pulled into her driveway, Pastor was on the porch waiting! He was not happy, to say the least. He accused me with, "Young man, your car is nothing more than a bedroom on wheels!" In a sense, I guess he was right, but that was the end of dating Pam.

When the time is right

In the dining room was a large oak buffet that matched the dining room table. It was a great place to put things for later. Mom knew it was there. Was probably a little excited about it. Also, a little protective of it. Anticipation. It was an expensive gift representing a new beginning. It was small and would be easy to misplace. Every time she opened the drawer, she was glad to see it was safe, but it was still there. She couldn't take it any longer. "Ralph, for heaven sakes, please just give that diamond ring to Mabel." And he finally did.

Déjà vu

Dad and Mom Buzzell, Jack and Sheila, Mom and Dad Barry

Jack was a good-looking guy and had a number of girlfriends as a young man, but there was one that was almost the same dating story as his dad in Maine. Story has it that he was driving through West Brookfield, saw a pretty girl, and stopped her on the common. Who knows what kind of opening line he used, but conversation was going well until he asked her name. It was Buzzell. It seems way back when the original Buzzells came to the New World in the 1600s, some moved to northern Massachusetts, which is now Maine. Some moved to New Hampshire, and somewhere along the way, descendants from both families moved back to Massachusetts, some to North Brookfield, and some to West Brookfield. Who would have thought after all these years you would run into a long-lost cousin, in the next town no less! However, in time there was a girl who stopped him in his tracks, and she wasn't a distant cousin. Sheila would become his wife.

Farm Boys

Milking it

Milking cows is a routine that runs like clockwork. Early morning and late afternoon the cows are ready to be fed and milked. They would see you coming, and you could hear them bawling impatiently to be allowed in as you put a mixture of feed down. Then we opened the door, and they would file in, finding their stanchions and the feed in front of it. A stanchion is a couple bars that lock together around a cow's neck to keep them in place while you milk them. They don't mind because they are busy eating, and actually milking them relieves the pressure a full bag of milk creates. It can actually be painful for them to endure if you are late to milk, and they will be very tender to touch, especially the heavy milkers, those that give a lot of milk. We had three milking machines to milk three cows at a time. Each machine would have to be assembled piece by piece in the milk room before each milking.

    Once you have put down their feed, let them into the barn, and lock them all in their stanchions, you start by wiping down teats and udder, cleaning away any dirt and debris, looking for any cuts or irritation. Bag balm might be applied if necessary and massaging the teats and bag to encourage the cow to relax and let her milk down. There is a wide leather strap, surcingle that goes over the cow's back, and adjustable metal rod attaching to the strap underneath becomes a sling to hold the stainless steel container called the milking machine in place by a kind of hooklike handle onto the metal rod. The milking machine is only a part of the whole mechanism, which is hooked by a hose to a vacuum system of pipes and nozzles to create suction by a central motor that turns on and off by a switch and runs all the machines at once. A machine hangs in place under the cow with four teat cups attached to the top of the machine with short rubber tubing. The teat cups slip up onto the teats and suck rhythmically like a calf would nurse his mother. Through the teat cups and tubing, the milk flows into the machine. You had to pay attention because each cow milks a little differently, slower or faster depending how much milk they give, and with time you could almost recognize by the sound when they were almost out of milk or maybe the machine was getting full. You could also pinch the tubing to feel how much milk was going through the tubing into the machine. This was important because if you didn't take the machine off when they were done, the suction would suck the meat down and ruin the quarter (the teat and that section of the mammary gland/udder). Cows weren't milked as they were lined up, but there was an order. You would choose a cow who took longer to milk with another cow that didn't take as long to make the routine easier to manage. When milk stopped, you pulled the teat cups off, took off the machine from the strap, releasing the top to pour the milk into the stainless steel pails to carry to the milk room. Take the strap off to put onto the next cow to start the process all over again. Each cow took between five and ten minutes, and after you milked and they were done eating, you would open the stanchion, and they would back out onto the floor behind to walk the corridor out to pasture.

Machines made it possible to milk fast and efficiently. Hand milking took longer, and it was a real workout for your hands and arms, not to mention you were leaning into the cow with your head turned sideways, squatting on a low stool. It was killer on your back and knees. You started by massaging the bag to help the milk come down and then grasping the teats with your two hands. You squeeze and pull down in a back-and-forth rhythm for several minutes. As the first two teats emptied, you had two more. And then you would make sure all the milk was emptied by *stripping* each teat one last time. It was important to strip because that helped keep milk production high. The more milk left behind, the less they gave. Nature's way of saying not to make more milk.

Each cow was different, but they all knew which stanchion was theirs. Even when they came in out of order, they would head right where they belonged, but there was always a couple who would grab a bite of feed from each stanchion until they reached their own. There were some that would love to whack you with their tail as you bent over to check the machine. There's nothing like a tail moist with manure whacking you on the side of the head! Others might kick at you when putting on the machine, but leaning into them would keep them off balance. That was a way to prevent them from kicking, but that was only if you had enough weight to push into a one-thousand-pound cow. You had to learn their temperaments and treated each one accordingly. One Jersey looked like a sweet deer and any loud sudden noise, even a yell to someone over the noise of the machines could scare her, and she would lay down on the machine and what a mess that would cause.

In addition to milking, you carried the milk up the stairs to the milk room to the front of the barn with just enough time to make it back to change the machine before a cow was done and started kicking the machine off herself. We tried a pipeline dumping station. After milking each cow, you would dump their milk into the station, and it would pump it up to the milk cooler in the milk room. It didn't last long. In the winter, the milk would freeze in the line on the way to the milk room, and you would have to carry milk anyway. After milking was done, you would fill it with hot water and an acid detergent and pump it through the line to clean it. One time Larry forgot to unhook the pipeline from the milk cooler, and all the detergent went in the four hundred pounds of milk. The whole milking had to be dumped. Larry felt awful, but Pappy said, "Just a mistake, boy, be careful not to do it again." The bacteria count with the pipeline started going up, so it wasn't worth the hassle.

Milking time kept you busy and on your toes. Spring, summer, and fall all the cows would be crossed to the day pasture from the night pasture adjacent to the barn after milking in the morning. In the afternoon, one after another they ambled through the gate across the road to the entrance leading to the barn. They knew right where to go most of the time, but there was almost always one or two that would see a patch of green and need to be redirected. At the end of haying season, we would let the cows pasture off the hay field. It was loaded with clover topped with sweet white clover flowers, and the cows loved it. Instead of standing in the road to the left directing them across the street from the night pasture, we would stand to the right, and the older cows knew! It was always amazing to watch the cows' reaction. Their eyes would get big, and some would run with awkward delight for the hayfield, while the younger ones would follow somewhat confused by the change in the routine.

The milk room

After moving the cows to pasture, there were the *milk dishes* to wash in strong detergent, taking each and every piece of the milking machine apart to wash, rinse, and hang to dry for the next milking. Mom would sometimes help out with the milk dishes. As you walked in the barn, the milk room door was on the right. From what we understand, originally it was a room used for slaughtering. The milk room was about twelve-by-fifteen with a cement floor having a drain in the center and two windows. It housed a large deep stainless steel double sink on one wall. In the center was a refrigerator milk tank the size of queen-size bed, which meant we had almost no room to move around the milk tank. The tank had a hinged cover, and the cover had portholes to insert strainer baskets where we would dump the pails of milk we carried up. The strainers were sort of like enormous colanders twenty inches around and could hold twelve quarts of milk with coffee-filter-like papers clipped in to strain any foreign particles. When the strainer was taken out, there were little stainless-steel covers for the portholes. The end of the tank facing the front of the barn was a valve on the bottom of the tank. When the milk truck came to pick up the milk, there was a small hole in the barn wall where they put a hose through to connect to the milk tank. (Not like a garden hose but like a fire hose.) Then it would be pumped into the truck to be taken to the milk processing plant. Then of course that queen-size tank had to be cleaned before the next milking. The tank cover came off, and it was sort of like cleaning a swimming pool with a long handle brush and detergent. There was a garden hose connected to the sink to rinse it out the tank. One of the companies who bought our milk was Meolas. When Russ was milking, we were still using the milk cans, and he would have to load all the forty-gallon cans and deliver them to Charlton. After Larry and I were married, there was no shower in the house, so the milk room was my favorite place to wash my long hair. The long hose allowed me to wash and rinse my hair over the drain in the floor.

Winter watering

We didn't have water for the livestock in the barn. There was water in the milk room, and we could carry pails to any of the horses housed nearby, but the cows had to get their water from the brook. There were too many to carry water for and no access to bring it closer. Even if we could get water piped closer, there would be a good portion of the year that it would be frozen. We tried using a milking station that would pump the milk up to the milk room, but the line was so long the warm milk would freeze and clog the pipe in the short time before it got to the milk cooler, so piping water down wasn't even considered. Water in the brook that curved through the night pasture ran clean and clear most of the year, and they could get all they needed there. Winter was a little different. Snow wasn't much of an issue. When a herd of fifty to eighty cows trudged through the snow, there would be a well-cleared path, but there were times when it was really cold, below zero, when the brook would freeze over. That was when we would have to take a double-edged ax and go chop a hole for them. They would follow us down and wait patiently until the hole was opened, and one by one, they would drink their fill before heading back to the barn. It was so cold, and often a cutting wind made it even worse, so this was a dreaded chore, and it only happened in the worst of weather. Chopping the hole meant we would often get splashed as the ice broke away, freezing pant legs and gloves. We would get back to the house for a hot cup of cocoa and time near the woodstove in the kitchen to warm up before heading back out to finish chores.

THE ARTIST, THE FARMER, THE HUNTER, AND THE GOOD GUY

No time to be sick

Everyone got sick from time to time, but on the farm, there really wasn't much in the way of backup. Larry noted that there were times when he was sick, and he had to do his best to just work through it the best he could. Sometimes he would go crash for even a half hour, but cleaning the milk dishes he found was harder when the milk dried on them, so no matter how sick he was, he would wash up those dishes before going to rest.

Gas and hay

Make hay while the sun shines. An old saying but it is truth through and through. You can't make hay on rainy days or cold weather, so when you make hay, it's under a hot sun. It's hard work in the heat and often humid too, usually long hours as well with lots of sweating and the hay chaff sticking to you. There was one time Larry got in four hundred bales of hay by himself. That's loading a truck with about forty sixty-pound bales, driving to the barn, and stacking them in the mow and going back to the field to start over until it was done. Then putting in about three to four hours of milking chores. On a hot day of getting in hay, anything wet looks good even if it's not cold. So when Larry spotted that two-quart glass bottle of ginger ale on the shelf in the milk room, he didn't hesitate, just assumed Mom or Dad had left it there just for him. He had downed most of it before realizing it was gasoline. Yes! The gasoline you put in cars. For months he burped gas and joked about not lighting a match near him. It ruined the taste of food, and he says he never will do that again! I'm not sure why he didn't die! Now to explain why the gas was there. Pappy had rigged up a tractor to run the milking machine vacuum motor if they were without power. Power wasn't always dependable, and any kind of storm could knock it out. It wasn't unusual to lose power from even a thunderstorm back in the day. Milking fifty cows by hand would take far more than the four hours normal for milking and very labor intensive. This was pretty ingenious of him to create this alternative method, but he needed the gas to put in the carburetor to get the tractor started to run the vacuum.

Very corny (as told by Larry)

I came up the stairs with two pails of milk, and just as I came around the corner, Ralph threw a whole pail of corn for his chickens, hitting me and the two pails of milk. While I was spitting corn and shaking it out of my hair and clothes, he was rolling in the floor laughing. And then I had to change the milk filters about three times for all the corn that was in the milk. I'm sure I must have looked funny to Ralph spitting corn and shaking it from my clothes, but I itched and scratched the rest of the time I was milking.

Spring cleaning

Our cows spent most of their time outside, but during milking time, cows don't care where or when they relieve themselves, so there was a scuttle that opened up behind them to scrape down manure with an old hoe into the cellar below as needed. Once a year we would clean out from under the barn. Neighbors brought their manure spreaders, and we would spend the day, Roy on the loader under the barn filling the spreaders with a constant parade of tractors and spreaders covering all the fields with the natural fertilizer and returning to the barn for another load until it was all cleaned out. Dad was on hand to mend and weld because inevitably something would break and need mending, and Mom would feed everyone. Another yearly chore was whitewashing. The boys would clean and clear out the barn and then sweep down the walls, stanchions, troughs, and floors with a big push broom to prepare for the fellow who went from farm to farm to spray down everything with a white lime mixture. Clean and bright for another year. When Pappy moved to the little farm, he always had us spread manure on the front lawn in the fall. It would sit under snow all winter, and we would rake it out in the spring, and we had the greenest lawn all summer.

THE ARTIST, THE FARMER, THE HUNTER, AND THE GOOD GUY

Off to a good start

Ralph started milking by hand in Spencer when only seven years old. His first cow was Rosie, a brindle. She was an easy milker and probably why she was the one he was given to milk. They had about fifteen cows and milked all by hand. Chaney Wamback, Uncle Wendell, Kenny Newville, and Marty Warner were helpers. They didn't have milking machines until 1943, starting with Dealer Valve machines, so milking was by hand until then. The family moved from Spencer in 1946 to the farm in North Brookfield. Pappy obtained three Surge machines for the farm around that time. At that point Ralph was eleven and milking about thirty-five cows. Junior was one of the homemade tractors Pappy created, and he adapted a sulky plow (horse drawn) to hook to it. Ralph plowed the old farm field behind the house with Junior. The Tucker kids started hand milking at six or seven, and they each had a cow to milk.

Cranking it up (as told by Russ)

I was eight years old, and Dad wanted me to harrow a field. It was the first time I had driven the Farmall. He drove me around the first row, and there was a low part that was wet area. He showed me how to pull out the throttle as we went through that patch, and he told me if I got stuck or stalled it to just leave the tractor right there and come get him for help. I went around, and I got to that wet patch, and before I knew it, I needed to pull the throttle. You had to lift and pull, and I was little, and it wasn't easy. I did my best to hurry and pull the throttle, but I was too late. I was stuck and stalled. Well, I wasn't about to let them think I couldn't do this, so I got off the tractor. I could see them up by the house watching me, but I was determined to do it myself. It had a crank handle to start it, but I was just a little guy, and those hand cranks were really hard. I gave it a crank, but it didn't start, so I sat down under tractor to rest. It took me a couple times, but I finally got it started. I climbed on the tractor and pulled that throttle and finished the field. I did it!

DIANE BUZZELL

What about Russ?

Making ends meet in any family of seven can be a challenge, but add fifty cows, calves, and more horses than they needed can really strain the budget. With so many mouths to feed, Pappy had to work off the farm to supplement the income. His big concern was always how to do both. A job would take time away from chores that had to be done, particularly milking. Cows have to be milked. You can't decide to milk them later or tomorrow. Milking has to be done twice a day about twelve hours apart or you run the risk of mastitis, a painful infection in the udder and teats, and quite simply it isn't healthy for your cows. It will also affect the amount of milk you get, and selling milk is what pays the bills. Young Russell overheard Pappy and Uncle Wendell talking about what to do about who could do the milking when Pappy couldn't be there now that Ralph was off to the Marines. Gloria Whitman had stepped in and helped out, but there had to be a more permanent solution.

"What about Russ?" asked Wendell.

"What about Russ?" responded Pappy.

"You really think he could handle milking on his own?" he added thoughtfully. "I think he can handle it. He's good with the cows, been helping to milk right along," encouraged Wendell. Pappy thought it over and gave Russ the job of milking by himself, which meant about three hours before and after school, milking thirty cows, and one cow, Nancy, had to be milked by hand. But there was more than just milking. Putting feed down before bringing in cows meant scoops of grain and a bushel basket of silage at each stanchion. Silage was shoveled from the silo into a basket and carried and dumped for each cow, and a sticky can of molasses slopped on top. After evening milking, he would put down bushels of silage to save time in the morning. Mom did help carry milk and do the milk dishes for about the first year, but Russ at only about eleven years old had to handle all the rest.

Playtime with the calves (as told by Larry)

Each boy took their turn as they grew up to feed the calves. We had to bring warm water down from the milk room and then divided it into smaller pails, adding a cup of powdered milk special for calves and mix it up. Sometimes if we had a cow treated with antibiotics, we couldn't ship the milk, so we would give it to the calves, or when a cow freshened, we would split her colostrum between the calves. The calves would be blatting impatient to be fed and hop and bump into us anxiously as we delivered their pail. As we fed the cows, we would give them a little cow grain once they finished their milk, which didn't take long. They could suck down a pail of milk in no time! Sometimes after milking, I would close all the doors and untie all the calves and let them romp around the barn floor. It was fun to see them buck and run back and forth and gave them some exercise and freedom.

Character shows

Dad used to take Larry everywhere he went. He was like a little shadow and a quiet companion to share treats and keep him company when he traveled about. I think from habit, Dad went to talk to people face-to-face instead of the phone, a habit developed before the phone was a convenient method of communication. This day he went to see friend Walt Nykiels. They were in the barn with the cows. Nykiels had Brown Swiss, which were really pretty cows, if a cow could be pretty. Their coloring was a soft caramel with darker hair on legs, ears, and around their eyes similar to Jersey cows with a quiet temperament. As Dad talked with Walt, Larry wandered to the cows, stroking their faces and talking quietly to them. He thought they were just beautiful. Walt's mother, an older Polish woman, watched him as he moved from cow to cow. When Dad called Larry to leave with him, Mrs. Nykiels spoke up, saying, "This is a good boy. I don't know him, but I can tell he is a good person." And Dad agreed. In addition, Chief Delude said, "If every kid in town was like Larry, we wouldn't need police." Dad said, "I don't ever need to punish Larry. I couldn't hurt him any more than he hurts himself."

> A good man brings good things out of the good stored up in his heart.
> —Luke 6:45

Multipurpose barn

    With a barn as big as ours, there were many options to its use besides cows and hay. It's sad more kids don't have the opportunity for the fun a big barn offers. I think every kid should have a barn. Our Barn was an enormous post and beam structure, and down the center of the barn front to back was a middle aisle about twenty-five feet wide called the barn floor. In the front of the barn was the milk room to the right, a grain room, and a tack room and an area for storage and the silo. There was a chute in the barn floor by the silo that went to a hopper below to have access to the grain where we milked the cows. Another trap door was a hole where we threw hay down to the cow barn floor. That hole was more than a trap for hay but the site of a couple rapid descents. On the left was a stairway to the loft, horse stalls, and chicken coop. Our barn was like an enormous indoor playground with a rope we could take turns swinging and drop into a pile of hay. We played hide-and-seek and made forts of hay bales. As we got older, we created an indoor basketball court.

Haying

    During hay season, we backed the trucks down the barn floor to pack hay in the mows. The mows were long sections of bays in the back of the barn on either side of the barn floor and went floor to second floor ceiling. Originally, they would have had loose hay pitch forked into them, but we used it for baled hay. One summer after haying, we had to move all the bales, hundreds of them, out of the mow because a support beam was kicking out under the barn. After jacking that part of the barn and fixing the beam, we had to move all that hay back into the barn. A lot of work!

    It was important to properly dry hay. One of the fears a farmer has is the spontaneous combustion of green hay. It could go moldy, or as it was packed in the mow, it would heat up, begin to smolder, and explode into flames, taking the barn and contents with it. We had one pile we knew was green and left it in a stack in the field next to the fence. In the sun, the green hay cooked within and began to burn, exploding with flames so high they saw it from the Quabbin Reservoir field tower in Belchertown, twenty miles away. Pappy kept a supply of rock salt, and we would stack the bales cut side up, sprinkling the salt over it as a preventative, and the salt was beneficial to the cows as well. There were nine bays in the mow, five on one side and four and the silo on the other. Two bays had smooth pine floors about sixty by twenty-five feet probably worn smooth over all the time hay had been shuffled in and out. We would purposely use that hay up first, sweep up the floor, and hung a basketball hoop. It was a pretty good indoor basketball court. Russ hung lights so we could play into the night, and kids came from town to have some competitive games. Pappy had no use for sports but let us do this without comment as long as our chores were done.

Down and out

It seems that trap door was left open sometimes. Larry running full speed down the barn floor fell victim. It was meant to be closed but for whatever reason was open. Larry, not paying attention, fell through. Another time he was knocked out cold. Near that trap door was the court where they played basketball. There were many games played there, and the haymow beyond was as good as any bleachers you could get. Jack was walking a girlfriend down the center aisle past the court where the boys were playing when she suddenly disappeared. Larry had left the trap door in the floor open after throwing bales down to the cows, and she didn't notice the opening as she was greeting and waving at boys playing. Jack stood there looking down. Fortunately, it wasn't a far drop to the floor below, and it was cushioned by loose hay, and thankfully she didn't bang her head or any other body part as she departed the barn floor.

On the left of the barn floor as you came in was a narrow hallway beside a stairway that went to a second floor over the horse stalls where a mow for the horse hay was. Under the stairway was an outhouse, a single holer, with a hen that nested right beside it to keep you company when you did your business. After the stairs were several horse stalls coming next and a chicken coop. Ralph used a chainsaw to cut windows out because he decided his chickens needed a view.

As told by Larry

The barn was an awesome hide-and-seek place and not just for little kids. We often played in the dark, and the shadows kept the seeker guessing. Roy knocked himself out when he thought he saw someone. Lunging forward, he called out, "Now I got ya!" With full force he tackled headfirst into a beam. If we weren't playing hide-and-seek, forts were built from the bales, and wars were fought with a supply of tiny crab apples. We made trenches three bales high to fight from. Between the bales, my friend Tony thought to make a small porthole so we could see our enemies to take aim. We would rise and shoot and duck. His brother Louie, a very good pitcher, threw a crab apple right through the hole, catching Tony in the eye and knocking him on his back like he was killed. He rolled in pain and over time won a worthy black eye. As we were the younger of the group, we thought we had the right to go to the apple tree on the hill with the big apples before the next battle, filling our supply bucket. We saw them coming and jumped up from our foxhole. I fired off this apple the size of a softball, hitting Jack in the forehead. He was not happy we had changed ammunition so that was the end of apple battles. We figured Louie being the pitcher he was, we didn't stand a chance.

Darn squatters (as told by Larry)

I went up into the hay mow to get hay down for the cows. I was pulling out bales and putting them down the hole when I realized there were small, I thought, flies flying all around me. Then they were landing on me, all over me! They were tiny bees, tiniest bees I'd ever seen, and they were all over me. I ran down from the loft and grabbed the hose and sprayed myself all over to get the bees off. Those pesty little bees had a whole barn and built a nest between a couple bales. In all my life I'd never seen that before.

THE ARTIST, THE FARMER, THE HUNTER, AND THE GOOD GUY

Just a bump in the road (as told by Larry)

We were going up the road to Tuckers to help bale some hay. It was not that far, but I was just a young teen, and I jumped on the back of the baler so I wouldn't have to walk. On the back end of the baler was a long chute where the bales came out, so I was sitting sideways, facing the side of the road. I often rode there because when we baled sometimes, the knotter mechanism would fail. My job was to feel for the strings on the bale as it was moving through the chute. If there were no strings, I would have to wave my arms and yell to stop so we could fix it. At the bridge down by the little red house, there was a huge hump, like a speed bump where the culvert for the brook went under the road. Dad was moving at a good clip to get to Tucker's field a short distance up the hill when the baler went over that hump. It went about ten feet in the air, and I went flying, landing in the road. Amazing I didn't break my neck. I did get a little bruised and some scrapes, but thankfully Dad stopped so I could climb back on. Dad yelled at me, "Hang on, boy." This wasn't the first time I fell off the baler, but usually it was in a hayfield. In the field, if we hit a rock or woodchuck hole, it would jolt me off, but it was a much slower speed and much softer landing. Often when we helped each other out, we would pay each other in hay. So we had loaded the truck, and I was sitting about fifteen feet up on the truck load in the sun. It was a really hot day, and I was so thirsty. I asked Joe if he had a soda or something to drink. He went into the house, coming back out with a bottle of beer. Apologizing it was all he had, he threw it up to me. I was so thirsty. It was cold and wet, and I was on the top of the load in the hot sun, so I drank it right down. Dad and Joe chatted for a bit, and by the time we were ready to head the quarter mile to our barn, my head was spinning. I slipped my feet under strings of the bales and held on to strings with my hands spread eagle like I was being crucified. You could say I was tripping on the longest ride of my life. I'm not even sure how I got down from the load.

DIANE BUZZELL

Timed out (as told by Larry)

I don't remember why, but I needed help with milking, so Russ came down to help. It might have been a time when he was working nights or maybe trying to get some artwork done. This was one of those distractions that interrupted his day, but regardless, milking was going along pretty good, and I appreciated his help. On the wall, midway down the row of cows, we had a radio. It was always full blast because you couldn't hear it otherwise over the milking machines and various cow noise. Next to the radio was a small cheap alarm clock we used just to know the time if we had to be somewhere and were running late, which was usually the case. For some reason Russ, in his frustration, grabbed the clock and hurled it down the aisle behind the cows and smashed it against the back wall. I stood silently looking at him as he turned around and noticing me, he said, "I'll buy you another clock." I guess he just needed to do that.

Cow in the scuttle (as told by Russ)

Ralph called me to the barn one day. There was a cow in the scuttle. (The scuttle is the trough behind the cows that flips open to scrape the manure into the cellar below.) I was concerned because I didn't know how we were going to get her out. As I looked at her lying with her hind legs down that opening, I could tell she was about done. Animals, when they realize they can't get out of a situation, give up and die, and she was about ready. I was thinking in my head how to rig up a pulley to lift her, but I knew first we needed to make more room to get her legs out. Ralph and I started working to rip out a few boards behind her. All the while she was lying there watching us. I'll never forget that look in her eyes. I still wasn't sure how we were going to lift her. She was about one thousand pounds, but as we pulled back those boards, she heaved a big sigh and rolled onto her side. She started working and struggling and darn if she didn't get her back legs out and then got to her feet. We had to help steady her a bit, and I'm sure she was sore, but she was okay.

Coulda, Shoulda, Wooda

Keeping the home fires burning, boys!

We were up early. Mom wasn't up, the stove was out, and it was cold in the kitchen. The woodbox was empty (our fault), and we needed kindling. Shivering and cold, out of frustration Russ made an executive decision and took an old chair, broke it in pieces, and shoved it in the stove and lit it up. "There, by golly, we will get a little heat!"

Share the warmth

We are so spoiled with turning up the thermostat when we are a little chilly or sleeping through the night and waking to a warm and toasty home. These days everyone has their own space complete with TV and computer. Sharing a room is unheard of, never mind sharing a bed with your siblings. But it wasn't always so. Bedrooms were exactly that. A room with a bed in it, or beds. You were lucky to even have a closet, and those bedrooms seldom had any heat, so sharing a bed with a sibling meant you could share the warmth as well. The boys grew up sharing a bedroom, a full bed for Russ and Larry and a twin for Jack. There was no bedside table or lamp, just a light bulb hanging from the middle of the ceiling with a pull chain to turn it on, which is maybe why Jack slept with a knife or hatchet under his pillow. Never can be too careful in the dark.

As told by Larry

Jack's bed was against the wall, so I had to turn off the light, and to do that, I had to stand on the footboard, which was just thin metal edge. As I stood on the end of the bed, I reached up to grab the pull chain and lost my balance. As I was falling, I could swear I saw a huge sword protruding out of the floor as I tumbled forward. I let out a scream of fear. It startled Russ and Jack, and they both jumped up. I wasn't hurt, and I tried to convince them I saw that sword. Of course, it was only my imagination, so you know how that went. Never lived that down. In the winter Dad would come in and throw the buffalo robe over us to keep us warm. You had to be ready in your spot for the night because it was so heavy, there was no moving once it was on. It was warm, but man, it was heavy. That buffalo robe came in handy the night it snowed in the broken window, and we woke under a blanket of snow as well.

Uncle Ken with Max and Major

Cutting wood

Storing enough wood for the winter was a big job. It had to be done way before winter, like the winter before because wood burns best when it is *seasoned* or dried out. In the summer it is too hot and too much brush to contend with, as well as bugs and poison ivy, but sometimes if we didn't have enough wood laid by, Dad would cut some trees down to *lay* for the winter. Dad said the heat and leaves would suck the moisture out. That wood would be saved for the end of the winter or into early spring to give it more time to season. So generally, it would be late fall after the corn was cut and the leaves were off, sometimes even into winter, we would head to the wood lot to cut our supply of wood for the next year. First, we would choose out trees. Managing a wood lot is more than just chopping random trees. We wanted to encourage other trees to grow and mature, so we weeded out less desirable trees first. It's amazing how fast shoots pop up and grow when managed right. We also took the ones dying and damaged by wind and weather. One year Dad told Larry to go and cut all the dead and dying trees as well as any downed limbs. He cleared out eleven wagon loads of just dead stuff.

Cutting down trees can be dangerous if you don't know what you're doing, but Dad did most of that because he had years of experience. It took skill to look at a tree, the shape and twist, the landscape, and where to fall in the desired direction, avoiding other trees. Then there were different techniques to get it to fall in a certain direction. Once the tree was down, we would limb it, cutting off all the limbs as little as an inch around into lengths, which made good kindling. We couldn't afford to waste anything. The eight- to ten-foot logs would be loaded onto the wood wagon and hauled home. Once home we used a cordwood saw, a large circular table saw to cut the log into stove lengths and required someone to put the log on the table, help feed it, and someone to take away the cut length. Next, depending on the circumference, it was split before throwing down into the cellar to be stacked. There was the wood furnace that took bigger, longer pieces, and the kitchen stove that took much smaller wood, so it was sorted into separate stacks. And of course, the kindling. Once winter was in full force, heaven forbid you let the stove go out, and the boys were expected to take that responsibility whether heading to the cellar to feed the furnace or bringing wood up to the kitchen woodbox. Each step was a workout, unlike what you got in the gym.

As told by Larry

One time cutting a tree with Uncle Ken, I was halfway into the trunk with the chainsaw when he grabbed my shoulder and wrenched me sideways just as the hollow trunk split apart and would have decapitated me if he hadn't moved me away. He could tell by the sound of the saw that the tree was hollow or completely rotten and from experience knew the tree would split as it fell. He then showed me how to notch and cut so if it was hollow, it wouldn't split like that. He also taught me to cut some four-inch limbs and lay them on the ground where the tree would fall so they would keep the tree high enough off the ground to make it better for my saw and easier and safer to cut up. So thankful to God Uncle Ken was with me that day or I would have been a goner. We had a good friend taken by a similar tree called *widow makers*, when the tree trunk split, hitting and killing him. Even worse, he was cutting alone, so no one knew until it was too late to help.

Let me show you how

Sandy and Diamond with Dad on right. Unknown friend

We weren't the most enthusiastic students, but Dad tried to teach us. One particular day. he wanted to show me just how it's done. He pointed out the tree and what he was going to do and where it would land. He notched it and started cutting. Unfortunately, it didn't go quite as planned and fell smack on the wood wagon. We were both silent in disbelief. We didn't say a word as we limbed it out and cut it away from the wagon. The wagon was pretty well busted up and not fit to bring anything home. We limped home, and as we pulled into the farmyard, Uncle Wendell was there. Taking one look at the wagon, he asked before I could stop him, "What happened to the wagon?" Not a good thing to ask! I couldn't even look up because I knew how disgusted Dad was with himself. Years later, a friend asked me to cut some wood, and he would help if we could split the wood. I thought it was a good way to help each other out, but I became very aware of what Dad must have gone through teaching us to be woodsmen. This guy knew nothing about cutting wood. He did the best he could but was in the way more than anything else. We got the job done, and I hope I was able to teach him a few things.

Wood heat warms you three ways. When you cut it, when you burn it, and when you clean up after it.

THE ARTIST, THE FARMER, THE HUNTER, AND THE GOOD GUY

Backup?

Dad had his own way of doing things and an independent spirit that didn't take well to being told what to do. When he needed to do something, he would think of a way to get it done and do it, but it didn't always impress others. For whatever reason, he was alone and needed to get a tree down to the house from the wood lot. It wasn't that far, maybe a half mile, but who knows why, he didn't limb out the tree but just hitched it to an ingenious contraption he rigged. He made a cart with a winch on it. By backing up over the end of the tree and wrapping chain around the log end, he could drag it anywhere, which was what he did. He just dragged the whole tree down Tucker Hill Road. There isn't much traffic on this back country road, but of course this day he met his neighbor Myrtle Hanson. Myrtle wasn't one to mince words and was quite upset that he was dragging a tree and taking up much of the road, so she told him, "You need to back up, John!" Really? He really had no right to drag a tree down the middle of the road, but there was no way he could back up.

"I can't back up with a tree. You will have to go around." So there was a little standoff, but in the end, she went down the dirt road and around the big square to get to her home at the top of Tucker Hill.

As told by Larry

I was with Ralph watching as he was cutting down a tall pine tree in the backyard. It started to lean but didn't fall. Hoping to help it fall, Ralph started running up the tree. So I ran up the tree behind him. Then it started to crack, and Ralph turned around, and we both ran back down the tree as it fell. Not one of our brightest moves.

Chim Chimeny
A Diane memory

The first time I heard of a chimney sweep was when Julie Andrews as Mary Poppins flew onto the stage to dance and sing with

Dick Van Dyke. I never saw my family clean a chimney. Not saying they never had the chimney cleaned, but I certainly didn't know about it. It was a little different at the Buzzells. Pappy had an interesting philosophy about cleaning his chimneys. Let her burn! As a neighbor stopped to inform him of sparks and burning embers flying from the chimney, he calmly thanked him and drank his coffee. On second thought, he sent Larry to the attic. "Make sure the chimney isn't too hot, boy." Exactly how hot was too hot is a good question for sure, and Larry guessed if his dad sent him to the attic that maybe he was a little concerned. While living at the Cider Mill farm, he had rigged a cast-iron pipe as chimney for the living room woodstove out front of the house. Cast iron unprotected from the cold encouraged creosote to build to a point the smoke was backing into the house. His solution was to pour fuel oil down the top of the pipe. There were flames shooting several feet out the top of the pipe, and the house filled with black, greasy soot that covered everything inside, but it sure cleaned that chimney! Dick Van Dyke he was not.

When we put on the addition for Pappy at the Cider Mill farm, we cut lumber from the woodlot and milled it for the floor joists and beams. Larry with the Major and a load of wood.

Grandfather Oak (as told by Larry)

Ralph was cutting down a big oak, a grandfather oak. I really liked the tree and wished he wouldn't cut it but knew he needed the wood. As he was cutting, I was cutting the pucker brush. Pucker brush is the brush around the tree that gets in the way of limbing it out when I hear him yelling and screaming at me. I turned around, and the tree was coming right at me, but I was able to get out of the way. We didn't say a word. We just picked up our saws and tools and left the tree lying there. I climbed on the wagon, and he climbed on the tractor and drove home. It was a windy day, and we both should have known better than to be out there cutting a tree. The wind had caught the upper limbs and spun it, and that's why it was heading for me. We got home, unloaded our tools, and went in for a coffee. I quietly told him, "You almost killed me. I thought you liked me."

Boy Toys

Pappy grew up at a time when horses and oxen were still being used as a common mode of operation for planting and harvesting, actually even transportation. Becoming the bus driver with his team after graduating the sixth grade, it wasn't surprising that he started out farming with horses. Preparing the ground by plowing, harrowing, planting, harvesting, cutting, and raking hay and dragging hay wagons with horses was common to him, but he also wasn't immune to the advantage of the motor-driven tractors, trucks, and cars. On the farm, the boys growing up were exposed to both. Pappy was somewhat of a genius, mechanically changing motors from one vehicle to another. I mean, who does that? And taking spare or scavenged parts and building new. Junior, Popeye, and Popeye II were tractors he built, one with an old Buick motor on a tractor frame and used for years on the farm. He was the epitome of Yankee ingenuity, jack of all trades, and pretty much a master of them all. He even invented a sidewalk plow while working for the town highway department. So he made sure there were always vehicles the boys could tinker with and learned to drive at a very young age. Ralph was only eleven when he started driving Junior, and it wasn't for fun either. He was to mow, rake, and bale hay.

Signs of the times

So the sixties and seventies were a time of change and turbulence. The civil rights movement, antiwar sentiments of Vietnam, the feminists were burning their bras, free love of the sexual revolution, and hippies high on LSD, miniskirts, bell bottoms, and go-go boots all revolutionized youth and society. During chores, the radio

THE ARTIST, THE FARMER, THE HUNTER, AND THE GOOD GUY

blared the rock-and-roll tunes over the hum of the milking machines. The Beatles gave us the "Yellow Submarine," the Animals' popular hit was "The House of the Rising Sun," and the Rolling Stones were celebrities visiting our town at Long View recording studio. On TV the Green Hornet was the new superhero over the old superhero, the Gray Ghost. All had influence to encourage the youth to do stupid things, like they needed any help in that department. The barn was nicknamed the House of The Rising Sun, partly named for all the parties and romance. It was a happening place. If the barn could talk, what stories it could tell! So with the influence of the times Larry had the Yellow Submarine '56 Chevy, their '49 Chevy became the Grey Ghost, and the Scorpion was a tricked-up '39 black Ford pickup with yellow wheels and cow horns on the front. Pappy didn't have much good to say about Fords. He was a Chevy or Buick man. When Ralph bought his red Ford convertible after he was married, Dad told him when he came to visit, he could just leave it at the bottom of the hill.

Ralph and Red with the Flying Scorpian.

Eat My Dust

Jack had an old jalopy he drove around the farm joyriding with his friends, a '48 Chevy retired after Ralph went into the Marines but good enough for the boys on the farm. One day he threw the keys to Larry to let him drive, who was only about eleven and had only driven a tractor. I'm not sure if Larry asked to drive or if Jack just wanted his little brother out of his hair, but sending him off in a car seemed like a good thing to do. Hey, it was just in the field, and the experience was good for him, right? Keep in mind that automatic transmission was pretty much a rarity, so he had to learn clutch and gears and gas. Did I forget brakes? Driving farm equipment was almost second nature to them, and from an early age they learned how to make them go.

Larry on the Super C, his favorite tractor raking hay at 10 years old.

Jack instructed Larry to go as fast as he wanted up the hill but take it easy coming down because the brakes weren't good, pretty much nonexistent. Larry started off from the bottom of the field behind the house. It was a large ten-acre piece sloping up to a magnificent view at the top of the hill behind the house. Experimenting with the gears, he putted along, enjoying his newfound sense of power and freedom. Getting to the top of the hill, he slowly circled around while taking in the expanse of the farm below and headed back down. As the car started down the hill, it picked up speed. He pushed on what could have been the brakes, but it didn't slow down at all. Different from the tractor whose brake was on one side and clutch on the other, he could have been slamming the clutch, which would prevent the gears from holding the car back to a degree, and it whined over bumps and hillocks. Too inexperienced to down shift, he did all he could to just aim for the entrance out of the field, quickly formulating a plan to just steer it down the road until the car slowed down over by Coltey's farm about a half mile away. At the bottom of the field, the car was moving at about forty miles per hour, and Pat Lazarik standing by the dump truck on the road leading out of the field leaped into the truck, fearing Larry was aiming for him. Hoping to slow it down, Larry slammed into a pile of cedar fence posts stacked high before exiting the field. Continuing on, to his horror, there was a large hay wagon in the way, so his plan to head down the road was foiled. Cutting the wheel to the left, he broadsided the wagon, flipping it over, and the impact destroyed the wagon, while the car was forced across the road in a circular direction around the right side of the house. When it came to a stop halfway up a large elm tree, the windows of the car were all broken by the crash, and smoke was pouring out from under the hood. Larry was afraid it was about to blow up. Unable to open the car door, he frantically climbed out a broken window, cutting his finger in the process. Larry and the car were consumed in a cloud of dust so immense Jack and Pat didn't know where they had disappeared. Pappy was way down in the bottom field behind the barn on a tractor, heard the crash and, seeing the cloud of dust plume upward, came up to see what was happening. Mom sitting in the kitchen was oblivious to the whole scenario. (Probably a good thing.)

All is well that ends well. Larry wasn't any worse for the wear, sustaining only a cut finger exiting the car and earned a valuable driving experience. Amazingly, he lived through it at a time when there were no seat belts, but on the other hand, cars were built to sustain and protect the occupants. I would guess maybe his angels were working a little overtime as well. Pappy spent days with Ralph Whitman rebuilding the hay wagon. Larry expected his father to be furious with him, but he never said a word to him. Didn't even ask if he was all right! I think Pappy was probably more upset with Jack for letting him have the keys.

In the driver's seat

One rite of passage is when a young man gets his license. Back then there were no driver ed classes. The boys grew up driving tractors and hay trucks from the time their feet could reach the pedals, so getting a license just made you legal. Essentially, knowing your hand signals and being careful not to pop the clutch was all it took. If you haven't driven a standard, the clutch is the third pedal and is used to change gears, and you went from first gear from a stop through second, third (and maybe fourth depending on your transmission) as you moved faster. Some shifters are on the column and others on the floor. It was always interesting to work the clutch and brake on a hill from a stop. You really haven't learned to drive until you could do that. Parents or older siblings taught you the basics of the road, and when you turned sixteen, someone went with you to the registry and you got your license, or maybe not. When it came time for Larry to get his license, his first car was a '55 Chevy with a four-barrel carburetor painted gray primer with pink fenders. Older brother Ralph thought it best for him to take his new Pontiac, just a slightly better impression for the registry inspector. Larry was unfamiliar with the car, and nervous as he was for the test, it made it even worse that he couldn't find the slot for the key to start the car. Off to a bad start, he then proceeded to take off without looking. He failed his test, barely getting out of the parking lot. His second test, he took his old Chevy and passed with flying colors, the inspector even asking how it was he failed the first time around. Sometimes old and comfortable is best. Word of warning from Larry, don't tell anyone when you are taking your driving test.

Luck would have it

Boys and their cars at some point involves a brush with the law. Russ was milking, lugging pails of milk to the milk room, when Ralph skidded his car into the barn, slamming on his brakes, and killing the engine. Jumping out of the car, he slammed the barn door shut just as the blue lights reflecting in the milk room windows whizzed by heading down Tucker Hill Road. That was a close one! Who knows what he had done? It was the days he doesn't remember. And Russ had an experience coming home from the movies with Larry sound asleep in the passenger seat. Coming through Spencer at the curve on Route 9, he was frustrated by a slow driver. He saw his opportunity to pass, and he did, about nine cars. Unfortunately, he didn't see the state cop who saw all nine cars that he passed. While the officer was talking to him, Larry, disturbed from his sleep and startled by the blue lights, jerked awake. His actions looked suspicious, but Russ explained he had been asleep and didn't see any of it. The police man told him, "This is your lucky day. I am out of tickets."

THE ARTIST, THE FARMER, THE HUNTER, AND THE GOOD GUY

Very foggy night

When Larry and I were dating, he was on his way to pick me up. As usual, he was tired from a long day and on the way fell asleep at the wheel. He wasn't driving fast and slowly went off the road into a telephone pole. The impact woke him up, and he got out of the truck and walked to a nearby farm. The family heard the crash and, unconcerned, assumed it was their decrepit old silo had finally fallen down. Larry called Pappy to pick him up and then let me know he wouldn't be coming that evening. Larry didn't realize leaving the scene of the accident was a no-no. He figured no one else was involved, so what did it matter? But the police didn't see it that way. The chief in that town called him and accused him of drinking, which Larry truthfully hadn't been, and his dad verified, but he still had to come to the station. When he got there, the chief wasn't there, but another officer was, and he took Larry's info and said to him, "It was very foggy last night." Larry was confused, but Pappy nudged him, and he agreed with the officer. A few years later we were at a square dance in that town, and as we were leaving, he took Larry by the arm and told him, "Drive careful. It's foggy out there."

Partners in crime

Now don't get any ideas. Jack had a motorcycle. He and his friends would often feel the need to best one another. Coming down North Main Street from school would often find them trying to prove just who was the best. But just as often, one of North Brookfield Finest would be at Brown's Mobile where Grove Street splits off, and to avoid being stopped or at least one of them being stopped, they would just split off there. You can't follow both at the same time.

Honestly

They had to race. Who gave the challenge? Who knows, but they were coming down South Main and picking up speed when they were caught in the act. Pulling them both over, Chief made his way to Russ first. "So how fast were you going?" and Russ honestly replied, "About fifty." So then he made his way back to Jack with the same question, and Jack "honestly" answered, "I think about thirty." Can you just picture the eyeroll as the chief questioned, "Really, and how is it if he is going fifty you are right behind him only doing thirty?" Good question. I would love to know what his answer was.

Hot wheels

Larry had several cars during his teen years. The '55 Chevy with the pink fenders, Pappy had put a big Buick engine with four-barrel carb in it. It was a hot car, and brother Jack loved to race with it in other towns, getting a reputation unbeknown to his younger brother, which often got Larry race challenges he didn't want or expect. Jack would also borrow it to go incognito dating girls. That also brought trouble on unsuspecting Larry. There was a group of guys from Spencer who wanted to beat the tar out of him for supposedly dating a girlfriend of one of their group, and Jack had to get his friends to straighten that mess out. The car had a rather short life when Larry succumbed to a peer pressure challenge to go airborne, all four wheels off the road over Tebo's Hill (Bates Street). Punching the gas pedal, they were in the air when Larry spotted Marty Warner's station wagon letting off a bunch of kids just below the crest of the hill. Mr. Warner luckily heard the four-barrel carb kick in and knew to hurry the kids out of the way, jumping in his car to also get out of the way. With only split seconds to react, Larry did the only thing he could think of. Closing his eyes, he cut the wheel as hard as he could, hoping as the car landed it might avoid hitting the station wagon by going out into the woods. On contact, the car, slamming unto the road, did a 180, the back end of his car ramming into the station wagon. Somehow no one

Chick Magnet

was hurt, the station wagon sustained minimal damage, but the '55 was totaled. He was however able to drive the half mile down the hill to home.

Mr. Warner asked, "Should we call the police?"

Larry couldn't feel any worse than he did at that moment, nearly killing a bunch of kids and totaling his car in the process. He responded, "No, they can't do anything more to me than my dad will, and he will take my license for sure."

"Who is your dad?"

"John Buzzell."

"I know your dad. I'll take care of this," Mr. Warner replied.

By the time Larry got home, which was just down the street, Pappy already knew the whole story. He only asked "You all right, boy?" and never said another word about it. Mr. Warner and Dad had worked together at Sibley Dairy when Pappy moved to Massachusetts in younger days some thirty years earlier and it appears were quite wild together. I think Mr. Warner must have reminded Pappy of the good ole' days when they were young.

Larry's next car was the Yellow Submarine, a '56 yellow-and-black Chevy. Russell had the Gray Ghost, a '49 Chevy, and his best friend Tim Woods had the Green Hornet. He remembers his Chevy had an enormous steering wheel and piling kids in to go have fun. One time they were all at the town beach in West Brookfield, and there was nothing to prevent you from driving up to the water's edge, which they did. Jokingly it was suggested to drive the Yellow Submarine into the water and test it. Larry didn't take that challenge!

A knock off

Another time, driving the Yellow Submarine, Larry had stopped at Roy's Blue Plate after school. One of his friends sitting on the hood kicked off the license plate. He didn't think much of it and threw the plate in his back seat. On the way home, he passed a state trooper on South Main who immediately turned around to follow him. Youthful ignorance kicked in, and he tried to avoid getting stopped by turning down McCarthy Road, a dead-end street to hide out on. At the time the pasture alongside McCarthy Road was clear of brush, and the trooper, even after having to turn around, could easily see where he went. Larry drove to the end and parked, his plan to make his escape after waiting a bit. Lo and behold who comes down McCarthy Road but the state trooper, who coolly exits his patrol car and comes to stand beside Larry, who was leaning against his car.

"What are you doing?" he asked.

Larry thought fast and replied, "Waiting for my girlfriend." (Who wasn't me at the time.) "She rides down here on her horse."

"I think I'll wait with you." They stood there leaning against the car several minutes, and Larry was getting nervous because of course his girlfriend wasn't going to show up, and of course the trooper knew she wasn't either but let him sweat a little.

"It could take a while." Larry hoped he sounded convincing.

"That's okay, I have time, and I would love to see this horse."

Deep sigh. After several more minutes, Larry suggested, "I guess she's not coming."

The trooper responded, "Is there a reason why your license plate is on your back seat?"

Another deep sigh. "It got knocked off."

"The next time I see you, that number plate will be on your car, right?"

"Yes, sir."

And with that, the trooper got back in his car and left him at the end of McCarthy Road. Truth was, his girlfriend did have a horse, and her farm was the field adjacent to McCarthy Road. She could have shown up if she only had known he was there, but that was before cell phones. A few weeks later, the trooper ran into brother Jack and told Jack, "Your brother is almost as good as you are." Jack asked Larry what he had told him and, hearing the story, thought it was pretty funny.

Face Time

Another Yellow Submarine story was an accident in the school driveway. After school coming down the long drive, Larry had to stop suddenly when a kid ran out in front of his car. He heard a crash, and his friend Tony slid face-first over the roof and down his windshield. Larry could tell he wasn't hurt because he was smiling and waved at him through the window. Larry, startled to see his friend sprawled in front him, exclaimed, "What the heck are you doing, Tony?" Tony, on his motorcycle had been busy waving to a girl and not paying attention to what was obviously in front of him, never stopped, just crashed into the Yellow Submarine. Larry was glad it was a good friend because he was thinking of all the ways he could be at fault. On the other hand, he was glad his friend wasn't injured, although Tony's motorcycle lay in a crumpled heap behind it. When Chief Thomasian showed up, he walked around, looking at the scene, turned to Larry, and calmly commented, "Well, Larry, you can go." Larry relieved said, "Thank you very much," and left Tony to answer for the accident.

Feel the Burn

After the Yellow Submarine came the '57 Chevy, a black convertible with red vinyl interior. It was a really sharp car. Because his birthday was in January and started school later than some, Larry was older than many of his friends and had his license before they did, not to mention a car. So of course, he was a popular ride for all his friends, especially in a black convertible. Larry liked piling in as many as he could and would tell the kids during school, "If you need a ride, meet me in the parking lot." After school they would typically squeeze into his car. With top down, he could seat several across the back and more in the back seat. It was a veritable minibus before there were minibuses! They all enjoyed waving to friends walking along the way as he drove through town, dropping them off one by one or stopping at Roy's to get a soda. I'm sure it wasn't safe, but again that was before seat belts, and we were free to take risks. At that time people weren't sue happy. If you did something stupid, you admitted it and moved on learning from the experience. Unhappily, the black convertible caught fire in the school parking lot one day.

Leon Mimeault ripped off his mohair sweater to smother the fire, but the car (and sweater) was a total loss.

I can see clearly now

Russ was driving, and the snow was coming down hard and fast. He looked back, and snow covered the rear window. He looked in his rearview mirror, and unable to see behind the car, he reached up and swiped at the mirror like that would clear away the snow blocking his view. As Larry observed his brother, he said to him, "I don't think that's going to help." Such a smarty-pants. Another time he drove where he was looking, and he was looking at a lovely young lady with short shorts. The telephone pole stopped him rather suddenly.

A bend in the road (as told by Larry)

Tony and I were coming home and saw red flares down the bend in the road on Route 67 just past Cider Mill Road, so we decided to go see what was happening. As we came closer, there was man putting out flares as a warning for drivers to slow down. There had been a terrible accident. Police weren't there yet. A motorcycle had hit a car head-on, and a motorcyclist was crushed in the grill of the car. The man putting out flares asked us to go check what was in the road about one hundred feet ahead. As we walked up, it looked like a pile of laundry, but to our horror, blood was oozing out from under it. The passenger of the bike had flown over the car, landed, and slid into a crumpled heap. Obviously both motorcyclists did not survive, and as we walked back, we recognized our friend, the driver of the car, running back and forth on the road. As I grabbed his arm, it was stiff like a piece of wood, and his blank stare just registered shock. All three in the accident were friends we knew. I have been told motorcycles are able to maneuver out of the way to avoid accidents, but that wasn't the case this day. Another friend would have been the passenger of the bike if he hadn't had a full milkshake he decided to finish. If it wasn't for that milkshake, he would have been that pile of laundry in the road. We heard the father of the passenger, upon realizing his son was gone, knelt in the cornfield at the edge of the road overwhelmed with grief. Back then I swore I would never go see flares again, but over time I realized, I will go. It means someone needs help. I will do what I can to help.

Smoked

Most farms have hand pump fuel tanks for their trucks, tractors, and equipment. Jack had a '55 purple (dust plum) Chevy. He needed some gas and helped himself a few too many times, thinking no one would notice. Pappy had an idea who but set him up by exchanging the gas with diesel fuel. When Jack fueled up, he drove off, leaving a cloud of white smoke, and there was no mistaking who was taking the farm gas. Billy Brown also had hand-pump fuel tank, and people were stealing his gas, so Pappy gave him that advice. You will know who took it by the white smoke.

On the other hand, Russ had a car that was running terrible, rough and spitting. Pappy instructed Russ to mix a five-gallon can, half gasoline and half diesel fuel. Russ thought he was crazy, and Pappy could tell. "Just do it, boy!" was his command. Against his better judgment, he followed his dad's instructions. He took off in his car with white smoke billowing out as he drove up Tucker Hill, and lo and behold, the diesel cleaned out what ever ailed that car and ran beautiful afterward.

Cracked block (as told by Russ)

I started out working at Reed and Prince with a welder, Norman Ledoux, a great guy and good person to learn from. He could weld anything! It didn't pay much, about $1.20, but turned out to be the best place to learn, and Norman was a great teacher. Norman had learned to weld in the Navy in Siberia. The work they did gave Russia what they needed to win the war. Ralph Whitman got me the job there. I was going to Worcester Trade at night at the same time but not for long because the teacher told me I had learned everything he could teach me at my job. Cast iron is hard to weld and needs a special nickel rod, and Norman showed me how to weld cast iron. He would take a cast iron part and "vee'd it out" (create a cavity). The welding rod for cast iron was a thick square rod. You would heat up the whole piece of cast iron with a big blowtorch to get it cherry-red hot and take the rod and dip it in the flux and fill the cavity with rod. Let it cool and do it again and then touch up the surface so you couldn't tell where it was welded. Norman taught me how to stitch, make a pass and stop to let it cool, repeating the process. It kept the cast iron from getting too hot and cracking after it cooled. Dad bought the Super C Farmall with cracked block, and I was able to fix it with the stitch welding I had learned from Norman. Later on, someone sold Dad a '51 Chevy cheap because it had a cracked block. We cleaned it and vee'd it the best we could and welded the engine right in the car without taking it out. Dad ran that car for a long time, and it ran great. They don't use this technique now, and it's a shame. It's not hard to do and saves money, but it's a throwaway society. They don't fix things now. They just throw them away.

I don't need a reason

Russ and Jack have the mechanical gene passed down from Dad. When something goes wrong with a car, truck, or tractor, they are the ones to call; however, they sometimes approach things a little differently. Russ was helping Jack by working on the frame of his truck. They had it all apart, and Russ had all the bolts laid out on cardboard and was painting them. Jack asked him what he was painting the bolts for, and Russ answered, "Because I want to." And that was reason enough.

Alternative alternator
A Diane memory

Boy toys aren't limited to just boys. I remember in 1980 being very pregnant, and Pappy needed help fixing the alternator on the big red farm truck. He couldn't see very well and needed someone's eyes to do the work. No one else was around, so I was elected to do the job. I donned some big overalls and a red kerchief to keep my hair out of the way. Climbing up on the fender, which was kind of a feat in my condition, I sat with my feet in the motor with the hood over my head and he guided me through the operation. I can say I replaced an alternator! Okay, gentlemen, how many of you have replaced an alternator? (But please don't ask me to do it again.)

Fire it up

We had the old Ford Major at our house. Not sure why, probably for plowing because it was winter, but we couldn't get it started. Cold weather and diesel don't go well together, but Pappy had a remedy. He brought his galvanized washtub and some kindling and started a fire. He let it burn down so it was just a little more than red-hot coals and slid the washtub behind the front wheels under the motor. Then he came back in the house for coffee. By the time he was finished with his coffee, the Major was all warmed up and started right up.

Lock and Load

Our farm was over a hundred acres. Much of it was productive open land, unlike open land of today. There were no trees and scrub brush except where they were meant to be, along pasture fence lines and woodlots. Growing up, we seldom saw much wildlife, maybe an occasional fox or skunk, and if anything, woodchucks because they liked the fields. Woodchucks were a nuisance. They always seemed to create their burrow in the middle of the field. It's a huge mound and would jolt the tractor when you didn't see it coming, and worse, it could break a horse's leg if they stepped in it. We saw no deer, bear, or coyote and definitely no beaver! The only real wild animals we saw were the rats and mice that were unavoidable in the barn, but even those, the cats kept their population to a minimum. We felt comfortable taking a blanket and pillow to sleep out up on Buck Hill. People believe we see wildlife now because we are usurping their habitat. Where were they sixty years ago? The answer is there are far more today, and we see them because the land isn't productive or hasn't been managed properly, and with all the undergrowth, they come closer. They have become less fearful as they rummage our bird feeders and trash. They are as comfortable with our coming and going as we are with them. We do little to control their numbers. In the 1950s, there were over fifty working dairy farms in North Brookfield, and at the time of this writing, there is one. When you see stone walls, they were mostly surrounding fields, garden, and pastures. Today stone walls snake throughout unproductive woodlands. I think of all the hard work our forefathers did to clear the land of those stones to build those walls for this generation to allow the land to go fallow. It also saddens me to see scrub trees growing up, crowding out larger growth, so the land can't sustain it all. Now we see mature trees breaking for no apparent reason. I am not an arborist, but I've read articles about the trees needing to be taken down around reservoirs because they were sucking up the water. Of course, they need water and soil nutrients, and the burden of overgrowth is rationing those nutrients between scrub and mature growth. When you see unmanaged forests, you see scrub and trees starving each other out. With all the dead, rotting, and dying trees, we are becoming a forest fire waiting to happen.

Of the boys, Jack became the hunter, but they all had guns mainly meant to protect the livestock. Shooting any predator was not fun. It was necessity. Many times, it wasn't a wild animal but some stray dog harassing the cows or killing chickens or a nasty feral tomcat killing chicks and kittens. There were packs of wild dogs in the area, but by law, any dog that went after the cows could be shot. Dogs would chew the cow's tails and bite their legs. It would upset the cows, and their milk production would be off as well as injure them. All the boys learned to be good with guns to keep predators at bay when needed. They would go to the dump and hunt rats. They liked to target shoot and learned to respect and how to handle guns properly. Well, at least they didn't shoot each other or anyone else.

Two mistakes (as told by Jack)

Russ and I were camping up in Vermont. A bear came into the camp and took all our supplies, even our toilet paper. That was his first mistake. We went into town and bought some steaks. We were going to put them out for the bear, but neither one of us had much money. We figured the bear wouldn't be back and said the heck with it and ate the steaks ourselves. His second mistake was coming back to our camp.

Jiminy Crickets!

The house was big with lots of rooms and three doorways leading outdoors. At night it could be just a little spooky especially if you are young kids home alone. Add a movie, darkened doorways, some creepy creaking noises common to an old house, and you have imaginations running wild. They were home alone, and to be on guard as any kid would, or at least Jack and Larry had their bows and arrows ready to protect themselves. They had to be paying more attention to the movie because they didn't hear the car drive up or see the lights, only footsteps. Quick! Get armed and the boys were ready aiming at the door. And Roy opened the door to come in just like he did most times, but seeing the arrows aimed at him, he slammed the door shut. "Jiminy crickets! It's only me!"

Hard lessons (as told by Larry)

As young kids, target shooting was fun. As a kid I remember getting a BB gun and feeling pretty good about shooting cans and other targets we set up. If I could do that, I began to wonder if I could hit a smaller target, like a barn swallow high on a telephone wire. Taking aim, I pulled the trigger and watched as the bird flipped off the wire. Brother Russell came up behind me as the bird fluttered to the ground. "How does that make you feel?" Realization set in, and I didn't feel good. I never shot another living thing just for the fun of it again. Hard lesson to admit and learn, but it was a lesson that has shaped me. Like any other tool, guns have a purpose, and just as we needed to know how to use an ax or saw, they can be useful but also dangerous and necessary to use your head and learn to use them properly.

As told by Russ

The reason I said that to Larry was because when I was a kid, I had a BB gun. I was in the front yard laying under the apple tree shooting up into the tree at the leaves. There was a bird way up in the branches. I wondered if I could hit it and aimed and shot several times. Then it suddenly stopped chirping. The BB went right through the head, and it fell to the ground in front of me, and I felt awful. I hated myself for doing that. Vowed I would never do that again.

How it's done

We decided to target shoot behind the house by the apple tree. It was a good place because whenever we missed the shot, it would go into the ground of the hill beyond. We had taken string and tied little white fence insulators to hang them from the tree, and we had chairs from the kitchen to steady our guns on the backs as we took careful aim. We were missing far more than what we were hitting, but we knew when we did hit it because it would swing a wide arc. We thought we were pretty good when it would swing because it was just a little target, and we were acting kind of cocky. Pappy could see us from the kitchen window and decided we needed a little demonstration. We had never seen Pappy shoot before, but he walked up, took a gun, and fired from the hip seemingly without aiming, and the insulator went flying. Setting the gun down, he said, "There, boys, that's how it's done," and he went back in the house. I guess that's how it's done.

Not how it's done (as told by Larry)

We were sitting on our beds talking. Jack had his .22 in his lap. Not sure how or why, but the gun went off. We both jumped and were shocked. Not expecting that one! The shot went through our door down the hall into Mom and Dad's bedroom and into the wall beside their mirror. Jack puttied the wall. We didn't own up to that one, and as far as we knew, they never noticed. By the grace of God, we are still here to tell about it. Another hard lesson we learned: no loaded guns in the house!

A hare off

    Russ had a new .22 and had to try it out. It's important to get comfortable with a new firearm. There was a rabbit running around his car, and he took aim. *Bang.* Missed the rabbit but dead center on the tire. Undeterred, he aimed again and killed another tire. After the second tire, he quit. I guess that could be one good reason why Russ never became a hunter.

Ready, Aim

    Varmints can be troublesome. They sneak in, steal, and kill and mostly at night. Raccoons, woodchucks, mink, bobcat and fox, possum and skunk, coyote and wolves, and rats, even tomcats and dogs. Feral tomcats, although valuable to kill rats and mice, would often turn on each other as well as chicks, hens, and even kittens. Woodchucks, although fairly harmless, would make their holes somewhere in the middle of the field where it wasn't visible. Livestock could get a significant injury if they stepped in the hole, often needing to be euthanized, and machinery would take a beating, causing breakage and expensive repairs. The rest were more nuisance than personal risk. It was often after several raids we would be on the lookout for them. Keeping watch, setting traps, changing routines were all part of the plan to catch them in the act, and it wasn't often we caught them red-handed, but when we did...

    So Pa was ready for this fox who had been in his henhouse and boldly taking claim to what was not his. Taking aim, he fired. But his aim was just a little off, and the varmint took off. A few choice words and then he hears *Pssssst.* The shot had ricocheted, and he took out an $800 tire on his farm tractor. All for a nasty little thief in the henhouse!

Preyed upon

    Ralph was kneeling on the ground, changing a tire, when suddenly out of nowhere a red-tailed hawk swooped down on him talons outstretched to take hold. Waving his arms to ward off this attack, he was stunned that a bird would be so bold! He stomped around, looking at the sky and thinking he was safe, took to working at changing that tire again. His attention on his work, he didn't anticipate another attack, but sure enough, out of the sky the hawk made a second attempt to make Ralph his prey! Who would have thought a hawk would consider a human a worthy meal? Of course, Ralph consulted Russ, and they checked with the wildlife authorities, and the consensus was this was extremely rare, but then Ralph was a one-of-kind rarity himself.

No trespassing

The Cider Mill farm had a long driveway, and coming across the bridge, people often mistook it for the road when they were unfamiliar with the area or had been drinking a little too much. One night a truck came up the driveway, slowly turned around, and headed back all the while dragging a sapling under his truck. It was particularly annoying to Larry to have someone waking us in the early morning hours before he had to be off to work about 4:30 a.m. Several times in succession we had people come up the driveway late at night and the headlights shine in our bedroom window, waking us. In angry frustration this cold winter night, Larry jumped out of bed, grabbed his rifle, and headed out to stand on the stone wall beside the driveway, taking aim. As the car came past the tree, they saw this apparition in long white underwear aiming a gun at them. In panic they jammed the car in reverse and backed down the driveway in record speed, missing the turn and jumping the ditch before righting themselves and headed down the remaining driveway. If it was you who came up the driveway that night, let me apologize and assure you the gun wasn't loaded.

On a late spring night, we had a similar experience, but these wise guys deserved the threat. We had a brook running through the lower pasture, and in spring the suckers run. They were kind of a catfish, and they were spawning, breeding and leaving eggs. Why you would fish at night I don't know. I'm not a fisherman, but they came to catch suckers. Now we don't mind fishermen, but late at night with their flashlights reflecting in our windows and the damp night air carrying their voices like they were in the room with us is another thing. They were loud, and the language was foul. Larry took a walk out on the front lawn with his gun and called out to them to please keep it down but only to get a "F—— you" in response. Not the respect Larry expected. So he bolted his rifle and the *click, click* echoed through the valley. Suddenly he heard "He has a gun!" and flashlights could be seen bobbing frantically, and you could hear thrashing as they raced for the road. That is respect. (Again, it wasn't loaded.)

Just one of those awful times

The rider was riding through the swamp way too fast, and the horse stepped in a hole. The leg snapped, and horse and rider went down. The rider didn't get hurt, but the horse… It was awful. Compound fracture. He stood there on three legs, moaning and gritting his teeth when we arrived. The policeman stood there staring at the horse. Pappy was furious.

"Can't you see the animal is suffering. Shoot the poor thing!"

Trembling, he stood, gun in hand. "I can't, John."

Pappy grabbed the gun and shot the horse, ending his misery. That was an awful, traumatic memory but most humane for the horse. Because of their size and weight, horses don't survive even simple fractures, and it was the only thing we could do. Just an awful time.

Good men

Good men cut baling twine, pick out stones from hooves, tighten a screw, cut weeds away from an electric fence, emergency mechanical tool, slice open mail envelopes, clean battery cables, whittle a switch, open grain bags, cut fishing line, filet the fish, fix a denture, so much, much more. A *good* man always has a knife. Pappy had a red Swiss army knife, a prized possession he carried everywhere, and he could dig a stone from a horse's hoof or whip it out at a restaurant to cut his steak better than any steak knife. I know, eewe! But he was sure to wipe it off his pant leg to clean it. Every good man had a knife. It was good to clean crud off battery cables or as a screwdriver and for stripping electrical wiring. Every *good* man had a knife. When Larry got his new teeth and the back edge was cutting into the roof of his mouth, yup, Pappy took his teeth and carved it with his knife to fit better because every *good* man has a knife. (By the way, that's not the only time he fixed a denture. Mom broke a tooth biting into an apple, and he took some superglue and fixed it good as new.) Growing up on the farm and back in the day, most boys had a jackknife. It was big deal to get your first jackknife. Kind of a rite of passage and you learned to be careful and not cut yourself. It was handy for cutting baling twine when feeding out hay, whittling a stick for cooking a hot dog or marshmallows at a campout, or cutting kindling to make the fire to cook them. Kids carried them to school, and no one thought twice about it because every *good* man has a knife. It was spring, and a cow's tail laden with mud and other stuff was nasty to get slapped with, and most often it would be your face. So a common practice was to tie the tail loosely with baling twine to a beam above the cow to prevent getting slapped. The Tuckers had their cows at the farm while rebuilding their barn. Margaret had tied a cow's tail up and then without thinking turned the cow loose with its tail tied up. The cow was bawling and tugging against its tail tied to the ceiling. Margaret couldn't release the taut knot and frantically screamed for help as the cow struggled. Larry ran and drew his knife to cut the rope and release the cow. *Every good man has a knife.* When Russ got his first knife, he was so proud. Then he lost it, and Pappy told him a good man keeps track of their knife.

Get a grip

It had been a long day, and he was tired and hungry. Pappy was on the way home with the big horse truck, and he pulled into Friendly's to get something to eat. As he swung into a parking space, he bumped the car next to him and put a dent in the fender. As he got out to apologize, he was met by a long-haired hippie type in full rage coming at him. The man, some twenty-plus years his junior, wasn't ready to hear apologies or even how to come to a reasonable solution. He came swinging and caught Pappy in the jaw. At this point, Pappy had no choice but to defend himself, but the raving maniac had no idea who he was up against or that he had just the vulnerable attribute that would bring him to his knees. Pappy in split seconds grabbed his long flowing red locks and swung him down, bashing the head attached to those locks into the side of the truck. Pappy maintained his grip on those long locks while the hippie continued to attack, repelled with another head slam to the fender. Finally, he cried uncle, but before releasing him, Pappy gave him another bash for good measure, and then let him stumble away. By the time Pappy arrived home, his jaw was swollen, black-and-blue, a battle scar of victory.

Fair warning

It was the usual Saturday evening in dead of winter at the local barroom. Patrons were laughing and chatting over their favorite beverage and enjoying one another's company. They didn't pay attention at first as the farmer entered, but slowly everything went quiet as they noticed the shotgun he had by his side. Looking around, he announced, "The next one who cuts through my fences or leaves my gates open will answer to this." He holds up the shotgun, looking intently into the faces around the room, turned, and slowly exited the bar. This wasn't the Wild West. It actually happened in North Brookfield. Farmers work hard at great expense to care for their property and livestock. It is frustrating when others have no respect for property, and you have to repair repeatedly the damage they cause. I'm sure it was not the first time he made those repairs from snowmobilers crossing his pastures. The difference was the timing. Today he would probably be in prison or at least lose his license to carry, but in that day, it was just fair warning.

Fur Family

Field Study by Russ Buzzell

Fur Family

On the farm, pets were pretty much a luxury that was unaffordable. Almost everything had to serve a purpose or pull their weight. But there were dogs, cats, chickens, rabbits, and lots of baby everything.

The dogs

Larry and Lady

We had a couple dogs. Lady was a black-and-white collie. As much as we loved her, she never came in the house. Her domain was the barn, and she helped bring in the cows. After Lady was Angel, another collie dog, mostly white with black face and ears. She also held court in the barn, overseeing who came and went. Friendly and good companions during milking but not the spoiled, pampered pups we think of as pets today.

A Diane memory

Wendy had been my dog before I married Larry. She had been a rescue from a situation of neglect. My older brother Dennis brought her home as a half-grown puppy and between work and college, he didn't have much time for her. A German Shepherd, she grew to be about eighty-five pounds and bonded to me and really didn't take orders well from anyone else in my family. When I got married, we had a small apartment upstairs in the farmhouse, but we had to go through the house to access our apartment. It was clear she would not be allowed in the house. In fact it was pretty clear she wasn't wanted period. They were afraid she would chase the cows or kill chickens. I was beside myself when my father showed up one day and said, "Either you keep her or get rid of her. We don't want her." She was definitely my dog, so I was stuck. I snuck her upstairs crying my eyes out, worried about what I could do. I was warned if she so much as chased a chicken, they would shoot her. I know it sounds harsh, but dogs often wreak havoc on livestock, and livestock comes first over unruly dogs. Well thankfully, Wendy turned out to be better than everyone expected. She never chased any of the livestock, following me everywhere and actually guarded the farm loyally. Cousin Mike came to borrow a shovel once when no one was around, and she wouldn't let him out of the barn with it. At first Mom was scared to death of her, and I did my best to avoid her at all costs, until one day Wendy bounded in the door with me. Mom didn't expect her and screamed, sending poor Wendy cowering under the couch. Another time she was laying on the back step, when Mom with little Stephanie, about four at the time, approached the house. Mom wouldn't go near her, but Stephanie walked right up to her, bumped her with her toe, and told her to move. Wendy got up and slunk off to one side. When Mom realized if little Steph could push her around, maybe Wendy wasn't so bad. She soon warmed up to her becoming best of friends and actually enjoyed her company, feeling much safer with Wendy around. Whenever we had to go somewhere, Wendy stayed with Mom, lying at her feet as she sat at the kitchen table with her coffee and cigarettes.

Wendy

As I said, Wendy was my dog, very perceptive and protective. I remember one time sitting on a box while we were milking with

Wendy beside me. The motor running the milking machines was loud enough that you didn't hear people coming, but Wendy could. There was one farmer that used to come around, kind of a hippy type, and I think used a little weed. As far as I know, he never was a threat, but Wendy didn't trust him for some reason, probably the weed. As we sat there waiting to remove the machine from a cow nearly done, I sensed her tense a little, and then the hair stood up on her back. Slowly the barn door started to open, and she leaped, and I threw my arms around her just as this guy started to come in. Seeing her in my arms, he slammed the door shut. She was fine once I assured her it was okay, but I'm not sure he was too confident. She was ready to serve and protect.

    I didn't routinely allow her on the bed, but I did like her in the bedroom when Larry wasn't around. You know the Johnny Carson thing with his brothers happened more often than I care to mention, and I was too tired to stay up. The big old farmhouse was kind of creepy after dark, so many doors and room upon room. Without him there, I was glad she was with me. If I fell asleep, sometimes she would crawl up onto the foot of the bed, and that was fine with me. One night she was on the end of the bed, and I was in a dead sleep. Larry came home really late, and she wouldn't let him in the bedroom. He stood at the door softly calling me to wake up as she softly growled her warning. Served him right. Go sleep on the couch!

    We did have another dog briefly whom we named Chuckie. He was a little pup dropped off in the road by the barn one winter night. It's so maddening when people do that! He was some kind of terrier, cute little thing, so cold and shivering. I took him in and cleaned him up, and he was so covered with fleas they were floating in the water of the bath I gave him! Wendy and he became friends. Unfortunately, as he grew, he didn't follow Wendy's good example and went off on a chicken killing spree. He didn't come home that night.

    Annie was a sheltie. I went with someone who was getting a puppy. I didn't really plan to get another dog after Wendy, but there she was. She kind of sat to one side observing the other pups and looked at me and gave a little bark. I decided we needed her. She was a like Wendy, a valuable addition to the farm. Pappy wasn't impressed when we came home and expressed his dissatisfaction, but she would talk back to him, always getting in the last word. He really came to respect her when not much more than a pup she woke us tugging on our blankets to alert us of a chimney fire. Another time she dragged us outside, insisting we come out to the barn. One of the cows had calved next to the fence, and the calf was on the wrong side of the fence where momma cow couldn't get to it and probably would have died if not for her. She was a great little dog, smart as a whip.

Annie

Cats

Everyone thinks farmers need cats, and a couple cats, maybe a few, can be helpful to keep the rodent population at bay, but so frustrating the number of cats and kittens dumped at our barnyard. Although we were never unkind or abusive, they never got special treatment, and a housecat used to lounging in a temperature-controlled home with meals laid out for them were in for a shock. It often didn't go well for them. They became feral and impossible to keep their population to a manageable number with all the kittens they produced. They sometimes became as much a problem as the rats. Heaven forbid you try to pat one. If you did manage to corner one, it would snarl and lash out at you. They were mostly on their own, but we had a hub cap we turned upside down and would dump some milk there for them. One of these feral cats Ralph found impaled on a spike we used to hang harnesses on. He gently took her down, and she took off. He was sure she wouldn't live, but she lived for years with a big scar and earned the name Gramma Cat. We have no idea how she ended up on that nail. Maybe fell from one of the beams chasing mice or a fight with another cat. Who knows? And it probably sounds awful she wasn't rushed to a vet, but it wasn't in the budget for a feral cat who was going to fight you tooth and nail all the way, and we couldn't catch her anyway. We kept the horse grain in barrels in the tack room. Tried to keep a cover on them to keep the rats out, but they would often find their way in. As the grain got used up, we would have to reach deep in the barrel to scoop it out. One day Pappy went to reach in, and big rat was at the bottom. He was eating his fill and couldn't get out, so Pappy went and found a cat and put it in the barrel. What a ruckus! Cat-1, Rat-0.

Rabbits

As a kid, Larry had rabbits. Ralph gave him the chicken coop for them, and he had fun with them at first. It started out with just two, but in no time he had more than he could count. They were hard to catch, and when you did, they would bite and flip over and scratch viciously with their hind legs. The coop had about a foot of hay chaff on the floor, and they created burrows through it for their own little world. When he tired of them, he went to the little old man in Spencer on Route 9 and worked a deal to sell them to him. The little old man was Polish I think, spoke broken English and had coops and hutches and little sheds full of just about everything you could think of, from rabbits, hamsters, guinea pigs, white mice and rats, goats, and a variety of birds to banties, pigeons, ducks, and geese. Ironically when I was growing up, long before I met Larry, my father used to bring us there, and we would walk through the narrow, slimy paths between the sheds littered with cages. Today the health department or animal protection would probably have shut him down because they were crowded into cages and coops and not very sanitary. I have to wonder if the Easter bunnies we got from him back then were any of Larry's.

Romeo

There was a steer named Romeo. A steer is a castrated bull. To put it politely as possible, castration removes the testicles, which changes the hormones in a steer, making them more docile, safer, and easier to handle. He was probably meant to be butchered but became somewhat of a pet, and they liked having him around. When it was time to get the cows in for milking, many days they were at the door waiting, while other times they would need to be herded up to the barn. Russ and Jack would take one of the many horses to round them up, but Larry liked Romeo. I wish I had a picture, but I can just imagine Larry plodding down through the field on Romeo. He didn't need a saddle or bridle but just climbed on Romeo's back and, leaning back to grasp his tail to steer him, would amble down through the pasture gathering the cows. It could have taken less time if Larry had just gone on foot, but the two of them got the job done. Romeo wasn't fast on his feet, took his time, and made it a pleasurable ride.

Chickens

Ralph had chickens from the time he was a little boy. Chickens weren't really pets, but Ralph loved his chickens, still does. Pappy not so much, especially when they would roost over the horses, saddles, and harnesses, dropping poop all over them, but he could tolerate them for a fresh chicken in Mom's pot pie. Chickens can be dangerous. One night Ralph climbed to the rafters near the roof of the barn to get a rooster sleeping on beam, slipped, and fell, had to be forty feet. Fortunately, there was three to four inches of hay dust where he landed, so he wasn't seriously injured. He did however get knocked out and woke with a few cuts on his head. It was just before he went into the Marines, and when they were shaving his head as they do to new recruits, he was questioned about his "wounds."

Ralph had about one hundred chickens when he left for the Marines, and he was surprised there were actually some left when he got back. Russ would throw them some grain, but they were mostly on their own. After the Marines, Ralph got his job at Aubuchon Hardware store. It gave him new opportunities to trade chickens. One time he brought a rooster to the store. He put him in the cellar until his contact would come to get him, which didn't come quite soon enough. The Aubuchon owners and supervisors came to the store and were welcomed by the sound of a rooster crowing. They knew that wasn't part of typical store inventory, and Ralph had some uneasy explaining to do. Ralph was a good employee, but the farm mentality influenced his view of this new work environment. At the grand opening of the new warehouse, he was impressed by the size and voiced the compliment, "You sure could fit a lot of hay in here."

Ralph later became known as "the chick man" when he went to work for Klem's. For forty years Ralph was the chick man at Klem's, ordering and selling chicks every spring and sharing his wealth of experience and knowledge. He was a fountain of information for customers, instructing them on care and feed and pointing out the different breeds. He was also very clear about their feelings and personalities. Yes, chickens have feelings! And personalities! And people believed him! Klem's had the perfect salesman when it came to chicks. When you went into the store, you would almost always find him down with the chicks. So when Larry stopped at Klem's, of course he would wander over to the chicks to say howdy. As he turned to go down the aisle to the chick section, he spotted Ralph and a coworker. Suddenly they started spinning arms in the air and bumping into each other back-to-back. What on earth? Of course, you can read Larry's face, and he was obviously confused by this behavior. The coworker dropped her arms and walked past Larry with a matter-of-fact comment, "Chick magnet." They actually paid Ralph to work there.

Duck!

Ralph tried his hand at raising pigs. They were growing really fast. Ralph and Larry were inspecting their progress one day and, leaning on their enclosure, watched as a couple of Ralph's Muscovy ducks flew by them and landed in the pen. Bad idea. It was just a flurry of feathers, and the pigs made short order of them. Nothing left but a few feathers. Ralph and Larry looked at each other and decided they best make sure Ralph's little boys didn't get in there. The pigs went off to slaughter soon after.

Udderly Family

Cutting Ice Cow

Udderly Family

On the farm there were hayfields, cornfields, woodlot, and pastures. Some land would be parceled off to family members for them to build homes as they grew up and got married. The pastures had various purposes. Night pasture was near the barn where the cows were kept at night and in winter. There was a place under the front portion of the barn that was a shelter from wind and the elements as well as shade in the summer but also allowed them freedom to roam and graze, even stand in the brook for relief from heat or bugs. Most mornings the cows would be lined up at the door to come in ready to be milked. Across the street in front of the barn was a day pasture. It had a long run or wide path along the edge of the cornfield to a lower field. Through the property brooks ran, and portions leached out across the low lands, making swampy areas before gathering again to a wide brook to go under the bridge and wind its way along the cornfield and down through the day pasture to join the brook that ran through that field. The brooks were important water sources for the cows and were clear and clean. The brook was even stocked with trout, and fishing was a common pastime, not to mention a cool place for kids to wade, swim, and explore on hot summer days. Years later Boston would interfere again to prevent the trapping of beaver. Beavers, which are nothing more than big rats, are the worst pollutants and ruin the ecology of the brook and swamp, making it stagnant and filthy. Fish and other water dependent critters lost a clean environment when the beavers were allowed to overrun and make a mess of it, and we lost a good place to fish, swim, as well a watering place for our livestock. Beavers in the process also destroyed the lower part of Tucker Hill Road, making it impossible along with flooding a field we had hayed for decades. Ironically Boston now even insists that cows must be prevented from "polluting the brook" with fences to keep them out when the brook is so polluted by beavers it's not fit for them to drink. There was another side hill pasture known as Victor's side hill across Tucker Hill Road side of the barn for dry cows, not in milk or getting ready to freshen (give birth). The brothers knew when to expect a calf partly by the gestation period, but as their time grew near, you could see the bag (the mammary gland sack where the milk comes from) starting to fill up, preparing for the birth of the calf. The momma cows would seek out private places to give birth, and then Larry had to go find them to bring them back to the herd where the calf would be put in front of her stanchion, and she would begin the daily morning and night milking process.

> God blessed them and said to them, "Be fruitful and increase in number; fill the earth and subdue it. Rule over the fish in the sea and the birds in the sky and over every living creature that moves on the ground."
> —Genesis 1:28

A stone's throw

This day, Larry ventured out to find a cow and her calf seeking out the places he knew she might be in the night pasture down near the swamp. Upon finding them, he hefted the calf over his shoulder to head back to the barn with the mom following behind. Keep in mind calves weighed between fifty and seventy-five pounds and not thrilled to be hanging over someone's shoulder, so he was blatting and struggling some, and Larry was trudging through some of the swamp where the footing wasn't that great either. I should also mention that the calf relieved himself, so his shirt had now become a diaper soaking up his pee. He had already trudged all over kingdom come to find them, it was hot, and here he was with a hot body draped over him like a fur coat with the calf blatting his displeasure when Larry heard the bull, a low, soft, threatening moan.

Bulls can be placid but never an animal you can trust. Too many times I've heard stories of the "gentle" bull turning on and killing

THE ARTIST, THE FARMER, THE HUNTER, AND THE GOOD GUY

farmers when they've become complacent. It doesn't take much. One farmer had a bull he led down to drink at the brook every day, and one day only the bull came back. They found him gored. Another "gentle" bull crushed his owner against the wall of his stall. Bulls can be very aggressive, downright dangerous, but at that time if you wanted milk, you had to have a bull so cows would calve to make milk. Now artificial insemination eliminates the need for a bull on the farm.

Before going in the pasture where the bull was, the boys would look for his location to avoid a confrontation. He was big, mostly white Holstein about 1,200 pounds. Larry remembers hearing this bull bellowing loud roars standing in the middle of the pasture one afternoon. One by one, all the cows came and stood in circle around him as he kept up his roars like he was some kind of god. It was creepy as he stood there puffing and pawing and the cows all paying homage to him.

Larry didn't remember he was in this pasture, and the bull wasn't happy to see Larry in what he thought was his territory and had an attitude for sure. Larry knew he was in trouble. Looking around, he dropped the calf and headed toward a well. It was an old dry well, or at least not producing good water, full of frogs and snakes about twenty feet around and low, but at least it was something he could keep between him and that bull. They circled that well round and round until Larry was running out of steam, but the bull wasn't. He noticed some stones about the size of a big softball on the ground. Staring that bull down, he slowly bent and picked up one of the stones. His hope was to discourage the bull from advancing or even send him packing if he could hit him, giving him time to get away. Thankfully, Larry was a decent athlete, played some baseball, and knew how to throw hard and fast, and that was exactly what he did. He caught that bull in the forehead between the eyes with a hard fastball throw, and the bull dropped to his knees seeing stars. Larry took full advantage of that moment to scurry, pick up the calf, and get to the barn double quick.

Weeks later as Larry and Ralph were going through the pasture, that bull challenged them again. Concerned, Ralph looked around for some place of protection, knowing the trouble they could be facing, but Larry stopped him and said, "Watch this." He slowly reached down to the ground *like* he was picking up a stone to throw, and the bull stopped dead in his tracks. There was no stone, but that bull was smart enough to be wary and prevent being the victim of another headache. Larry and Ralph knew better then to press their luck and left the field, keeping an eye on the bull, but he just watched them and didn't venture after them. Good memory! The bull, I mean, he had a good memory.

Larry had a similar experience another time while searching out a cow and calf in a neighbor's pasture. They often shared pastures, and this one was a little overgrown with brush and a thick alder grove and a winding brook running through it. The brook had some shallows but also some fairly deep sections. Larry didn't know the neighbor's bull was in the pasture until he heard thrashing coming through the brush. He did know it was a Jersey bull, small and compact but aggressive and nothing you'd want to tangle with. He headed for a section of brook that was deep and set the calf down, waiting for the phantom causing the ominous stir to appear. In the meantime, he found a rock about the size of a football and prepared for battle. As the bull burst through and made his way into the brook on his hasty mission, Larry hurled that rock and caught him in the head just between the horns and, like the time before, stopped him in his tracks. The bull floundered in the deep water, while Larry picked up the calf and made a beeline for the fence and safety.

Larry's comment: "As I look back on these times, I can't help but thank God for his protection and provision. It was by his grace I learned to throw. I had no one to really teach me. I mean, I had big brothers and friends but no real coaches like today. Then there was the well and the deep part of the brook as well as those stones placed for my protection decades before, right where I would need them. God is just amazing."

> For he will command his angels concerning you
> to guard you in all your ways.
> —Psalm 91:11

THE ARTIST, THE FARMER, THE HUNTER, AND THE GOOD GUY

Cruising by

Getting a bull in that has escaped the pasture can be a challenge as well. Larry was on the dirt road and could see their young bull coming down Tucker Hill and needed to divert him through the open gate opposite the end of the dirt road. He knew he couldn't get there in time and didn't want him getting past the gate, so he picked up a good-size rock and took aim as the bull came in range. However, he did not know the chief was in the town cruiser slowly following the bull. Country cops are used to playing cowboy on occasion. Larry fired off the rock just as the cruiser pulled out around the bull to force him into the gate, and the rock flew over the hood, just missing the windshield, hitting the bull in the neck. So the bull went in the gate by team effort, and by the grace of God, there was no damage to the cruiser. Chief Thomasian told Larry, "Awesome throw but you almost got to buy the town a new windshield!"

No bull
Conversation with Larry

Recently we were driving on South Main by what used to be a pasture just before McCarthy Road. Deep in thought Larry peered at the passing scenery.

"I didn't throw rocks at just bulls you know."

Thinking there had been some animal in that pasture, I had to ask, "Really, what else?"

"Tony and I were walking home right here from the movies one night. It was pretty late, and a car came up behind us. Some kids I didn't know got out of the car. Had to be out-of-towners. Tony and I started down McCarthy because they looked kind of suspicious. When I saw them with a lighter, I yelled at Tony to 'Run!' We took off, but they had lit cherry bombs and threw them at us. I could really run, but Tony, not so much. One blew up in front of Tony and got him in the chest. He was bloody and burnt, and I got mad, really mad. I turned and started hauling rocks at them. I dinged up their car pretty good before they jumped back in and took off."

"Did you call the police?"

"Naw. By the time we got anywhere to call the police, they were long gone. It was just stupid kids. It did feel really good to hit their car, let me tell you."

Taking the bull by the horn

Pappy had a run-in with Tucker's bull. One morning this thousand pound guernsey bull was in the front yard making known to the world his power and might with grunts, bellowing and pawing the ground just looking for someone to challenge. Just a little too much testosterone going in his head. He had whacked the barrel of kerosene on a tripod out front, tossing it in the air and rolling that barrel around like a toy. He came around back and was pawing at the back door. There were windows in the top half of the door and was not heavy-duty by any means. The family felt trapped in the house by this raging monster. Dad was working at the highway, and Mom called him, telling him she was afraid the bull would try to get in the house. He came storming home, angered he was taken from his job "just to chase a bull." He pulled up in front of the barn, grabbing a lead pipe nearby, as the bull ran at him. Pappy stood his ground as the bull advanced, swung the pipe at the bull, coming in contact with a horn, whacking it off the bull's head as he came at him, and then a second swing got him in the nose. Taking a horn off is *not* easy and extremely painful for the bull, but it was in total self-defense and what he deserved. Bleeding profusely and bellowing miserably, the bull ran off down the road. Pappy-1, Bull-0.

Being bullied (as told by Russ)

I was about twelve, and Dad sent me to check on Sanella. She was foaling, and I was going up one side and down the other of Buck Hill looking for her, and then I heard the brush moving. It was Tucker's Jersey bull. Margaret and George Tucker both got attacked by their bull and tossed in the air. I didn't like him, and he didn't like me. Course he probably didn't like me because I had thrown rocks at him, but anyway now, he was coming after me. I ran for the big rock on Buck Hill, and my heart was racing. Running full speed, I leaped on that rock. Usually, I had trouble climbing that rock, but by some miracle, I scrambled up to the top, and that bull circled round and round. He kept me there for quite some time, and I was a little nervous to get down even after he left, but I had to find Sanella. It was really fascinating when I did find her. She was in labor, and all the horses were circled around her. She would lay down and then get up and walk about and then lay down again until finally the foal dropped, and all the horses stood around like they were protecting her. Nature is a beautiful thing.

Took a licking

Ralph unloading grain at the train station up town

When Ralph got out of the Marines, he started out working for George Hanson at Eastern States getting $1 an hour unloading one-hundred-pound bags of grain from the train uptown onto trucks for delivery. Then unloading it from the trucks at the farms it was delivered to. At the chicken farm he had to sling them over his shoulder to bring them up a flight of stairs. Ralph was a slim build at that point, but from being in the service, he was in peak condition and could sling a bag on each shoulder to get the job done.

As told by Ralph

I was working for George Hanson at Eastern States delivering grain. We would have to unload the grain bags, and at one place, we carried these one-hundred-pound bags through the cow barn to the bin. We would try to carry two, sometimes even three bags to get the job done, so I was walking with a bag on each shoulder. As I went past the bull pen, this big old bull reached out through the bars with his big long tongue and wrapped it around my arm and knocked me right over. Course I wasn't expecting it, carrying quite a load, and I wasn't a very big guy, so it wasn't hard to knock me over with two hundred pounds of grain weighing me down. But by golly, it was his tongue! Long enough to reach out and grab me!

Birdie
A Diane memory

    Years later I had a run-in with a crazy little heifer. A heifer is a young female cow and called a heifer until she gives birth to her first calf, usually about two years old. Birdie wasn't even a yearling, and being a heifer, I didn't think twice to be wary because it's very rare that a heifer would go mean like a bull. We had bottle-raised her until she was old enough to turn out with the other heifers and, like our other heifers, was used to being handled. Ralph had come to our farm with a new calf, and we needed a collar for her. Corey, my son, was a little more than two years old at the time, and I told him to stay with Pa in the barn while I went to get the collar off Birdie. (The kids called Ralph "Pa" like their cousins called their dad). This was one time I was thankful he didn't do as he was told and followed me out to the pasture.

    I had jumped over the gate to the back pasture and started calling Birdie like we often did. I walked out past the thick soft ground where the cows gathered where we put their feed down. It is mucky and almost sucks your feet into the muddy goo. I could see the cows coming up from the lower pasture in answer to my call. Birdie was in front, and as she came through the break in the stone wall, she was moving. She had her head down, bucking and heading right for me. She wasn't acting right and looked like trouble. I tried to get back to the gate, but in the thick mushy area, the poor footing slowed me down, and she got to me before I could get out. She was only about four hundred pounds, but that was still about three hundred more than me. I know it sounds strange, but when a large animal wants to maul you, the best thing you can do is get as close as you can, so I grabbed an ear and one of her stubbly little horns and did my best to hug her to keep from getting any impact from head, horns, or hooves. She whirled around and around, and I clung on as best I could, yelling to Corey to "Go get Pa!" By the time Pa came out and got to us, she had flung me off. I was down on the ground on my back in the muck, kicking the best I could to ward her off, but she was winning the battle. Those short stubby horns battered and bruised my thighs, butt, and arms. Pa jumped in, whacking at her while I crawled onto a pile of fence posts nearby to recover, but she went right around him and after me again. He grabbed a post and beat her off again until she got the message and took off for the lower field, and I crawled over the fence. She was shipped to Ralph's the next day. With kids around, we couldn't take another chance she would try that again. And she did! That winter Pa was out feeding his cows hay, and she tried it with him. Fortunately, breaking through the crusty snow slowed her down enough to allow Ralph to run on top of the crust and get away. She went to a bigger farm, and they lopped off her horns, but she was psycho, and finally, she was shipped off to become a Big Mac or Whopper, which was what she deserved. I tell this story because if a half-grown heifer calf can do that damage, think what a thousand-pound bull can do. She really was a rare case, and we have no explanation for her actions. Ralph first thought I did something that made her react like that, but I hadn't, and when she went after him just months later, we knew she wasn't right in the head or safe to have around.

Willie (as told by Ralph)

I was only about thirteen when we had Willie. He was a good dairy bull. Pappy had gone to Maine, so I was milking on my own, all thirty-five cows. Willie had a stanchion in the barn, but this day he didn't come in the barn with the cows to his stanchion until I was milking. When Willie came in, I quickly realized he was coming after me. After a lot of dodging in and around the cows, I was able to escape through a stanchion and out through the silo. I went right to the house and called Abraham Aframe, the cattle dealer, to come get him. By the time I went back to barn, Willie was in his stanchion, and I was able to close his stanchion, keeping him captive until Mr. Aframe came. He blindfolded him, loaded him, and trucked him away, and I was happy to see him go. Pappy was mad at me that I got rid of him and told me I could have beat him. I didn't think so. I knew Willie didn't like me, and at that point I didn't like Willie either, so it was best we didn't have to deal with him anymore. Willie had also run off some fishermen, so I wasn't his first challenge, and it wasn't going to get better. You just can't trust them bulls."

Fun fact: Bovines are said to be colorblind, so the red of the bullfighter's cape has nothing to do with causing a bull to attack.

Physician assistant

Sometimes livestock need to be doctored. Farmers do their best to keep their herds healthy and handle vetting as much as possible themselves, but there are those times when the vet has to be called in. Such was the case with a cow with milk fever. Milk fever happens right after giving birth. They lay down too weak to get up and stretched their head back like they were dying. They need IV treatment, so for this case the vet was called. Larry came down to milk to find Pappy helping the vet, holding an IV bag. Pappy instructed Larry, "Go get a pitchfork, boy!" Larry was a little confused why the vet would need a pitchfork but hurried to get one because his father was pretty adamant about it. He quickly came back with it to hand to his father, asking him what he needed it for. Almost angry, Pappy commanded him, "Keep between us and that bull!" Larry turned to see the bull head down and snorting at them. Skinny little Larry protecting the vet, Pappy, and the cow with a pitchfork! I bet you don't learn that in vet school.

There's another time the vet is called when it's more than something they could handle. It was called casting their withers. It happens when giving birth, and the uterus is expelled along with the calf. Treatment was physically difficult and draining for all involved. The cow in the stanchion standing up with Larry having to hold a washtub containing all the internals pressed against her backside to keep her from lying down while the vet cleaned them and pushed them back inside. It is pretty gross. Most cows didn't recover well and would have to be shipped. Hard enough to treat the cow, but knowing it's all for naught is depressing.

Insides out (as told by Russ)

I came upon a cow who calved, and she was in trouble. She had cast her withers, expelled her uterus with the calf. At that moment Billy Brown happened to come by and flew into action. He urged me to get pails of water as hot and as fast as I could get them and call Doc Smith while he grabbed grain bags and laid out all the innards on them. As I fetched pails of hot water, he rinsed and splashed the hot water on the cow's organs, keeping them warm until the vet came. It was imperative we keep them warm to reinsert them back into the cow. His fast action saved the cow.

Artificial insemination fail (as told by Russ)

In school we had Future Farmers and agriculture courses. I wanted to do all I could to improve our herd and make the farm more profitable and learned that the bull and breeding can make all the difference. We couldn't afford a "good" bull, but Mr. Frizzell, our teacher, helped me learn about artificial insemination. I went through a catalog, and we picked out a beautiful bull with excellent breeding, and we purchased the semen to breed our cows. Our herd were just run-of-the-mill cows, and hopefully this would improve the herd. Unfortunately, we didn't take into the consideration the size of the bull, and when the cows started calving, it was disastrous. The calves were huge, way too big for our cows to birth safely. Many of them cast their withers, and with others, sadly the vet would have to butcher some of the calves within the cow to get them out. It was a gruesome process having to support the cow standing up while he aborted the calf in the attempt to save the cow. She would have died otherwise, but we lost several good cows along with their calves despite everything we tried.

What's in a name

When I asked Larry if he named the bulls, he said, "No… But I called them a lot of things." On the other hand, the cows were different. Their personalities, markings, and habits often determined their name. Some were named for people or family we knew, and it was a great honor to have a cow named after you. Ralph had cows like Susan T, named after Mabel's coworker at the hospital, and Mary Magdalene. Some cows were placid and nondescript, but others were memorable.

The Traveler, the Elephant, and the Smurfs

Traveler earned her name. She was spotted black-and-white with very cool markings (that really dates us, but I'm quoting Larry), and it was her habit of roaming the roadsides that pegged her the Traveler. Particularly at night, Traveler had a habit of leaving the pasture, and she had a unique method of escape. The fences were mostly barbed or electric wire strung between cedar posts about ten feet apart. She would walk up very close beside the fence, lay down on the fence, and get up on the other side. She would spend the night roaming the sides of the roads, eating her fill, and be back at the farm in the morning ready to come in and get milked. It was unusual that she didn't bring any of the others with her because that's usually the trend. One gets out and the others follow, but she was kind of a loner and didn't invite the others to join her.

Elephant was another memorable cow. She was a huge red-and-white cow probably guernsey cross with a bag the size of softball and gave hardly any milk. We often wondered why Pappy kept her. She also had a unique escape route. We knew she was getting out but not sure where. One day Russ was fly fishing in the brook with a steel rod Uncle Louie gave him and followed her down the brook to watch where she would go, curious to see where she was getting out, and she wallowed right down the middle of the brook and under the bridge! After evening milking in the warm weather, she would go down the cow path to the brook, walk into the brook, and drink her fill and then amble through the water under the bridge to the other side. On the other side was a path, most likely one she made that led to the back of a big field belonging to our neighbor Billy Brown. That field was thick with alfalfa, and Elephant would graze all night to her heart's content and come back the same way she went arriving with a belly bloated like she was pregnant with her secret indulgences. All that alfalfa and big belly and almost no milk, but you had to admit, she was no dummy. We never fenced the bridge, and no other cow ever tried that. One night Elephant wandered up through Billy Brown's field, crossed the street to his house. It was a warm summer evening, and Billy was sitting by an open window in his living room watching TV. It must have caught Elephant's eye, and she leaned into the window and gave a loud moo. Startled Billy so bad he almost fell off his couch! It was a moooving experience for both.

Then there were the Smurfs, Smurfette and Smurfelle. They were Holstein crossed with probably Hereford. They were black with white face but with milk cow conformation. Herefords are meat cattle and have "more meat on their bones" than a dairy cow, which tended to put their calories into milk production so they would look bonier. Brother Ralph got the pair from Ralph Whitman but didn't have room for them, so they came to the farm on Cider Mill. They were small for milkers but still gave more milk than we needed for the family. We raised some veal calves off

Smurfette and Smurfelle

the extra milk and even sold some. They were quiet, easygoing cows, didn't need as much feed as a bigger dairy cow, and didn't test fences. They were quite sneaky when they happened to find a hole in the fence and would daily meander into the neighbor's field and eat their fill. Larry found a beaten path that led to their wanderings, but they never went farther than that and came back when we called them for milking. They were at the scene of a terrible accident. Larry was working at Norton Company by this time, and one of the guys had bought chicks for his kids at Easter. Well, one grew into a boisterous rooster, and the neighbors weren't impressed, so he needed to find a country home for him. Larry reluctantly agreed to take him. Many roosters end up in the pot, but he couldn't in good conscience do that to some kid's pet, at least until he knew they wouldn't come for a visit, so the Smurfs had a new roommate. We had him a couple weeks, and we called him City Rooster. That obnoxious little rooster always met Larry at the door, flying at him when he came to the barn and pecking at his feet, so Larry thought it odd when he wasn't there one morning when he came out to milk. The Smurfs were lying down, so he bumped one of them with his foot to get her to stand up, and lo and behold, there was the rooster flatter than a pancake under the Smurfs. He had to be a city rooster to be so foolish to hang out under a cow at bedtime. Eventually the Smurfs went to Ralph's farm to join his herd. Smurfelle birthed out a set of twins among others in following years, but Smurfette, while birthing a calf, was attacked by coyotes. The remains of the calf still had the partial birth sack. We will never know the terrible trauma she experienced, but Smurfette never conceived to have another calf after that.

Mandy—pain in the butt (as told by Russ)

Mandy, Mandy! She was a black as the ace of spades Angus Jersey cross. I used to take my pony Ned out to round up the cows, but Mandy did not want to be rounded up. She would bellow like a bull and lower her head and paw the ground. Ned was scared to death of her, so I would just leave her alone. Ned wouldn't go near her anyway, but once the other cows were in the barn, she would wander up in her own time. You didn't want to go near her if she had a calf because she would come to meet you. You wouldn't dare get close. We would have to wait for her to come in to get milked when she was good and ready and while she was in the barn, then we would go get the calf. She conformed at her own pace. Once when Ralph was milking her, she turned around and bit him in the butt, the only cow I knew that ever did that!

THE ARTIST, THE FARMER, THE HUNTER, AND THE GOOD GUY

Silk (as told by Russ)

Silk was a little heifer I raised. She was what we called a reindeer. A reindeer to us was anything that was a combination of breeds, but she was most likely a Shorthorn Holstein cross with a little bit of something else. She was a mottled red-and-white, pretty little thing, and I wanted to show her in 4H, but there was never enough time to go to meetings and get to the events. She grew up into a big cow. She never gave much milk, but she was my cow.

Outstanding in their field

Cotton was a big white Holstein, incredible milker, and we had her for years. Her distended bag drooped so that the teats almost touched the floor, and we didn't need a milking surcingle for her but just set the machine on the floor beside her. When she freshened, she gave so much milk sometimes she would fill the machine, and we would have to dump and reset to finish. She was one of our best milkers, and we got good stock from her as well. (Freshen means having a calf, and right after calving, they give the most milk "fresh." Gradually over time, as you milk cows, they start out giving a lot and then less over time until they dry out and time to calve out again.)

Then there were the twins. They were so similar, same size, same black-and-white markings, were almost identical. They stood side by side in the center of the row and were together most of the time. Larry remembers one of the Twins, after calving, figured out that if she made a hard right coming in the barn door through the narrow hallway to the center barn floor, she could get to her calf. It was such a small space and two hard turns, but she made it because she wanted to get to her calf. Kind of makes you realize that animals have feelings much like we do.

Nancy named for Nancy Wilson (she lived at the farm in Spencer where Dad was renting) and was a hard milker. She had funnel-shaped teats, and the teat cup wouldn't go on, so Russ had to milk her by hand. It was hard work to milk her and took a lot of time, but every day she filled a twelve-quart pail morning and night, so we kept her.

She once kicked Ralph in the forehead, knocked him right over and almost out cold, but he said it was his fault. He surprised her by reaching down for her udder when she wasn't expecting it.

Dumb Dora was a big cow named after Mom's Aunt Dora. Aunt Dora was a very nice person, and Dumb Dora was not a reflection on her at all. She was named after Aunt Dora, but Dumb was added later by some of the little things that made her unique. There were twenty-five stanchions per side, but Dora knew her stanchion, and no other cow dared go in her stanchion at both Spencer and the farm. She would drive them out hard and fast. She was also at the top of the pecking order out in the pasture.

Popeye had a watch eye. Good milker, big cow. Sylvia was not a friendly cow. She beat up on Rip. He fell asleep milking her, and she let loose kicking and bucking. Machine, stool, and Rip went flying, and he landed facedown in the gutter. Getting kicked by the cows wasn't uncommon, but you did your best to avoid it, obviously. Larry once got kicked in the middle of his back and flattened right out on the ground, leaving a big black-and-blue hoofprint on his back. Pa got kicked in the knee so bad he thought he broke his leg. You never really knew what or when something would set them off. Flies, noise, sudden movements, or someone they didn't know coming in the barn. Larry learned his lesson not to yell at them. It was shortly after getting his new denture while letting one cow out. She let loose with manure going everywhere when she had a whole pasture to poop in beyond the door. He was telling her what he thought of her, and it wasn't "nice cow." As he put some emphasis into his salutation to "Get out of here!" his teeth flew from his mouth and slid down the gutter. He pulled the milking machines off that were in progress and went straight to the house to clean them. Still not sure if I could have put them back in my mouth after that no matter how well you cleaned them.

End of an era

Popcorn was a heifer we kept when we sold the farm. She was a big black Holstein, and Stephanie named her for the large white

THE ARTIST, THE FARMER, THE HUNTER, AND THE GOOD GUY

Popcorn, 1980

popcorn-shaped spot on her face. She was a good, dependable cow. She gave milk to Pappy and Mom and ended up with Ralph. Ralph wanted her because she was a brush eater. Most cows graze on grasses, but Popcorn would reach up and clean branches and brush. She helped keep his fence lines clean. She became the "boss" cow in his herd, setting all the others straight as to the pecking order. I learned that she was the bell cow. Most people think a cowbell is a cute ornament, but the cowbell had an important use. On a farm with acres of pasture, the bell would let the famer know where to look for his cows. Generally, there was only one bell cow, and she was kind of the leader of the pack. When it was time to be fed or milked, all the other cows would follow her to the barn. I'm told that each bell has a different sound, and a farmer would know just by the sound of the bell which cowbell and cow he could hear. It could also alert him to trouble because most cows just amble along, but if they were running from danger, that bell made a racket, and the farmer would know to go help. Popcorn lived a good long time (twenty years), having mostly bull calves and never causing any trouble. In the end she went blind. It was really hard to see Popcorn go. She was the last of the herd from the old farm, but Ralph still has her cowbell.

Mumsy was Frank Partridge's cow. Frank was the little old guy with thick glasses renting the little farm Pappy bought on Cider Mill when the farm sold. He was a good friend, and Pappy let him live rent-free in the little red house until he passed away. The little red house was part of the old farm that was divided off and kept when the rest was sold. It was always called the little red house, but I never ever remember a stitch of red paint on that house. It had a little barn, and Frank kept a driving pony and Mumsy out there. Mumsy was a pretty little Jersey with front legs so crooked I'm not sure how she could walk, but she was another really good cow, almost a pet, and her milk was almost pure cream. She would definitely raise your butterfat count if she was in your herd. She lived with us on the little farm for a while after Frank passed, and I will never forget the time I went out to check on the cows. Not sure what prompted me, maybe the good Lord, but I saw Mumsy coming up through the break in the wall running and bucking. Now that was really unlike the slow ambling she was known for, until I saw the German Shepherd latched onto her hind leg. I have never had any desire to kill anything until I saw our Mumsy stumbling and fighting off that dog, and it's probably a good thing I didn't have a gun in my hands at that point. I ran like a crazy woman screaming at that dog. It let go, took off, and I chased it into the woods before going back to a panting and bleeding Mums. Thank you, Jesus, I was there to prevent that dog from doing too much damage, and a call to the neighbor made it clear what would happen if he showed up in our pasture again. She ended up living out her days at Ralph's in his herd with Popcorn.

Kind of Corny

Corn harvest is in early autumn. It is one of the necessary jobs that starts with tilling and planting in the spring and praying it grows enough all summer to feed a hungry herd of cows all winter, supplementing their hay and grain. Driving a tractor hauling a harvester up and down corn rows as it gathers the stalks, leaves, and cobs to chop it all into feed, then thrusting the mixture up a chute and into a dump truck to be hauled back to the farm is a process that took hours of monotonous time. There was one big cornfield across the street from the barn, but there were others around town as farmers co-opted land. At the barn, the driver would back up to a hopper. As the dump body of the truck tipped up, silage would slide into the hopper for the auger to suck the silage into a chute up and into the silo. Pappy had created a pitchfork kind of tool with a long ten-foot handle, and the long tines bent flat to rake the silage out of the truck body reaching the farthest corners of the dump bed to get it all out of the truck. Corn harvest was kind of routine seasonal task. Sort of mundane except for the comradery that hard work brings. Some good conversation and joking around made the job a little more enjoyable. One thing many farmers do, and Pappy did as well, is plant a few rows of sweet corn around the outside edge. Sweet corn is very different from feed corn, sweet being the operative word, but it is also smaller ears with tender kernels. Cow corn is much coarser. The sweet corn was given to friends and neighbors, but you had to pick your own. One fellow came to the farm thankful for the free corn until he realized he had to pick it himself and went away kind of sour. Pappy stopped planting the sweet corn when he found out someone was sneaking in, picking, and selling it.

Some silos are tall round structures with a roof and attached to the barn. The one at our farm was actually inside the barn reaching three full stories high. That's a lot of chopped corn! There was a window opening at the top on the outside where the chute inserts to fill the silo. Inside the barn at the bottom floor where the cow stanchions were, there was a door to access the silage to conveniently feed out at milking time. Over the winter it packed in, and some fermentation would take place that preserved it. Sometimes Ralph's banty roosters would get in there to get their fill and come out pretty tipsy with wings out to keep their balance and making funny low crowing noises.

There were also trench silos that were just long trenches. The driver would just back the truck into the trench to dump the silage there. When the old silo became unusable, Pappy made a trench silo. It was just a tarred base with earthen sides and tarps with tires placed on top to keep the tarps in place. There was a small bulldozer that the boys would use to push, level, and pack the corn into the trench. Larry always hated driving the bulldozer, fearful he would roll it over. He was grateful when another family friend, Roy Green, would show up, step in, and expertly level out and pack the mountain of chopped corn. For Roy, it was playtime driving the bulldozer, and he looked forward to helping out that way. The trench silo became kind of a popular place for pheasants to seek shelter as well as drown their miseries. They would exit such as the roosters would, wings down, and walking sideways.

To feed out the silage, we used a tractor and silage feeder, driving around the edge of the pasture, blowing out the silage in a trail of feed for the cows. That was a one-man job to load it up from the trench and spread, but it wasn't always that way. From the barn silo, we would shovel a peach basket full and serve it up to each cow in their manger in front of their stanchion, adding their grain and a can of molasses. That's fifty baskets to shovel morning and night. When niece Christy was little, she used to like to help Larry feed the "stinking stuff." It was stinky, but the cows would lick it up like candy. The old mangers would be almost shiny as they cleaned up every morsel.

THE ARTIST, THE FARMER, THE HUNTER, AND THE GOOD GUY

By the time I entered the picture, we were using the trench silo, and most of the farm was worked by Larry and Pappy. The brothers were called upon and still employed for the bigger jobs that required many hands or maybe some brawn, but Pappy would work with whoever was at hand, and that included me. He needed a driver, and I was all he had. I could drive a stick shift, sort of, but the stick in the 1949 Diamond T dump truck was a little challenging, not to mention I had never followed a harvester before. The truck was big, and stick was so loose you could roll it around in circles before shoving it in place and then just hope it went into the right gear. Larry warned me to keep the passenger side window shut. From experience, in the warm monotony, he got very sleepy, started to doze off, and didn't keep up. The harvester blew chopped corn in the cab and all over him. Woke him right up! Pappy would yell at him, and his response was "Just feeding the pheasants!" Nowadays we don't see pheasants, but back then they were pretty common, maybe because Larry fed them so well.

So Pappy and his new recruit went off to the cornfield. It was in October, and there had been a freeze, and the melting frost made the ground a little greasy. Pappy told me to line the front fender of the truck approximately beside the back wheel of the tractor, but I also had to keep an eye on the dump body through the little rearview window about the size of a number plate to see where the corn was landing in the dump body. The field sloped up from the entrance at the road, and he had advised me to load the rear end of the dump body to give the truck traction on the slippery ground. It was a farm truck, and the tires were less than perfect, so it needed all the help it could get. Round and round we went, and we were getting a pretty good load. At first, I was really nervous about doing it right, and once I got too close, and the fender collided with the tractor tire with a loud *thudder* as the ridges on the tire caught and skidded under the fender. With a look from Pappy, I rectified that quickly, and we continued on. We had about a quarter of the field chopped, and I was feeling pretty good seeing that mound of corn filling the dump body until we got to the top of the hill where I had to stop and wait for the tractor to pull ahead to make the turn at the end of the field. As I stopped, the whole front end of the truck rose up off the ground, plunking the back of the dump on the ground. What a feeling sitting in that big truck so high above the ground, and I was panicked! This wasn't supposed to happen! What do I do now? Not to mention what would Pappy say? He could really call you out for doing something stupid, but not in my wildest imagination would I ever believe a mound of corn could tip a big heavy dump truck on end! Pappy only shook his head, stopped the tractor, unhitched the harvester, and pulled around front of me. He chained the tractor to the front of the truck and pulled the front end down and headed me downhill. All he said was, "You might want to put a little corn up front now." And I did!

Two horsepower

Pappy was cutting corn in the big field across the street, and Billy Bissell was helping him. The high side of the field went fine, but as they got to the back of the field where it sloped down near the brook, it was wet, really wet. It was so wet that Popeye and the chopper sank up to the hubs. Billy looked at the tractor and said, "Well, I guess we're done." But Pappy looked at the situation as a problem to be solved. He had to come up with a solution to eliminate the heavy tractor and think of something to power the corn chopper. He hitched Sandy and Diamond to pull the chopper, rigging a mechanism to power the chopper, and he was off and running to the amazement of all. Two horses to power the chopper and finish the field. Waste not, want not.

Yip in the Thilo

Rip was one of the many friends that gravitated to the farm. He was a smart young man, could have done almost anything he wanted, but liked to work on the farm. He became like family helping where help was needed, as well as joining in on family time like meals and resting up under the apple tree on the front lawn between chores. There were the horses and trail or hayrides that were part of farm life too.

THE ARTIST, THE FARMER, THE HUNTER, AND THE GOOD GUY

It was an autumn day about 1952. Pappy was in the tall barn silo leveling it as silage came in through the chute. Ralph was milking the cows just beyond the silo. Larry was just a little guy following around wherever the big guys were working. He probably had been riding with Rip in the truck following the harvester cutting corn. Rip was raking the corn down the truck body as it tipped up for the silage to slide into the auger. He straddled the hopper, using a long metal fork Pappy invented. He reached up to pull the silage down. He never should have been on the hopper and didn't count on the surface of the hopper to be slippery with slimy corn juice. His sneakers slid, and he lost his balance, slipping into the auger. He screamed for Larry to pull the lever to stop the auger. Larry tried desperately but was just too little to have the height or strength to leverage the handle and went running to the house. Mom couldn't understand his frantic lisping "Yip in the thilo!" and besides the silo was a common place to be at harvest time, so she didn't understand the meaning of his message. The machinery was so loud Pappy didn't hear Rip's screams for help, only realizing something was terribly wrong when a bloody shoe hit him in the head. Dropping his rake, he raced out of the silo, yelling for Ralph, who was milking nearby to come help. When Ralph saw Pappy running, he knew it couldn't be good and pushed between the cows and slipped through the stanchions to follow him. It was just around the corner and out the side door to shut down the machinery and pull Rip from the auger, his legs shredded from just above the knees. Pappy took him under his arms, and Ralph took what was left of his legs and carried him to the front lawn calling for help. Aunt Esther, seeing the bloody mess the three men were, ripped curtains from the living room windows, and she and Pappy tied torniquets on Rip's legs as a desperate call was made to Doc O'Boyle. The line was busy, so Pappy threw Ralph his car keys, and he raced uptown to Doc's office. Walking in with blood all over him, Doc didn't even ask. Leaving his patient on the exam table, he grabbed his black bag and must have made record time two miles to the farm. There were no EMTs, no emergency squad, and there really wasn't much Doc could do for him. Rip never lost consciousness and lay bleeding on the lawn and, in time, asked for an aspirin for the pain. Pappy told him he didn't think aspirin was going to help much. His body also begging for hydration from loss of blood, Rip downed water by the glassfuls, which kept young Russ running back and forth from the house for more.

Can you imagine the pain and horror waiting for help to arrive? It must have seemed like an eternity. When state troopers arrived, Rip was loaded into a car, and they headed off to the hospital sirens blaring. Police called a warning to the towns en route to make way for them, speeding through on their way to the hospital. Pappy with state troopers drove from hospital to hospital getting blood for Rip. At home Ralph was left to finish milking. Later the auger needed to be cleaned and contaminated chopped corn buried while they waited for news from the hospital. Just writing this memory is traumatic enough, but why there isn't PTSD for the whole family is a miracle.

The happy ending is that Rip recovered, and unlike nowadays, there was no lawsuit. The Buzzells offered to take care of Rip as long as he needed, and he lived with them as family for years. Larry remembers as a little boy his job was to bring Rip his legs every morning. He went on to make a life for himself despite being legless. Occasionally we run into people who knew Rip and of course are surprised to hear the story of how he lost his legs on our farm.

Mane-ly Family

Mane-ly Family

Horses were a major part of the Buzzell Farm and family. This book wouldn't be complete without mentioning these major players, and there were far more than listed here. Horses are like chocolates. You can't just have one.

Bay State Sandy

Bay State Sandy was bred at the University of Massachusetts equine program government breeding farm. He was Pappy's pride and joy. I think he loved him as much as his kids, maybe even better sometimes. He was a registered Morgan stallion sired by Niles out of Marigold and had offspring all over central Massachusetts.

Dad, Larry, and Sandy

Pappy got him as a weanling in 1950, and he lived until 1967. I remember when I was a young girl growing up in Holden, and in our 4H club, one of the other girls had a bay pinto mare named San Calico who was sired by Sandy. Many of Sandy's get (*get* is the term used for a stallion's offspring) had San in their name, like Sandell or Sanella. Sandy was teamed up with many different horses but paired with Diamond for so many years they became a well-known team. Pappy said Sandy was willing, and Diamond was willing to let him.

As told by Russ

Of the five dairy farms in the valley, only one had running water in the barn. Our farm wasn't that one. If the cows wanted a drink, they had to get it from the brook. Sucker Brook wasn't very big, but it was clear, had trout in it, and every winter it would freeze up from time to time. That was where we came in. Every day during freezing-cold weather, each of my brothers and I took turns cutting a hole through the ice so the cows could drink. It was the only time the cows wouldn't fight or push each other around but stand patiently while the hole was cut, then each would drink their fill and walk back to the barn, where grain and hay waited for them. One day when I came home from the art school on a weekend, Dad called me aside and said, "I have something to tell you. The other day I turned Sandy out, and after I let him go, I realized no one had cut a hole in the ice." He watched as Sandy went to drink, and of course there was no opening for him to drink. Now Sandy had a habit of stamping his right front foot when he was impatient with something. In the winter my father worked his team of Morgans, and their shoes had toecocks welded on their shoes to have traction on ice and snow. Sandy struck the ice and in a short time broke a hole and drank. After that, Dad said he would turn Sandy out first so he would break a hole for the rest of the stock to drink from.

As told by Larry

I'm not sure how old I was, maybe a young teen. I was going to bring a bucket of water into Sandy's stall. It was a big bucket and very heavy, so I was kind of bent over straddling the bucket as I came in through the stall door. I had my back to the wall when a hen, protecting a nest of baby chicks she had in the corner of the stall, flew up at my face cackling and flapping her wings. I didn't know she had a nest in there and was so startled I dropped the bucket. It rolled

THE ARTIST, THE FARMER, THE HUNTER, AND THE GOOD GUY

against Sandy's legs while a flock of baby chicks started running frantically around the stall. I had nowhere to go and pressed back against the wall of the stall as Sandy, also startled by the chickens, started dancing about, avoiding the rolling bucket, chicken, and chicks. I did get a cut on my leg but from all the commotion that hen caused. I'm lucky that was all I got. Sandy didn't step on one chick or the chicken, which was also short of a miracle. If it had been any other horse, I think I would have been dead.

As told by Russ

That hen had a nest under Sandy's feed dish and would eat any grain he dropped. When her chicks grew up, they would roost on Sandy's back. He was the only horse in the barn with chickens roosting, and I think it was because they grew up in his stall.

Sanella, Maverick, Sanesta, Wonder, and Bobby Horse

Maverick and Russ

These were all offspring by Sandy out of Whitman's mare Dolly. Sanella was sometimes used in a hitch with Sandy. She was a chestnut with a blaze like her sire. Maverick was a bright red-chestnut with a blaze. He was powerful and, if he was registered, would have made an impressive park horse in the Morgan shows. We did show him, and he did very well in open shows. Years later after he had been sold, he turned up in 4H. He had to be close to thirty and still going. At that point he had been renamed Blaze. It was so good to see him.

Redwing

Redwing was by Sandy out of Sanella, chestnut with a star. When she was a few years old, Dad decided Russ should ride her on the Vermont fifty-mile ride. She had never been ridden, and at the Green River where we all let the horses get a drink, she decided to get down and roll in the river.

Sanella and Redwing with Dad behind the barn.

Orient Dancer and Sally

Dad and Jean Hussey in the cart they made on the Vermont fifty-mile ride

When Sandy passed away, John found a Sandy colt, Orient Dancer, to replace him. He was a great little horse, but I don't think anyone could fill Sandy's shoes. I took Dancer for a ride one very snowy morning. There had to be a foot of snow on the ground, and we went up the hill behind the house. He was feeling kind of frisky, having been cooped up, and kind of crow hopped sideways. I was dressed for the cold in a snowsuit and overshoes. In the slippery suit and his hopping about, I slid sideways, and as I did, my boot went through the stirrup. Not a great position to be in hanging sideways, but as I slid sideways, the rein turned his head sharply, and he went down as well. Thankfully the deep snow cushioned us both, and I was able to get my foot free before he jumped back up. I wasn't taking any chances for that to happen again and walked him back to the barn. Dancer was teamed up with Sally. They were the team that drove Larry and me from the church when we got married. Sally's dam, Sandra, should have been registered but missed the deadline. Back in the day as the registry was becoming established, there was only so much time to get it done. Sally was by Bay State Torrence owned by Gil Scholls. Christy showed Sally at open shows as well as fun rides around the farm.

Colleen on Sandra, Christy and Sally

Select Ethan otherwise known as Diamond

Northampton

Diamond's real name was Select Ethan in the Morgan Horse Registry by Niles out of Select Lass, so he was half brother to Sandy. He acquired the nickname Diamond for the large white diamond spot on his forehead. He was kind of one of those outlaws that most people couldn't handle, but he was a good match for Sandy, and Pappy had no trouble getting him to do what he wanted. It was sort of a love-hate relationship. Diamond would obey but gave Pappy every reason to curse him. He was so smart and needed someone like Pappy who could match his intelligence. He had an annoying habit of turning

Phyllis Smith and Diamond

his head instead of facing straight ahead. In a team where the reins were connected to both horses, it made it so he could avoid the bit and also interfere with the other horse. Just one of those things that he was known for. He would chase the cows if he was turned out with them, but he could also herd them better than the other horses. And he could be really aggravating by blocking the door to the cow barn and not letting the cows in at milking time. Diamond was used in a documentary on Paul Revere. They had to trot through the covered bridge down at Sturbridge Village, and they needed the hoof beats in the bridge for sound effects. Diamond could flatten out his extended trot so fast that there were only a couple beats in the bridge, and the scene had to be done several times over until they had enough hoof beats to satisfy the director. The rider who was the stand-in for the acter in real life was a polo player and was impressed with Diamond, saying he would make a first-rate polo horse.

Diamond and Paul Revere

As told by Russ

Diamond was quick and agile and could turn on a dime. He was great for herding the cows. One day I took him up behind the house to get the cows. I didn't bother to put a saddle on him. We were over by the lower side by Bullard's house, and a cow came out of the brush. It wasn't expected and scared me. Diamond moved so fast in a side pass he left me in the air holding the reins. Course I didn't stay in the air for long.

The Diamond I knew A Diane memory

Diamond took great pleasure in scaring people. I came to know him in his twenties, and I loved him and got along great with him. He was a favorite of Phyllis Smith too. She knew him long before I knew him and would choose him over the others because he was smart, agile, and a smooth ride. He never tired out. Pappy said Diamond was good for us because he liked blondes. I would love to go out to call him and see him come running full tilt, ears flat back, mouth wide open, and the whites of his eyes looking like he had the intent to kill but slid to a stop right in front of me and put his head down to be rubbed. Most anyone else would have run, and he would have chased them. It was good sport for him when fishermen would walk the brook through his pasture. There is a story of someone stealing grain from the barn, and Pappy had an idea who it was but couldn't catch him. One night he left Diamond out, and as the thief came up through the pasture, the next thing Pappy saw was a flashlight hightailing it through the swamp with Diamond on his heels. The thefts stopped after that. Diamond, as he aged, was really all show and little action. We had a little goat who would curl up with him in his stall and eat out of his grain dish. The little goat would even steal hay from his mouth as he picked it up. But Diamond was still a rascal. Larry was building a peacock pen in the middle of his pasture and was on his knees nailing chicken wire to the base. Diamond snuck up behind him and picked him up by the back of his jacket, letting him hang swinging before dropping him on the ground and running off. Larry saw him peeking out around the corner of the barn, watching him. When he was about twenty-six, I took him up to the Morgan National in Northampton and entered him in the half-mile trotting race. That afternoon I was on the back side of the track, kind of warming up and getting the feel of the track. He flattened out in his extended trot flying about a quarter mile. When I brought him back to a walk and headed for the trailer to rest until race time, I was stopped several times, asked who he was and astonished he was in his twenties. In the race, we were boxed in and couldn't break through to extend out. Came in about fifth. I have a feeling the box was on purpose, and I had never raced before, so my inexperience didn't help.

Toby

Toby was a little Shetland pony gelding. (A gelding is a castrated stallion/male horse, generally easier to handle.) He was a brown-and-white pinto. Ralph Sprague was a big guy that used to pick up Toby and call him "his dog." Toby was a cute little guy, but like most ponies, he had a mind of his own. The kids thought it was pretty cool if you pulled on the reins, he would rear up and walk on his hind legs. Ralph riding Tony and Russ on Toby were heading out for a ride. All was going well heading out the gate until Toby decided to take off. Russ, initially surprised, had all he could do to hold on, and Toby wasn't taking any commands. Little creep went right under electric wire fencing, catching Russ in the neck and flipping him off. Russ had a red wire cut on his neck for a long time. Another time the brothers were riding, galloping full tilt in the field. Larry was on Toby between Russ and Jack. They came to a large clump of thistles, and Toby slid to a stop, dumping Larry into the prickery stems. Larry got pretty scratched and banged up and didn't ride for a long time after, not trusting him and hating horses in general because of that. There was a lady who often came when visiting family in the area and would pay Larry to saddle up Toby so she could lead her little girl around on him. Larry remembers the NY license plates and getting paid.

Russ and Toby, Jack on Tony with Dad and Uncle Lawrence

Carrying milk up the stairs to the milk room was not easy and time-consuming. Pappy came up with the idea to hook up Toby to a little cart, loading it with forty-quart milk jugs and driving him up the driveway beside the barn to the milk room. It was quite a load for the little guy, and he had to really dig in to get up that hill. This method was used until they switched to the big milk cooler.

THE ARTIST, THE FARMER, THE HUNTER, AND THE GOOD GUY

Tony and Old Nell

Tony was a quarter horse, dark dun almost black. Buck Hill rises up from the dirt road and extends back to the back side of Smith Hanson Road. As kids, the hill was clear of trees and brush and was a favorite place to ride. Ralph made a small corral up by the big rock and would take Tony supplied with blanket and pillow and sleep overnight like a real cowboy. He also loved to do trick riding on him. Running and vaulting over Tony's rear end and into the saddle for a fast getaway or running alongside would grasp Tony's mane and leaping on like the Indians did in the movies.

Old Nell and Tony

Old Nell was a Percheron Morgan cross. Pappy bought her to breed to Sandy because he thought it would produce Morgan type with good bone, endurance, and strength as well as a great disposition. She never conceived but was used extensively on the farm.

As told by Russ

I remember one time taking Mabel for a trail ride. Dad told me to put her on Old Nell. Mabel seldom rode, and she would be safe on Old Nell. We rode all the way to New Braintree for a trail ride and chicken fry. It was a whole day of riding before heading back home again. I'm not sure Mabel thought it was that good a time. Maybe a little boring, but Old Nell kept her safe and sound.

Comment: If you didn't ride much, it was probably painful by the end of the day. That could have been a reason it wasn't an activity you would want to repeat anytime soon.

Little Nell

Little Nell was a pinto mare with a watch eye. A pinto has any combination of white, with brown, or black, or both on the body, and a watch eye has a ring of white around it. Nell's Sire was Delgado, a black Morgan, and her dam was an Indian pony. She came from Mary Turgeon. She was about six hundred pounds, twelve hands, and Russ as a child

Little Nell in front of Tucker's Barn

thought it was special that she was just two years older than him. Little Nell was what you call bomb proof. She didn't frighten easily, always easygoing. She was as wide as she was tall and almost impossible to fall off of. When Larry would ride her on trail rides, he often would doze off, and Nell would weave back and forth, whichever way his body would lean to keep him from falling. You could put almost anyone on her, and she would take good care of them. She was the mother of Tigerdell, Mandell, and Sandell sired by Sandy.

Sandell and Mandell

Sandell was a pinto looking a lot like his mother. There was a group of riders that met in front of the barn to go for a trail ride. Pappy told Russ to put a saddle on Sandell. He had never been ridden before, but Russ did what Pappy told him. As Russ mounted, he felt Sandell's muscles tighten and then explode, bucking and twisting until Russ was thrown, hitting the recently paved road hard.

Russ and Dad with Sandell, Ned, Little Nell, and Toby

THE ARTIST, THE FARMER, THE HUNTER, AND THE GOOD GUY

Pappy told him, "Get right back on, boy!" which is good advice most of the time. Russ was a good rider, and you always try to leave a session on a good ending, but this was not an opportune time to continue. Sandell was hyped by the other horses, and Russ was hurting. Russ refused and Sandell was the only horse Russ never rode a second time. Mandell was a little bay. Bay is a chestnut color with black mane and tail and black points. Points are black legs, ears, and on the face. Jack used to like to ride him to get the cows. He would just set the reins down, and Mandell would cut the cows without any guidance, just seemed to know what to do. Mandell and Sandell were raised together and always went together. If you took one, you had to take the other. The pair ended up with Jean Hussey in Belchertown. Tigerdell was a chestnut like his father, Sandy. Pappy sold him, and we lost track of him.

Ned

Ned was just like Little Nell only a little bigger, but he didn't have the same good nature as Nell. He could have a little mean streak in him. He was Welsh weighing about seven hundred pounds, standing 12.2 hands. (Hand is a measurement used to describe a horse's height at the shoulder. Four inches is a hand. A pony was anything under 14.2/58 inches.) Russ used Ned to round up the cows for milking except for Mandy, an Angus Jersey cow who could act like a bull. Ned was scared to death of her, and so she was left to make it to the barn on her own accord.

Tom and Jill

When Dad got a job working at the Worcester Reservoir cutting hay, he bought a beautiful team of Belgians. They were huge at about seventeen hands and weighing about 1,500 each, powerful, gentle giants. Gelding and mare, they were well matched bay chestnut with black manes and tails and black feathered legs. They were quite a sight to behold. We used them at Salem Cross for the sleigh rides in the winter and hayrides around the farm throughout the year as well as parades and special events.

Max and Major

Max and Major was Pappy's next and last team. They were Haflingers, a small draft horse breed from Austria. Always a warm chestnut with flaxen white manes and tails and often white feathered legs. They are well-known for their easy temperament. Smaller-than-average draft horses at about 14.2 hands. They were about 1,100 pounds with blazes on their faces. Sweet team and strong for their size. They were also what you call easy keepers requiring much less feed than larger drafties. Pappy used them for hayrides and for the fifty-mile trail ride to Vermont.

The next generation—Toto, Sam, Ginger, and Freyja

Other kids had bikes. Our kids had ponies. Toto was Stephanie's pony, a little bay with a fluffy black mane and tail. She rode him and drove him wherever she wanted to go, often meeting up with cousins like Renee or Jen and their ponies.

Sam was like Little Nell. Bombproof. He was a seal brown, which is essentially black but under tones of brown. So many kids learned to ride on Sam. They even had a special trophy for Sam at the Hardwick Fair because almost every year there was a new kid on him. He

Stephanie and Toto

Nate, Sam, and Stephanie

knew the drill. I remember Nate riding him in the potato race, which was to run down to a barrel where three potatoes were, picking up a potato each time to bring back to the first barrel and back again until you finished. Nate couldn't reach the potato, so Sam reached over and grabbed it, munching all the way back! In the end he became Pappy's ride hitched to a little four-wheel buggy, driving around town, getting him home safe and sound every time they went out.

Ginger was our other pony, a chestnut with a flaxen mane and tail, blaze, and four white feet. He was the opposite of Sam. Not flighty, but he took great pleasure in giving kids a run for their money. Jalna and Ginger became a pair showing

Jalna and Freya State Show

Ginger and Jalna

at horse shows all summer long. As she outgrew him, she started driving him and continued to do well in driving classes.

Freyja was a Morgan cross dark bay with no white markings. She was a good step up from Ginger and then to Skye.

Horse of Another Color

Although most of the horses on the farm were Morgan or part Morgan, I would be remiss if I didn't mention Applesauce, King. And Tory. Tory and Applesauce were Appaloosa. Applesauce was just an easygoing plug. On one of the Vermont rides, a friend was having a terrible time with her horse, Tango, and Russ graciously offered to switch with her. Applesauce made her ride much more pleasant, and Russ could handle Tango just fine.

Stephanie and Tory

Corey on King

Tory

When Stephanie out grew Toto, she graduated to King and then to Tory. Tory was a sweet mare. I think Steph had a lot of good rides on her until we had to put her down with cancer.

King

King was Welsh cobb and hitched as a pair with Sam. Also a great little horse with the kids.

THE ARTIST, THE FARMER, THE HUNTER, AND THE GOOD GUY

Skye, 1969–2005

Heatherland Skye was my horse, that dark Morgan stallion dream come true. I bought him, before I started dating Larry, as a weanling (just weaned from his mother at six months old). I raised and trained him. I rode him on the fifty-mile trail ride from Colrain, Massachusetts, to Wilmington, Vermont. When I was pregnant with Jalna, I decided to lease him. I knew with a new baby, I wouldn't have the time to devote to him, and as I became a full-time mother, we wouldn't have my income, so it would be best to put him somewhere he could be used and become a sire. The lawyer advised me to sell with a first option to buy back for liability issues. I remember in shock as I opened a horse magazine and seeing "Champion Heatherland Skye" advertised at stud by a farm in New York. The buyer had sold him without telling me. So then I had to keep track of him to get him back. By then Jalna was

Diane and Skye—Colrain, Massachusetts, beginning of the fifty-mile ride to Wilmington, Vermont

ready to show him, and I was so proud of both of them. He taught her a lot and were a beautiful pair in the showring. He hated the rain or getting wet. One day I heard him in the pasture screaming, not a whinny, an obnoxious screech. It was a terrible sound, and I was alarmed, but only to find him standing by the brook angry because Freyja, who loved the water, was splashing him. As he aged, he took over the run of the farm. If I didn't get up soon enough, he would come and run his teeth across the screen on my window to get me up. And he would come to the back door looking for carrots. He didn't like apples. As he lost his teeth, we would have to cut them small so he could gum them. Granddaughter Lynnea adored him and would hug his leg, and he would gently nuzzle her. We put him down at thirty-six years old. There isn't another who could take his place.

Hold Your Horses

Sleighbells

Hold Your Horses

Hayrides

Today, most hayrides are with a tractor, and those are okay, I guess. As old-fashioned farming began to wane, horse drawn hayrides became a way to entertain and sometimes an opportunity to earn some extra income. Climbing in on soft, sweet hay and snuggling down wrapped in blankets with friends on a cold, silent, starlit night is an incredible experience. There is nothing like feeling the wagon move along, the sensation of the motion of muscular horses, and the soft clip-clop of their hooves as a team pulls the wagon. When the moon is full on dark dirt roads or wooded trails, you can hear a symphony of soft nature's melodies blended with the clink of harness, wheels in motion, and rhythmic beat of hooves.

Because hayrides were partly family fun and also employment, I'm not sure where to begin. I think, in general, hayrides began when horses were used to pull heavy loads of harvested hay to that barn, and whoever worked to pitch the hay onto the wagons would enjoy the ride on top of the load back to the barn. It

Wedding Day Chauffeur

wasn't necessarily fun, just part of the job. There is so much more to a hayride than just climbing on the wagon and off you go. It's daily upkeep. The horses have to be fed and cared for as well the harnesses and wagon. If you don't take time to take care of these, the horses will not be in the condition of strength to pull a wagon full of hay or people. Pappy made up special shoes welding toecocks on their shoes to keep them from slipping, especially in the winter. Long before the hayride begins, maintenance is key to keep harnesses flexible and prevent breakage, wheels greased, and shaft maintained. On the day of the hayride, the horses need to be harnessed and hitched. A work harness has a heavy collar with hames wrapping around the collar, girth, britching, and traces that hitch to the wagon. A bridle with blinders keep the horses facing forward with long reins attached to the bit used by the driver to guide and control the horses' direction and speed. The wagon would need greasing or tire pressure checked, but at very least getting a few bales of fresh hay to shake out for people to sit on. After the ride the hay needed to be cleaned out, generally not to be wasted, put over the fence for the cows to pick over. And among the leftover hay, all kinds of change, jewelry, or treasures could be found left behind. And not so pleasantly, occasionally the contents of someone's upset stomach depending on their beverage of choice.

A Proper Driver

People often didn't understand the time and effort involved but also didn't understand the expense we incurred leading up to the hayride. Feed, shoes, veterinary were just some of the expenses. Insurance became a big expense later on as people became more apt to sue for any and everything. One woman wanted a romantic hayride to celebrate her anniversary with her husband and couldn't understand why we would charge the same for just two people as we did for twenty. Unfortunately, it was still the same amount of expense, work, and time for two as it was

THE ARTIST, THE FARMER, THE HUNTER, AND THE GOOD GUY

for twenty. For family hayrides, anytime worked, but when we scheduled a paid event, it all had to be timed around other farm chores. We often had to rush through milking to get ready in time for a hayride. Hayrides could be just around "the big square" (Old West Brookfield Road to Smith-Hanson to Tucker Hill Road back to the barn), or sometimes we trucked the horses and wagon to another place. Just as Pappy drove us from our wedding, it was popular experience for others as well. Dressing the part and shining up the horses were extras we didn't charge for.

Going postal

Diamond, John and Sandy

One hundred sixty-three miles from Northampton, Massachusetts, to New York City. Twenty miles a day. Eight days of travel to deliver mail. It was a promotional for the Wiggins Tavern in the Hotel Northampton. Sandy and Diamond were fitted with rubber shoes to make the trip hauling a stagecoach with USPS mailbag to be delivered to the post office in New York City just like the route would have done one hundred years ago. Along the way the horses boarded overnight at various farms, while Pappy and Russ dined at great restaurants and hotels. The days were long, very long, starting at about 4:30 a.m. to get hitched and on the road until after 11:00 p.m. Russ followed the coach in a truck in case of breakdowns going about five miles per hour, sometimes taking short naps before catching up. (Russ said it wasn't hard to catch up or find them at five miles per hour.) All along the way people were curious until New York City. In New York City the people paid no attention, like a team and coach were part of normal traffic, except for one person. Russ watched them make their way down the street while a drunk standing on the sidewalk leaning against a lamppost watched them pass and scratched his head. "Well, son of a b———" and spun around and went back in the bar! I guess that old drunk couldn't believe his eyes.

A taste of history

Pappy worked Sandy and Diamond at Salem Cross Inn many years and later Tom and Jill, his Belgian team. Salem's liked to give their customers a full early American inn experience from candles and roasting in the big fieldstone fireplace, to the lovely old building and an authentic old-fashioned horse-drawn across the frozen fields hayride. Sandy and Diamond were well-known at Salem's. They were the first of many teams to continue the tradition. Uncle Ken also worked teams at Salem Cross, as well as Aunt Velma worked as waitress there. The first year of our marriage I enjoyed assisting him with Tom and Jill on winter Sundays.

Sandy and Diamond at Salem Cross Inn

To prepare, on cold days after the first snow fell, we would spend a day during the week watering down the road through the inn's fields. We had a big tank on sleds we filled with water, and someone would run behind to pull out the plug on the back of the tank to release the water onto the road so it would freeze and maintain a track we could use long into early spring. It was wet and slippery work on cold days but paid off in the long run because the roads would stay iced long after the snow melted.

Horsepower

It was winter, and the roads to Salem's sometimes were just as slippery as the sled tracks we created. One morning we loaded the horses with their harnesses into the trailer and headed the five miles to Salem's, but at the end of Hunt Road coming out onto Route 67, there was slight incline that was snow covered. We had to stop before proceeding, but with a trailer loaded with about three thousand pounds of horses, it wasn't going anywhere. Pappy got out, unloaded Tom and Jill and hitched them to the front of the truck and trailer and with me at the wheel to steer pulled the whole rig up unto Route 67 where the road was clear. We loaded them back up, and off we went the rest of our way to Salem's. Now that, my friend, is real horsepower!

Ready for takeoff

Pappy had a real sense of adventure, and that often rubbed off on his team and the people who loved his hay and sleigh rides. Even with a full load, Sandy and Diamond had spirit and power to deliver. As team and driver, they could act out a routine that felt like a one-in-a-lifetime experience, but Pappy probably should have let his stand-in know. Russ took a hayride for Dad, and all went well. Everyone was enjoying the ride snuggling in the hay, but as the ride came to an end at the bridge leading up the road to the barn, Sandy and Diamond took off galloping the last stretch to everyone's delight, that is, except for Russ. It was totally unexpected, and he was scrambling to keep his balance on the driver's seat and grasping the reins as Sandy and Diamond raced up the hill homeward. It was only later that Pappy admitted to Russ, "I let them have their heads and let them go. It's only a short stretch, and everyone likes it."

We have your back (as told by Larry)

Every hayride was different. Like Murphy's law, always expect the unexpected. One time when on the dirt road (we always called Tucker Cross Road, the dirt road) I was driving the Halflingers, Max and Major. There was a college football team in the wagon, and we came upon some teenagers who had built a fire in the middle of the road. There was no way to back up or turn the team and wagon around on that narrow road, and even though it was dirt, it was still a public way. I asked them to put the fire out so I could pass. I tried to reason with them, even told them they could light the fire back up after I went by, but they had been drinking and weren't in the mood to comply. The conversation was getting a bit testy when several of the team big guys stood up behind me and said, "Do you want us to handle this for you, driver?" The team had been drinking too, so I was between a rock and hard place, a place I didn't really want to be. Things were looking ugly. I strongly suggested to the teens they put out the fire, and those big guys standing behind me, I guess, were so intimidating the teens got the message because they put out the fire, and we went our way. With all the drinking going on, I was just happy to get out of there.

Automatic pilot (as told by Larry)

The hayrides we gave were most often in the winter in the cold. Again, I was driving the Haflingers. They were such a great little team, steady and dependable. Pappy had them so well trained that I hardly had to drive, and this night was proof. They knew when to dig into the collars and pull and when to let up and even when to stop as we often did and set the wheels to give them a rest and breather along the way. Setting the front wheels was turning them slightly as they stopped and would help keep the wagon from rolling backward and took the weight off them so they could rest. This night was sooo cold. The passengers were down below the wagon sides out of the wind with blankets, quilts, and even extra horse blankets to ward off the chill, but as the driver, I sat up top and got full force of the wind and cold. I had on Pappy's bearskin robe that cut the wind like nothing else and heavy gloves, but my hands were still so cold I couldn't feel the reins. We were only about halfway coming up the hill by Jack's on Smith-Hanson when I looked down and realized, I had dropped the reins. Driving without reins is like driving a truck without a steering wheel and brakes. I wasn't worried about the team taking off mainly because we were on a hill with a full load, and they were doing what they do best, just trudging on. I was more concerned what the people would think and didn't want them to panic. As I pondered my options, I decided to quietly step down on the single tree behind Max and onto the shaft between the horses as they were moving along. I steadied myself, leaning against Max's rump to reach the reins that were dragging on the ground. The fur coat made it really hard to maneuver, so I was moving slower than I anticipated, and before I could climb back up to the driver's seat, I heard, "Hey, where's the driver? The driver's gone!" So much for avoiding panic, and I quickly called out, "Everything is okay. I'll be right back." I think they were feeling a little warmth from the beverages they were sharing because they took me at my word and believed me! I could hear laughter as they welcomed me back when I finally climbed back up onto my seat.

Side note: When adults booked a ride, they often brought a washtub filled with ice (like you need ice in below zero temps) filled with their favorite beverages for the two-hour ride. They were often well warmed and feeling no pain by the end of the two hours.

I was Viking it (as told by Larry)

As usual it was freezing cold. All I could think of was getting home and in by the warm fire. On the halfway point, Max and Major stopped, set the wheels, and I sat shivering. Those few minutes seemed like forever. One of the passengers passed me a glass of something unfamiliar. Not wanting to insult them, I took a sip thinking I would tip it out when no one was looking. That drink slid down so smooth, and I began to feel the warmth spread through me. I drank it all down, craving the warmth it provided. In a few minutes, Max and Major stepped aside at the end of their break, and we began the journey back to the farm. Thankfully, they knew the way.

By the time we got home, I was all warmed up and happily waved to the group of passengers as they got in their cars and headed home. Not sure who unhitched the team or what tipped Diane off, but next thing I knew, I was sitting on a bale, and she was unbuckling harnesses from the team on the barn floor, ripping them off. "Boy, you're good!" I exclaimed, watching her haul those harnesses off, which were not only an awkward mangle of straps but weighed a good fifty pounds, hanging them on the hooks on the wall. Somehow, she didn't take the compliment the way I thought she would. She blanketed Max and Major and settled them in their stalls with some flakes of hay. She thoughtfully tossed me a blanket, shut off the lights, and said good night as she shut the door. My wife having grown up in a Swedish family knew all about Glogg, and the effects would wear off with a good night's sleep. After that, I learned to leave Swedish Glogg to the Vikings.

Dreams of tomorrow (as told by Larry)

Although I was not a drinker, mainly because it really didn't take much to get me drunk but also because I didn't think that was a good thing to do, there was another time when alcohol got the best of me, and thank God we had good horses. I went along to help Uncle Ken with a hayride at the college. Mike Hunter came along also. Uncle Ken, who is really a cousin, was much older than me and was Dad's nephew, but we always called him Uncle. He had a team of huge Percherons, Chub and Shorty. I wasn't much older than the kids on the hayride, and they were having a grand party, and the beer and Bacardi Rum was flowing bigtime. Uncle Ken and I joined in, and as the night wore on, our good sense went down the hatch. At one point Uncle Ken, who was driving, handed me the reins, saying "Take the reins, boy!" (In Maine where Ken was from, every younger male was "Boy"). His vision had become somewhat clouded, and evidently his team of two had become a four-in-hand. Handing over the reins of his team to me was like a driving instructor handing over the keys to a kindergartener, but Chub and Shorty knew more than I did, and Ken told me to "Just hold onto the reins. They know what to do." As we headed down one road, cars were parked along both sides. The wagon was mere inches going through, and those horses cleared the cars perfectly. Once in the parking lot, Ken managed to get down from the driver seat, and we unhitched the team, or at least I think "we" did. Chub and Shorty were so well trained that in typical down East drawl, Ken commanded them "Get up in there," and both horses climbed the ramp to the horse van, turned themselves around, ready to be hitched for the ride home. Thankfully, Mike was with me and driving. By the time we got home, I was pretty wasted as the rum had completely polluted my focus. He half carried me, half walked me into the house as I laughed thinking all this was incredibly hilarious. Diane, having been warned, met us at the door to help make it as far as the living room. As they laid me down, whatever was in my stomach projected out of my mouth. They didn't think that was so funny either and left me again to sleep it off. At least I had upgraded to the couch instead of the barn.

Trail Rides

There were a lot of trail rides. Some from the farm or other farms and some with the Western Riders or Brookfield Riding and Driving Club. Average trail ride was twenty miles, some more some less. Spring and fall everyone gathered to head to Wilmington, Vermont. It was a twenty-five-mile ride each way staying overnight at the Viking Motel, while the horses stayed at the fairgrounds. We rode the horses into the Green River to cool off and give them a drink. There was a clearing where we stopped about halfway for lunch and a rest. I'm not sure who found this route or when they started the rides to Vermont, but they were such a good time. For the most part, it was all dirt road and ran from a farm in Colrain, Massachusetts, to Wilmington. There was a lunch stop along the way where we shared a picnic meal, lounged on the grass with conversation around family, work, and of course horses and some taking short naps before heading the rest of the way. Some rode horseback, some in wagons and carts. One year I drove Sanella with Irene as passenger with me. I don't know what was wrong with Sanella, but she took the bit and

John and Jean with Sanella

wanted to fly. My arms were so sore trying to hold her back after only the first few miles, and she didn't give up the whole fifty miles. We were coming down one hill, and a huge truck was heading toward us, and I was sure we were goners. I headed her toward a telephone pole, and she went head first into it, but at least she stopped and sort of off the road. Howard Jackson had a sweet team of Saddlebreds with a beautiful four-wheel carriage and, seeing my exhaustion, told me to line her up behind him. She could only go as fast as he was going. He would lean back and stroke her face and talk to her, but the whole time she had her face pretty much pressed into the back of his seat. That was one ride I was glad when it was over.

Ken and Lorane with Max and Major and Pappy's wagon with car tires rode like a Cadillac.

Like father like son

First, I have to give a little backstory with this one. You know everyone has relatives you never knew existed. I grew up and got married before I knew I had a cousin on my mother's side, Nancy Anderson. Nancy had a horse named Copper, beautiful chestnut stallion, and he was a Bay State Sandy colt. The Buzzells knew my cousin better than I did! Just another coincidence? I think not. Amazing hand of God at it again.

As told by Russ

Dad and I went on a trip to Montana with Jean and Julian Hussey in their Winnebago. On the way we were in South Dakota and saw some bison on the side of the road. I jumped out to take some pictures. There were three bulls, and they were walking right along. I had trouble keeping up with them. I was trying to get some

THE ARTIST, THE FARMER, THE HUNTER, AND THE GOOD GUY

close-up pictures when the one in the back stopped, turned, and roared at me. There was a large tumbleweed nearby, and he threw that thing twenty feet in the air like a toy. They were done with having their pictures taken and me following them! Dad yelled for me to get back in the Winnebago, and I figured I better, so I did just

South Dakota Russ on the piebald on the left

that. We stopped at Jean's niece's ranch in South Dakota. The scenery was amazing and had the chance to ride their horses, real working ranch horses. We went on to see Nancy Anderson at her ranch. She told me I could take her stallion Copper for a ride. Copper was a Sandy colt, and he gave me ride just like his old man. It was just like riding Sandy. I could feel his muscles tighten up, and he did a little crow hop when he took off. Nancy said I could go as far as I liked. The ranch was miles of trails, and she said when I wanted to come home to just lift the reins and let Copper have his head, and he would bring me home. I was miles from the house, no idea where I was, and I lifted those reins, and Copper took me home just like she said. It was just like riding Sandy.

Nell and Larry (as told by Larry)

I loved riding Little Nell. I wasn't much of a rider, but we all went on trail rides with the Western Riders group. She was so wide that at the end of the ride, I would be so bowlegged I could hardly walk straight. As a youngster, some of the rides would be so long, and I would get so sleepy. Little Nell must have known I was asleep as she ambled along, knowing to keep up with the rest, and the other trail riders would come alongside and keep me from falling off as I bobbed along sound asleep. One time as I dozed along the trail, we came to a brook, and the other side was a steep banking. Little Nell didn't hesitate and splashed through the brook and right up the banking. I immediately came to as sprays of water rudely woke me, almost falling off and clinging on for dear life as we lurched up the banking. Another time, Little Nell and I were going at our own pace and had fallen way behind the rest of the group. We came to a fork in the trail, and I wasn't quite sure which way to go. It looked like the tracks went one way, and I tried my hardest to get Nell to take that fork, but she kept refusing, sidestepping and going in circles. Finally, Pappy came hurrying down the other trail looking for us. I should have just trusted Little Nell.

Another time I was with Susie. It was a moonlight trail ride, and we got way behind the rest of the group. Susie thought she knew where she was going, but we got so lost that we didn't make it into camp until after midnight. As we rode into camp, there were a bunch of guys drinking around the fire and laughed at us saying, "If we were with Susie, we would get lost too." I didn't understand what they meant, and Susie just rolled her eyes and told me to keep riding. We were so much like family that one time at a campout, the girls wanted me to sleep in their tent and our parents thought that was okay.

Hot footing

There are not many people who can say they have been stopped by police while riding a horse, but Larry can—and not only once, but twice!

Nell didn't get alarmed when the blue lights pulled up beside us. I looked around and didn't see a car and couldn't imagine he was stopping us! But the policeman got out of the car, and it was us he was after. We were on Route 9 in West Brookfield coming back from getting ice cream at Uncle Milty's and just going at a walk down the sidewalk. As I stopped, the police with hands on hips and quite disgusted with me pointed at the trail I was leaving behind. The sidewalk had just been recently paved, and in the hot afternoon, the tar was still soft, and we had left a trail of hoofprints all the way from Uncle Milty's. I apologized, embarrassed that I didn't notice, and promised to stay on the road the rest of the way home. He didn't ticket me, but I'm not sure what kind of ticket he could give me anyway. (Uncle Milty's is where Dunkin Donuts in West Brookfield is now.)

Horse thieves

I was with the McKenseys on the way back home going past the West Brookfield Elementary School. The sun was going down, and we had our flashlights ready to warn cars we were in the road when a cop came up and stopped us. There was a report of some horses stolen, and he was sure he had his suspects. But what does a cop in a car do with horse thieves? We tried to convince him they were our horses, but he wasn't buying it, so he wanted to follow us home, thinking for sure he would catch us in a lie. He told us to get off the main road as quick as we could. Again, we explained that it would be a lot longer, but he didn't believe us, so I decided if that was what he wanted, that was what he was going to get. So the next turn was Wigwam Road up and over by the West Brookfield Dump to the dirt road to Smith Hanson and down Tucker Hill. We walked along, and I didn't urge Little Nell at all even when he asked us "Couldn't the horses go any faster?" as he followed at a snail pace behind us. I explained it wasn't good for the horses to go any faster on the tar road, and it was getting too dark to safely go any faster on the dirt road. We didn't want to injure *our* horses. So we took our time getting home in *record* long time. Dad was in the barn with Sandy on the crossties in the process of shoeing him when we arrived with our police escort. Frustrated by the hour or so of following us, he impatiently asked Dad if these were his horses. Dad responded, "Yes, and this is my son." And off he drove having wasted all this time with the wrong horse thieves! Confused, Dad asked us, "What was that all about?"

Bearly home (as told by Russ)

It was going to be a beautiful evening, and Phyllis wanted to go for a moonlight ride. I told her I would go with her if she helped me get milking done. We got through milking and saddled up Sandy and Diamond. Phyllis loved Diamond, and Sandy was a good ride, so off we went around the big square, about a four-mile distance. As the evening settled, a mist was rising from the brook and across the valley. We were almost home coming down Tucker Hill Road. In the dark just up from the little red house and we could see something up ahead, something big and black emerging from the misty shadows. It was moving kind of slow and really hard to make out as the evening mist crept up from the swamp, veiling it in the moonlight. Sandy and Diamond started snorting and dancing some, so we got a little nervous. Actually we were scared thinking it must be a bear. We weren't sure if we should turn around or what to do, and then as it got closer and came out of the mist, we realized it was only a cow! It was just Mandy, our Angus Jersey cross, out roaming the streets. What a relief! Well, that made it a really memorable ride.

Never Gonna Grow Up

"Harry and Larry"

Never Gonna Grow Up

So as time goes by, the stories don't stop. Every week there is something going on with the brothers. Ralph and Larry as the oldest and the youngest have an interesting relationship. On average, several times a week the younger brother goes to see the older brother, just to check on him. Typically, they go for coffee (and maybe a donut), but sometimes over to EB's for breakfast or out to Belchertown for tractor parts.

Great comebacks

One morning Larry found Ralph on his tractor, but he was not doing anything special, so he climbed down and got in Larry's truck and off they went. They got to the restaurant, and the waitress showed them to a table and then noticed Ralph's pants. When he had climbed off his tractor, he didn't realize the seat was wet and had soaked his whole rear end. She kindly informed Ralph, "Did you know the back of your pants are wet?"

Anyone else might be mortified, but Ralph didn't miss a beat and quickly responded, "No! But thanks for noticing!"

Ralph had a habit of reading the waitress's name tags as they greeted them. He would greet them back using their name. He met a waitress who had a great comeback. As she met them at the table, he as usual reading her name tag said, "How are you today, Susan?" and she replied, "I'm fine. How are you, Ralph?" Caught him completely off guard, forgetting he had his name tag on his work shirt.

Another time a waitress asked, "What can I get for you gentlemen today?"

Ralph thought he would be funny and replied, "We're looking for some wild women!" and to their surprise the waitress proceeded to take off her apron and responded, "Well, here I am!"

Larry, a little alarmed, blurted out, "No, no, no. Not me. Just him! He's looking for a wild woman!"

Looking over the menu at one restaurant, Ralph saw "Soup in a bowl." When the waitress came to take their order, Ralph asked, "What is soup in bowl?"

The waitress hesitated and slowly responded, "Soup…in…a…bowl." Duh! It was really a bread bowl, but I agree with the waitress. It's kind of self-explanatory. And they all laughed.

Ralph and Larry often go for rides. One day as they headed out the door to lands unknown, Mabel asked Ralph where they were headed. I'm sure he thought this a generic vague answer, "Going to go look at cows."

Mabel quickly pointed at Ralph's herd and said, "Then just look out the window."

You don't always get what you want

How many farmers do you know who are lactose intolerant? Well, one of the Buzzell boys, namely Larry, has a terrible time with milk. He does however have to color his coffee and can tolerate a little milk, not cream or half and half. At every restaurant he asks for a pitcher of milk instead of the little creamers they generously hand out. At one restaurant when he asked for coffee and a pitcher of milk, the waitress was more than generous. She brought out a quart-size pitcher. They all looked confused by the large pitcher set at their table, and Larry had to ask. The waitress misunderstood that he just needed a tiny bit of milk in a little pitcher. There was some laughter as the confusion was cleared up. Her comment was, "I was wondering what you wanted a pitcher of milk for." Now Larry is more specific by ordering a "little" pitcher of milk and emphasis by holding up his thumb and forefinger.

Brother bonding conversations

I call their get-togethers brother bonding. Evenings watching games or movies, day trips to find things for Russ to paint, and sometimes a few days or a weekend excursion to explore history. Once I was able to sit in the back seat and listen like a fly on the wall to their conversations. They go back and forth about people they know or things they heard, and this time the comment was, "I didn't know that. You learn something every day."

Another brother responded, "Well, you must know a lot because you are old, John."

John hesitated and said, "Well, I don't know that much."

"Are you saying you don't learn something *every* day?"

"No, I'm saying I'm not that old!"

As they traveled along, driver John took a wrong exit and ended up in New Hampshire. He was not very happy with himself and even a little more frustrated because all the construction didn't allow for a quick turnaround. He was mumbling under his breath, and other brother John said, "This is a good opportunity!"

"Good opportunity for what?" Frustration very evident.

"Let's see if we can keep a positive attitude!"

If looks could kill. I would really like to keep a recorder on board so I could hear all their conversations.

Cooped up in a car, conversations can lead anywhere, and I can only imagine what they say! After a discussion about something that didn't go well, Ralph made the observation, "We aren't very smart."

Which Jack took some lighthearted offense to, pointing out, "What do you mean *we*?"

And Larry piped up, "It never bothered me."

To which Jack replied, "We could understand that." Brothers can be brutally honest.

How to bug Russ

There have been occasions when the brothers would go places and introduce themselves as brothers, and Ralph would seize the opportunity to speak up and add, "And we love each other." I know Russ loves his brothers but isn't always vocal about it. Russ would shake his head, responding, "Why does he *always* have to say that?"

As they were driving along, Russ saw a beautiful elm tree. Russ likes elm trees and often uses them in the paintings he does and rates the trees from 1 to 10. Russ exclaimed, "Wow, look at that elm! That is a nine!"

Larry questioned, "What's the difference between a nine and a ten?"

Ralph quickly answered from the back seat, "One!"

Russ also likes to take pictures of wildlife and several times told his brothers to keep an eye out for a red-tailed hawk. (FYI, a redtail is a kind of hawk.) So they were driving along, and Larry spied a beat-up old red-tail in a dead tree and pointed it out to Russ. "Hey, there's your red-tail. Do you see that? Up in the tree? You said you wanted a red-tail in a tree. There's one for you up in that tree!"

Russ stopped, quickly jumped out and snapped a picture, and jumped back in the truck. Ralph said, "That was nice to get a picture of that redtail."

Russ responded, "It's a mangey hawk. I only did it to shut him up. He would never shut up if I didn't stop and take a picture."

A Diane memory

We were watching a grandson play in a basketball game and noticed the coach speak to the referee. We also noticed how one of the players kept making comments to the opposing team. They weren't loud or rude, just making comments. We couldn't even hear what they said. Larry turned to me and said, "Oldest trick in the book, getting into their heads. It was the only way I could beat Russ at ball. He would miss a shot, and I would quietly say, 'Shot is a little off today.' If he did it again, I would say something 'You usually get those baskets.' And I would keep making little comments, and he would get so mad. Pretty soon he couldn't make a shot no matter how he tried, and I could beat him."

THE ARTIST, THE FARMER, THE HUNTER, AND THE GOOD GUY

On the road again

Driving along they often delegated one to be navigator, searching the map for scenic places off the beaten path and sometimes to find their way back from those scenic places. Driving along, Ralph was in the back seat with the map when Russ asked him if he knew where they were. Ralph confidently replied, "We are headed due east," as Larry and Russ shielded the late-afternoon western setting sun from their eyes.

Larry wasn't a whole lot better at navigating. As he perused the map, Russ just a little impatiently asked, "Are we going north or south?"

Larry flipped the map upside down and spit out, "South!"

(I really have to wonder how they ever find their way home.)

As the boys drove along at their age, a cup of coffee often needed to be off loaded. "Looking for a tree" was synonymous for letting the driver know they needed to stop somewhere to relieve themselves. Russ looked for a good tree, pulled over, and Ralph and Russ headed around the truck to be discreet. As they were standing there, they looked up the hill to see people sitting on the porch of a house set back from the road waving at them. Larry asked, "What did you do when you saw them waving?"

Russ answered with a shrug, "Waved back."

Door #1

The brothers went to visit the President Coolidge homestead in Vermont. As they explored the store, the caretaker marched in and announced, "Who the hell was in the barn?"

Larry answered, "That would probably be my brothers," as he pointed to his brothers standing next to him. They wanted to see the inside of the barn, being old-time famers, and didn't realize they weren't supposed to be in there. The door being really hard to open should have been a clue, but little brother throwing them under the bus made them sheepishly admit it was them. Caretaker certainly wasn't anything like Silent Cal.

Door #2

Brother bonding over a movie. Favorites are the old westerns, the cows, the cowhands, the cowboys! I think they identify with the trials and tribulations of the old west. In this scene the cowboy rides up to the big barn with a big sliding barn door on the barn, just like the one on the old farm. The cowboy dismounts, walks up to the barn door, and in the big barn door that is so hard to push open and in the winter lets in all the cold air, is a little door, a man-size door with a handle just like on a house. A door in a door. The three brothers look at each other as light dawns on marble heads. "Hey, we could have done that!" Nodding in unison. "Yup, why didn't we think of that?"

Face-plant (as told by Larry)

The phone rings and I hear, "Come over. I need you. Won't take long." That should be a red flag, but it wouldn't matter I guess, so I go over. Ralph has a tree trunk balancing on the end of his truck teetering back and forth in Tucker's driveway. "I need you to get up on that end of the tree and hold it down."

"And then what are you going to do?"

"Drive it down to my house."

It's only next door, maybe five hundred feet and downhill, but I look at this tree and think, *This is going to be some ride!* I'm hesitant but not sure how to say no. "All right, but if I can't hold it down, I'm getting off."

"You get on that end. Your weight will hold it down. I know it will."

I climb up on end of the tree trunk, and my weight is holding it down, and Ralph gets in the cab. What he didn't tell me is that he's going to put the truck in reverse and drive the trunk of the tree into the stone wall sliding the whole tree up against the front of the bed with me on it! So here I am with my face slammed up against the rear window, and he takes off down the road to his house.

THE ARTIST, THE FARMER, THE HUNTER, AND THE GOOD GUY

Big as a barn A Diane memory

I admire anyone who can use their mirrors backing up. Heck, I admire anyone who can back a big truck up, because I am not good at it. I take all the help I can get, but I think guys are little different. We had a load of hay on the truck, and I was guiding Larry to the barn door to unload. He was going slow and could see and hear me. I kept telling him, "You are going to hit the barn, go more to the left."

And of course, he didn't believe me and said, "I can see it. I'll be fine." So I let him hit the barn. He slowly backed up, placing the end of the bumper right through the siding of the barn. I hate saying I told you so, so I didn't. I was pretty sure the impact was telling enough, but Pappy standing on the porch let him know.

"You couldn't miss the whole barn, boy?" Precious! Just precious.

Hen hotels

These days everyone wants to be green, reuse, recycle… blah blah blah. If you look back in history, previous generations put us to shame. Clothing was handed down until it was too tattered to be worn, and it would be cut up, and pieces would be worked into quilts. Everything that was slaughtered was put to use, meat, bones, and hides. I have spoons my great-grandfather carved from bone, and I remember as a little girl the big gallon jug filled with bent nails picked up from job sites. Morfar would patiently spend evenings hammering them out straight to reuse. Lumber was at a premium in early days of our country, and it wasn't uncommon to carefully take down a building and bring it with you to rebuild. I think you could say that Pappy was pretty green because he could take parts from this and that and create whatever he needed.

When they sold the farm, he had built a small barn, and he wasn't about to lose that investment, so he figured out a way to haul it with him, and it sits today forty-plus years later at the farm on Cider Mill. Ralph followed his example when he had a chance to get some cabins perfect for what he needed. Turning to his father for help, Pappy devised a trailer of sorts from the rear end of a truck and a plank bed that hitched to the Major diesel tractor. It was quite an undertaking, but with the help of various and sundry friends and family, they raised the buildings and backed the trailer under them. Then under the guidance of the local police, they were off hauling them from West Brookfield on Route 9 all the way home to be placed safe and sound at Ralph's side yard. There they sit today, the Hen Hotels.

Only a minute

They always seem to get into trouble every time they get together. One time they went to bring Ralph's truck to Regin's to get it fixed. Ralph said it had "look out brakes." It went pretty well with Larry following until they came to a stop sign at the Silver Bridge, and Ralph's truck didn't stop. With no brakes, look out! He slid right into the intersection of oncoming traffic. With squeals of brakes and cars skidding out of the way, Larry thought for sure his brother was a goner, but thankfully the other cars had brakes. Someone should get that man a Triple A card!

This next one happened one day when Larry left me with the infamous words "Going to see Ralph. I won't be gone long." I've heard that before.

"Limb came down through my chicken coop in that storm last night. Need to get some shingles to fix it," said Ralph.

"Don't buy any. I think Artie has some leftovers from his shed. I'll check for you," replied Larry, and sure enough, Artie did and was more than willing to donate them to Ralph's chicken coop. What a good nephew.

Then a couple days later, Larry said to me, "Not sure what to do about Ralph's chicken coop. He wants me to take him to Lowes to get some plywood to fix the roof. Neither one of us should get up on that roof."

Hmmm, he was right for once. I thought this deserved a call to Tina, just in case he didn't tell them himself. I texted Tina, and she called me right back. "Oh my god. When are they doing this? Joey won't be home for a while!" I explained they hadn't done their shopping trip yet, but I wanted to give her a heads-up because at eighty-four and seventy, neither one should be on a roof, especially an old rotted roof. That chicken coop (hen hotel) was old when Ralph towed it to his place from West Brookfield fifty years ago. The whole thing could come down with them. A day later Larry stopped in to see Ralph, and off they went to Lowes. When they got back, the conversation went something like this.

"Now, John, you have to get someone to fix this roof for you." (Remember they call each other John.)

"Nope, I have a plan. Help me put everything on the back of my hay truck and I'll back it up to the coop. I have a ladder, and I'll stand it on the back of the truck. I can do this."

"You're eighty-four! You can't get on that roof. Not to mention a ladder on the back of a truck! That roof is so old you could end up going right through. You have to promise me you will call Joe or Jim to help you or least watch you so they can tell me how you got hurt!"

Ralph considered his younger brother's advice, and I'm not sure if he planned to wait until Larry wasn't around or was actually thinking about what he advised.

Then he asked Larry, "While you are here, can you follow me to Zagarra's? I need to get my tractor there. It will only take a minute." Larry agreed, hoping it will keep him off the roof at least for a while, and they slowly headed toward Zagarra's field, which was actually the field where the old farmhouse stood. They got about halfway there just past where the beavers have flooded Tucker Hill Road when Ralph steered off onto the side of the road, and the tractor died. Larry was not at all mechanically inclined and suggested, "I'll go get Jack for help."

Ralph shook his head and said, "Nope, I'm a dope. I know what's wrong. I'm out of gas."

Larry couldn't believe what he heard and scolded his older brother. "You mean you didn't check your gas? What if I wasn't following you and you had to walk? How would you get home?" I can almost hear the deep sigh. "Come on, we'll go get some gas."

Ralph responded, "Yup, I'm a dope. But I have some gas in the garage. Only take a minute."

"You mean you have gas in the garage, and you didn't check before you left?" Another big sigh. "Come on. We'll go get your gas." But when they pulled up the driveway, there were cows munching on the lawn. They looked at each other in disbelief.

"Can you help me get them back in?" asked Ralph. Larry was thinking about the "I won't be long" statement before responding but agreed. He couldn't leave his brother to do this by himself. And of course, they needed to find out where they got out or getting them in would be a little futile. So they herded them back in and set off to find a gaping hole in the fence up on the hill behind the house.

"Can you help me fix the fence? It'll only take a minute." Ralph could see that Larry was skeptical. "I got a plan. I have the old railing from the porch that will fill that hole in no time. I got wire and tools right in the garage" was his encouragement. So they dragged the railing up the hill, and Ralph had a pail with fence staples, wire, and tools. They got the railing in place and wired up and appeared it would hold as a pretty good patch. They packed up the tools before descending the hill, which was quite steep for a couple of old guys. Larry told his brother, "I'll take the tools, and you take your time coming down the hill." He started off picking his way down the hill toward the garage. He hadn't gone far when he heard a flop, and Ralph rolled right past him! Larry hurried to help pick him up at the bottom of the hill, anxious he must be hurt somehow. "Johnny! You okay?"

But Ralph was laughing and said, "I'm fine." Relieved, Larry helped him up, and they put the tools away. They got the gas to fill the tractor and after following him to the hay field gave him a ride home. Larry was getting back in the truck to go home now several hours later when he stopped and turned to Ralph. "You know how

THE ARTIST, THE FARMER, THE HUNTER, AND THE GOOD GUY

I told you anytime you need me, just call?" Ralph nodded his head. "Wait a day or two."

Have baler, will travel

Pa. otherwise known as Ralph, or John, is amazing. He continues to farm long after almost everyone else in town has given up. His equipment is almost as old as he is, well, not quite, but definitely in the vintage category. He has traveled as far as Sturbridge near the Mass Pike to get hay and continues long past the season, once even into December. There was a picture in the paper of him driving tractor and baler in a snowstorm! And was featured in the town parade as well. He is one of very few who can say they made hay with horses forking it in loose and then square bales with a tractor and from there round bales after that.

Fire…works

He was baling with the round baler in our field and looked back, and flames were coming out of it! The baler caught fire. There are belts on a pulley-type system, and sometimes they get caught, but the pulley keeps going, and as the metal gear gets hot, the hay catches on fire. It was contained in the baler and burned up quickly. Luckily the field didn't catch any embers!

Nathan was taking a nap on the couch when he heard a frantic knock on the door. Pa told him his tractor caught fire and was fearing an explosion. Nathan grabbed a towel and water and raced out to the tractor. Throwing the towel over the fire, he doused it with water. The fire went out. Whew! Pa decided it was safe to refuel, but as he started the process, the fire started up again. Nate threw the towel over the fire and put it out again! Evidently, he was using a metal funnel, and it was hitting the battery cable, causing a spark. When they figured this out, Pa said, "I am never using this funnel again. I'm throwing it away!"

Take the hint

Nathan and Dad (Larry) were driving on Wickaboag Valley Road in West Brookfield when Dad spotted a bear. "There's a bear! Go back!"

Nathan said, "It's just one of those plywood cutouts. It's not real."

"No, really, it's a bear." So they turned around in time to see the bear go across the road and down a driveway. "Pull in."

"We don't know these people. We can't just drive in."

"Just to see where he goes."

So Nathan pulled into the driveway. In the meantime, the bear had wandered behind the house, and as they pulled into the driveway, the owner came out, curious what they wanted.

"We just saw a bear go behind your house!" So the three of them walked around to the backyard, where there was a grove of blueberry bushes. (Hello? Bears love berries.) They didn't see the bear and kept walking, approaching the bushes, when they heard it in the bushes and backed off a little. The bear came out, considered his audience, but then wandered toward the woods over a stone wall. Unsatisfied with watching the bear wander off, Larry decided to follow it. Of course, it's perfectly safe to follow a bear on foot, right? As they got closer to the woods, the bear turned, stood up, and swung a paw and growled at him. He meant business! Now, he finally got the hint and headed backward to the car. Wildlife is fascinating but at a distance, boys!

You would think Larry would learn his lesson having dealt with a wild bear, but no. This time he spotted a bobcat on the side of Bates Street. It was behaving a little strange, running in circles around a bush. He decided to get a closer look and got out of the car. Of course. As he left the car and walked closer, watching the cat, it didn't pay any attention to him. He thought, how odd. But then out of the bushes came an even larger bobcat, and this one did see him and was not happy with his presence. Larry realized he was in a bad place. The cat could surely reach him faster than he could run to his car, so he slowly started backing away until he reached the car and both bobcats disappeared into the woods. When describing what he saw to Russ, it was actually a pair of lynx in a mating ritual. How rude, Larry!

Personal sacrifice

Larry and Ralph were on their way up to Buck Hill. Not many can say the place they loved and roamed as young boys is still a place to enjoy in their autumn years. On their way past Jack's, Jack flagged them down. "I saw a bear up there yesterday. Be on the lookout." As boys, the land was open, really open. Only a few trees and no underbrush. They never saw wild animals and were able as kids to have sleep outs on the hill with no worries. But times change, and with the overgrowth to hide in, wildlife is taking over. As they got to top of the hill and exited the truck to make their way to the clearing, Larry told Ralph, "If we see the bear, you run back to the truck, and I will sacrifice myself for you."

Ralph shook his head and responded, "I could never run and make it to the truck."

Larry raised an eyebrow and agreed. "Okay, you be the sacrifice. I'll run to the truck."

Believe it or not

One time the brothers were in Gettysburg on one of those brother bonding trips. Russ and Ralph were talking about chickens, of course. If it's not chickens, it's cows. Ralph said, "We're all different, and that's a good thing, or we would all like cows." But anyway, Ralph said those chickens are known for having red eggs. Well, Jack couldn't believe it. Thought he was joking but Ralph assured him he knew what he was talking about, and they laid red eggs. That night Larry noticed Jack lying awake and asked him if he was okay.

Jack responded, "Chickens don't lay red eggs. I'm going to go ask Steve."

Larry told him to let it go, but after returning home some days later, he was at the Hardwick Co-op, and Steve asked Larry, "What did you say to your brother? He marched in here, asked me if chickens laid red eggs, and when I told him yes, he turned around and walked out."

Gettysburg—Jim, Ralph, Sam, Larry, and Jack

A ladies' man

Gettysburg is a great place to explore, learn history by memorials and plaques and statues telling the story of the sacrifices made there. It's a lot of sights to see, and one of the places they checked out was a panoramic movie theater. It was about thirty minutes showing, and by the time it was over, Larry's stomach was giving warning signals it was ready to evacuate. As he came out of the theater, Larry questioned the first guide he saw for the whereabouts of a men's room. She pointed the way, "Outside that door and turn left." He quickly told the brothers he would see them outside and hurried out. His stomach was now in full-blown alert, and as he came around the corner of the building, he stiff armed the bathroom door in his haste to make it in time. As he entered the stall, he began to notice his surroundings. His first thought was *This is a really nice men's room.* Actually how lovely, it was decorated and scented with florals. Then he began to panic because he realized it wasn't a men's room at all and what should he do if another patron should come in. To make matters worse, he could hear the brothers outside laughing. By the time he was ready to leave, he was debating how he could crawl out a window, but alas, there was no window accessible, so he had to exit the door to his waiting family. When nephew Sam got home, his mom questioned what was the best thing about the trip, and his answer was, "When Uncle Larry went into the ladies' room!" Still hasn't lived that one down.

Up on the hill

Buck Hill was a favorite place for the brothers. Camping, exploring, sleepovers, cowboys and Indians, Army. It was their playground. As they've grown older, it was a dream for Russ to build a home there, and had he built years ago before all the building codes and regulations, it might have been financially feasible. Now for a road, electricity, cable, etc., it's not, but it is still their playground. The furniture is rustic, hand-me-downs that have seen better days. Ralph built a two-room shed housing an outhouse on one side and storage room on the other. Tiny but handy. Firepit and gas grill made meals easy and tasty. The hill made get-togethers, memory makers, and a place to share their memories. One of the chairs, a plastic low-back lawn chair, had an unsteady leg, sending Ralph over rolling in the grass. The initial response was one of concern, but when all was fine, it was good for a laugh. So not to make a habit of it, they resolved to get rid of that chair! The next time the brothers got together, Larry took a spill from the very same chair. Getting to his feet, he picked the chair up and threw it in the bushes!

"I thought you got rid of this chair!" he says to Russ.

"We did now!"

The number of days

God has a plan for us. When Ralph was diagnosed with prostate cancer in the 1990s, it was major surgery and long recovery with some unpleasant side effects, but Mabel was a nurse, and who better to take care of him? Ralph's diagnosis led to Russell's diagnosis, and his life was saved by the timely intervention, and Mabel stepped up to help him in recovery as well. The doctor said another six months, and Russ could have been dead. Time goes on and all is well. Larry stops in to visit Ralph one morning and finds him hanging his head. Automatically Larry is concerned and asks, "What's the matter?"

Ralph replies, "The doctor said if I had the surgery for my cancer, I would be good for another twenty years."

Larry looks at him curiously. "So?"

"Today makes it twenty years."

With a hmph, Larry laughs and tells him, "Well, that doesn't mean you're going to die today! You, knucklehead!" And it's been another ten years since then, so I guess the doctor did a good job. Since then, Larry was diagnosed with prostate cancer, like his brothers. Because of his brothers, he has been closely monitored, and it was found early and treated with much less invasive remedy. Will he have another twenty years? It would put him into his nineties, but moral of the story, Buzzell men, any man, get checked early and regularly!

Pre-GPS

Ralph and Larry are often lost, but that is okay most of the time. The plan was to go to Eastern States Expo in Springfield, and after getting off the pike, they had no idea how to find their way. There was a car that was covered with Eastern States stickers, so they decided it must be going to the fairgrounds and decided to just follow them. They followed the car through Springfield right to their driveway! The people got out of their car, and they sheepishly waved at them. So they were still lost in Springfield and had to keep driving. They did eventually find the fairgrounds, but I can tell you that even if they had GPS, they wouldn't have found their way. They don't know how to use it.

Marionettes

Eastern States is a great fair to go to. So many things to see and do, and over the years, we have gone there, sometimes to compete, sometimes to work, and sometimes just to see the sights. Who knew what they were doing at the fair this year, but guys saw the big banner advertising "The Marionettes"! They looked at each other and, raising the Buzzell eyebrow, decided they must be dancing girls. Now I won't say they are anything but good guys, but as guys, they don't always control where their minds wander. So they made their way into the big top, taking a seat. Looking around, they noticed the audience was much younger than them and were kind of puzzled, until the Marionettes came dancing out. Puppets! They were puppets on strings! Not dancing girls. Haha boys!

At the fair they also featured the Dallas Cowboy Cheerleaders. They put on a great show and after were autographing pictures. Ralph encouraged Larry to go get his picture signed. There was such a crowd around them Larry didn't anticipate getting one and just leaned against a post watching. He wasn't paying attention when a cheerleader walked up, stood beside him, and offered to sign his picture. Surprised and stunned, he handed her the picture, unable to say a word. Just a country boy. Dress them up but can't take them out.

The taste of fire
A Diane memory

It was a winter evening when I came home from a lady's meeting at church. As I walked up the steps, I noticed several blackened logs in the snow. *That's odd,* I thought. When I went in the house, Larry had the bedroom light on, which I thought was odd as well because he should be asleep to get up at 4:00 a.m. He was half sitting up in bed, and he told me, "Something awful happened."

I was so concerned by his face and couldn't imagine what it could be and asked, "What?"

He answered, "I threw my teeth in the woodstove."

I closed my eyes, momentarily imagining a melted, mangled mess, and sympathetically answered while thinking how quickly we could get new ones, "That's okay, hon, we'll get you new ones."

Shaking his head, he pointed to a glass of water with his teeth in the bottom slightly scorched black around the edges. "No, they are okay. They just taste really smokey."

Relieved, but dying to keep from laughing, I picked up the glass and told him, "I think I can handle that for you," and quickly left the room. Evidently, he had been cleaning his teeth before bed and watching the news on TV while drying his teeth with a paper towel, and he absentmindedly tossed both teeth and the paper towel in the woodstove. Realizing his mistake, he frantically roused Nathan sleeping on the couch to help save them. By putting on oven mitts, he dug burning logs from the stove, tossing one by one to Nate, who tossed them outside on the snow until he found the glowing dentures in the coals and could retrieve them. The dentist would never ever believe this one!

Not the only time he had dental issues. One time while driving a back road, he could feel his denture slipping. He thought he should apply Poligrip kept in the glovebox for just such emergencies. He didn't pull over. Talk about texting and driving. Well, as he slathered on the Poligrip, the car swerved just slightly but enough for the car mirror to hit a mailbox, pop the mailbox open, and mail flew out. So now we had to stop, pick up mail, and close the mailbox. No real harm done, but I couldn't stop laughing. Only Buzz could do something like this.

Talking trash

Now that he is in his eighties, in an effort to keep track of Ralph and keep him safe, his sons got a medical alert button for him, and they encourage him to wear it although he isn't always quite as cooperative as they would like, often leaving it at home. We received a call from the police one day that Ralph's button was going off, they couldn't find Ralph, and might we know where he was? Larry said, "I know right where he is. I'll go check on him." And sure enough, he was on the tractor baling hay. He flagged him down and told him the police were looking for him. The police had to physically see him for proof he was okay, so Larry waited at the gate for the police to arrive. In the meantime, Jack, who got the same message, came, drove into the field, and told Pa he had to go back to the house. He got him in the truck, and off they went driving right by Larry. Now the police came, and of course there was no Ralph, and Larry didn't know where Jack had taken him. Didn't look good to the police, but they tracked Jack and Ralph down back at Ralph's house. As it turns out, the old alert device was malfunctioning, and the sons had replaced it for him. Ralph had put it in the trash. Pushing down the trash in the basket set off the alert, so it was literally talking trash.

Sharing is caring

As you can tell, Larry and Ralph spend a lot of time together. So, this day Larry stopped to see Ralph, and as they wait for the coffee to get hot, Ralph helps himself to a banana right in front of Larry. Peeling it back, he took a bite and slowly ate the banana, right in front of Larry.

"Where's my banana?" asks Larry.

"This is the only one left," replies Ralph kind of sheepishly.

"You mean you're going to just eat that in front of me? If you really cared, you would have given it to me."

"I don't have another banana."

"That's okay. Now I know how you really care about your little brother." That happened years ago, and Larry still talks about that banana. Moral of the story, share your bananas.

Kale

On their many excursions to find barns for Russell's paintings, the brothers see lots of sights. On this trip, they were in Vermont and passed a large field. Not a typical field crop, Russ mused, "I wonder what that is?"

Ralph didn't hesitate and answered promptly, "That's kale."

I can see Russ rolling his eyes. "That's not kale." And a friendly argument broke out.

"Yes, it is."

"Naw."

"Yep."

"Who would plant that much kale?"

Their bantering is pretty common. If one brother sees a crow and announces it, the other will rebuke with "Naw, that's a raven." Or maybe one will see a llama, and of course, they argue it's an alpaca. Or maybe they drive by a pinto, and the difference would be a paint (color breed).

In the meantime, Russ was losing patience, understandably so. Anyway, driving a little farther they came upon a barn, and Russ stopped to ask permission to photograph the building. In conversation he asked, "How old is the barn?" It turned out it's not really an old barn but was an old barn taken down and rebuilt only a few years prior, just like the old days when they took barns down, moved, and rebuilt them. Back then it was done because it was hard to get the milled lumber to build, so taking a barn apart and moving it was the most economical way to do it. This barn was just rebuilt because he liked the old barn. But then Russ asked, "What is planted in that field?" and the answer was—wait for it—kale! Ralph was in the back seat puffed up like a little banty rooster. Russ said to Larry, "You have to be careful with that Ralph. Sometimes he's actually right!"

Bale me out (as told by Larry)

I was driving past Billy Brown's house. Of course, Billy Brown is long gone, and the house has had a couple owners since then, but it will always be Billy Brown's house to us. As I came up over the top of the hill, I saw Ralph's tractor. Not unusual because Ralph mowed the hay there, had been for years. But what was alarming was peeking out from under the baler attached to the tractor were Ralph's feet.

Stopping quickly, I jumped out of the car and raced, well, as fast as a seventy-year-old could race over to the tractor, sure that Ralph had met his maker. Thinking to myself, *This is the way we expected it would be and the way Ralph would want to go.* But as I got closer, there was some slight movement and a call, "Just in time! I could use some help." I didn't know whether to be relieved, angry, or laugh.

Look out! (as told by Larry)

Ralph needed to have his tractor picked up for a repair. It was parked over by his chicken coups and needed to be dragged over to the end of the driveway and down onto the road so the truck could pick it up there. I asked him if it had any brakes (because most of his tractors didn't), and he kind of smiled sheepishly and said, "Yeah. Not very good brakes." So we started out with him on the Ford tractor pulling me on the tractor that wasn't running. All went pretty well until we got to the end of his chicken road and headed down the driveway. That was when the chain started getting loose. I was getting anxious as he was in front of me, putting along, and I was standing on the brakes, trying to avoid rolling into him! We got there. We always do, but it's never easy! It had brakes, look out brakes, meaning you may not stop, so look out!

Dead flowers (as told by Larry)

We went to Amherst to get grain. There's a farm up there that grinds corn much cheaper than commercial grain and probably fresher. When we got there, they were grinding the corn, and it was coming out a chute into a bag a young girl was holding. I thought I would help her and said, "Better let me help you. It looks like it's kind of heavy for you." I grabbed the bag and held the open bag to catch the grain. The force of the grain coming out of the chute ripped it out of my hands and went everywhere. So much for being macho. The farm also had a flower shop, and Ralph wanted to get Mabel flowers for their anniversary. As they wandered around the shop, the lady asked them if she could help them. Ralph explained he wanted flowers for his wife but wasn't sure what she would like. The lady suggested a lovely dried arrangement. He looked her and said, "You mean they're dead?"

Secret Service men

As Larry grew "more mature," his knees wore out, and walking or standing for any length of time became a problem. That didn't stop him when he had the chance to go to a political rally in New Hampshire. He and his friend John (his name really is John) drove there, finding a place to park in a library parking lot right next to the venue. They walked a path to get in line. Standing there was getting pretty painful as he leaned heavily on his cane when a Secret Service person approached them. John and Larry were anxious that they were being singled out, but instead the men informed them, "Sir, we have special seating for you." And started leading him down to a handicap section.

"Wait, what about my friend? Can he come?"

The man turned and looked at John and said, "Are you married?"

To which John replied, "Yes."

Motioning over his shoulder for him to come with them he said, "You qualify." And led them down to the front row right in front of Sarah Palin. She opened with, "How is the moose hunting here?" which made the crowd go wild. Later as they headed back to the library, they were stopped by more Secret Service.

"Sorry, gentlemen. You cannot go down that path."

Surprised, they pointed to the car and said, "But that's our car right there," and the response they got from two big suits, "And that's Governor Palin's trailer right there. You are not going down that path." So the cane didn't help this time. John had to take the long way around to get the car and drive back to pick up Larry.

Larry told John, "I guess it was a good thing I didn't say anything. I was going to tell them they were messing with a Marine."

Go together

Whenever they go to Russell's together, they climb the flights to the third floor to visit. Larry goes behind to make sure he can help

THE ARTIST, THE FARMER, THE HUNTER, AND THE GOOD GUY

Ralph if he gets unsteady. After the visit, as they head back down, Larry volunteers, "I'll go first. That way, if you fall, we will both get killed." It was a little different one day when they were out riding about. I called them to warn them a tornado had touched down and maybe they should keep an eye out or even better seek shelter. As they headed for home, a large branch broke from a tree and flew across in front of them. Ralph looked at Larry and questioned, "What do you think we should do?"

Larry said, "If it gets any worse, we might have to find a ditch and crawl in it."

Ralph shook his head and replied, "I'm not climbing into a ditch. You can go climb in the ditch."

So much for togetherness.

Red, Yellow... Blue

Larry brought Ralph to get his license renewed, and looking into the camera, he was supposed to tell the colors he saw. "Red... yellow...blue!"

The registry man looked at Larry, "Is he all right?" Larry shrugged. What could he say? "Let's try this again."

And Ralph recited again, "Yellow, red, blue."

Hmm. The registry man was unsure what to do. "I'm going to give you one more chance. What colors do you see?"

Larry nudged Ralph emphatically. "What colors do you see?"

As Ralph looked carefully into the screen, "Red, yellow, green!" And two men sigh in relief (not Ralph).

"Great! You passed."

As Larry and Ralph walked out, Ralph told Larry it really was blue, and Larry reminded him, "The only blue lights you should see, should be behind you, and then, let's hope not very often!"

Take the boy out of the country

Larry and Russ were in Boston, the big city, at the hospital just a referral for some testing. It was loud and overwhelming. There were so many people and so many twists and turns. Standing in the lobby of the hospital, they gazed around to which direction to go. In the crowded lobby, a nurse kind of bumped into them, and they asked her how to get where they needed to go. She kindly led them to the elevators. She was about to go her way when Russell reached out and slapped the large yellow arrow painted on the wall pointing up. At that point she decided, "I think I will go with you guys." And pressed the elevator button to go up. She led them right to the doctor's waiting room and told them, "Stay right here. They will come find you." They thanked her very much. Another time in a large building in the city, there were several elevators to choose from. Some only went to specific floors, and trying to decide which elevator to take, Larry turned and asked a maintenance person nearby, "Which elevator goes up?" With a puzzled look, the answer was, "I think they all do." You can take the boys out of the country, but you can't take the country out of the boys.

Running for office
A Diane memory

We were only halfway through shopping, not nearly done, and it was taking forever! Larry took off to go find another item in hopes of "helping," but as I perused the aisles, I saw him talking to yet another person. He had talked it seemed to everyone in the store. How did he miss this one? He caught up to me, and we continued on only to meet someone else to chat with. Hoping to make it brief, I joked, "We do all our socializing here. Only two more aisles. We should be able to leave in an hour or so." We all chuckled, said our goodbyes, and headed on. As we turned to go down the next aisle, here comes another acquaintance he just had to say hi to. Continuing on again, we passed one we had already chatted with heading to someone new, and she commented with a smile, "There goes the mayor." When you live in town seventy-plus years, I guess it goes with the territory. You know everyone and it's especially important to Larry to make them smile with some funny comment and a little conversation.

THE ARTIST, THE FARMER, THE HUNTER, AND THE GOOD GUY

A distance memory

Larry liked running cross-country. When he wasn't running after cows, he would take practice runs along back roads. He was coming down the hill, and one of his classmates in a skimpy red bikini sunning herself on the front lawn waved as he was running by her home. His long legs tangled, nearly launching him into a headlong roll, but he managed to stay upright. Years later as he waves going by, he contemplates the memory and how different it is now. He can barely walk, never mind run, and she doesn't wear bikinis anymore.

Yankee ingenuity

While working at Klem's, Ralph had some flexibility in his job. He was trusted to do a good job, but one day he made a mistake. We don't need to know what he did, but he was called on the carpet and was asked, "Why did you do that?" His response was classic.
"Because I'm stupid!"
How can you argue with that? But he is far from stupid. When he decided he wanted electricity in his barn across the street from his house, he devised a great plan. He ran a wire from his house down the driveway through the culvert under the road down to the barn. It worked well for years—until the highway department dug up the culvert.

Oh, that face!

You can recognize a Buzzell. It is written all over their face, but there have been times when the face is unrecognizable, like the evening Larry got a call for help from Mabel. He arrived at Ralph's to find him sitting on a stump dazed and bloody. George Hanson was there to pick up one of his rams. As they were corralling this ram unto the trailer, Ralph slipped on some wet ground and met the ram face-to-face. His face was swelling and bloody, and some teeth had been knocked loose. George managed to get him to the stump, but he was in no condition to tackle that ram again. Ralph, against Mabel's insistence, refused to go to the emergency room. He was toughing it out. In the meantime, George was on a schedule and encouraged Larry with, "Let's get this ram. I've got to go."

And Larry answered, "Are you crazy? I'm not going in there." In the end they did manage to get the ram in truck. Larry will never forget how bad that face looked.

There was another time, just a few days before Easter. Ralph was cutting some wood with a chainsaw and was setting the saw down, and it bounced back into his face, cutting his nose and lips. He managed to walk to Joe and Tina's for help, but no one was home, and he couldn't figure out how to use their newfangled phone, so leaving a trail of blood, he trudged to sister-in-law Catharine's up the street. Also a nurse, she raced him to the hospital, where they stitched him up. I admire the handiwork of the doctor because he came away with barely any scarring. Larry tells him he even looks better than before, but on Easter, he was a terrible sight to behold.

That's entertainment!

On a recent brother bonding trip, the boys were exploring one of their favorite antique malls in Vermont. They always come home with some "treasures." But the story related to me about this shopping trip was the real treasure. After wandering the shop for some time, Ralph and Larry were getting tired and needed a place to rest their legs while waiting for Russ to finish his exploring. It was almost closing time, so Larry suggested they go sit at an old retro Formica kitchen set on display. They pulled out the chairs to have a seat and started a conversation about what they had found during this excursion. Ralph asked Larry where Russ was, and Larry replied, "Last time I saw him he was swinging an old ax, and you know the head of those axes can come off sometimes, so I figured it best to get as far away as I could." (Of course, Russ wasn't swinging an ax in the store, but this makes the story more interesting.)

"You don't suppose Russ fell down somewhere?"

"No, they would have found him by now."

"You find anything good?"

"No, the problem here is I'm looking for giraffes, fishes, and bulls, and all they got is horses, dogs, and ducks. Russ found me a hay hook, and guess where it was made? Bangor, Maine. We need a hay hook from Bangor." (The last time he used a hay hook was never but now he needs one.)

"You found anything?"

"Yessir! I found a good-looking rooster. Did you know this the first time in my life I have more fake roosters than real ones? When Russ and I were on the farm, we had close to a hundred of them. They were everywhere. We had upstairs roosters and downstairs roosters."

"You know we probably shouldn't get too comfortable sitting here because we are old, a couple of antiques."

"Yeah, especially since we are older than most of this stuff. They might look right at us and think we belong here and lock us up with the rest of the antiques. You don't suppose Russ is out in the truck waiting for us?"

"I can go check, but I don't think he would do that."

"It's almost closing time. Maybe we should go find our father?"

They got up to go look for him, and heading around the corner, there they found the employees manning the register. They were about in tears eavesdropping on Larry and Ralph's banter. Chuckling, they told them, "Thank you for the entertainment. The last hour in the store can be really boring, but you made the day. You can come back anytime!"

At that moment Russ came down the aisle. Ralph called out, "There you are. We were getting worried and coming to look for you."

And the employees again barely holding back their mirth, "You don't look like their father."

Russ shook his head. "You guys!"

Journey jingles

I like this trip between you and me as long as we can find a place to pee.

We've been here so long if we want to deviate, we will have to find another state.

New technology
Conversation with Ralph

"What can you tell me about the old wire baler?" asked Larry.

Ralph, surprised, answered, "I can't believe you remember that baler! That was in the early fifties, and you had to be really little."

"Oh, I remember it, all right."

"Yes, that old thing was a Case, one of the first balers after loose hay. Uncle Wendell loved it because it was bales and better than loose hay, but Dad said it took three men and boys to run it. Loten Whitman loved it too, and Dad would bale for him."

"You must have worn gloves handling that wire."

"No, you know us. We didn't have gloves. We got cut up some but not too bad."

"I remember Mom sitting on it. Wasn't there a seat on each side?"

"Yep, there was a tube about eight feet long by the chute. One person sat on one side and had to draw the wire out and feed it around the bale, and the person on the other side slipped the end through a loop to tie it up. Dad told Mom to get up there, and she was doing pretty good tying the knots. He had Russ driving Popeye, and he was only eight years old. 'Course, you know Dad. Had to be just right, and he started yelling at Russ because he was cutting the corners and missing hay. You know, Popeye wasn't an easy tractor to drive. Mom got mad at him for yelling at Russ, and next thing we know, there goes Mom out across the field. It was the last time he got her on the baler."

"Johnny, my friend Bruce has an old tractor like yours, and the clutch seized up just like yours. He said on the old tractors, you need to take a two by four, depress the clutch, and put the two by four to hold it down, and the clutch won't seize up on you."

Ralph replied, "I know that. Pappy told me that years ago. In fact, the old tractors, when you bought them new, came with a two by four."

"Really? I didn't know that. Pappy never told me that."

"Yup." Ralph continued. "I saved a bunny."

"How did you save a bunny?"

"I was mowing Zagarra's and when I came around, a little bunny was sitting on the swath I had just laid down. I saw this red-tail circling above and I could tell he had his sights on that bunny. I drove the tractor right across the field and scared the hawk off. I saved that bunny."

Next Generation

Skips a generation

As the brothers sit around the table talking, the conversation settles on their kids. Every parent is proud of their kids and bragging to one another the amazing talents and attributes from being smart, athletic, pretty, artistic, handsome, a hard worker, the list goes on. They look at each other in wonder, "How did our kids get so good?" A blank look is a response as they consider the possibilities.

"They must have got it from Dad because I'm not that smart!"

"You mean it must have skipped you?"

"I guess it did."

"Whatever our kids are didn't come from us. It must have skipped a generation."

"Yup, skipped a generation."

How do you spell relief?

They were on their way to the airport, and it was a long ride made longer by a crying, fussy baby Christy. Nothing seemed to placate her, and she was getting more intense as the ride continued. Grampa had just about all he could take, and finding a place to pull off the road, in frustration, parked the car and got out. Pulling his jackknife out of his pocket, he pulled the back door open, reached down, and slit the elastic of each leg on the rubber diaper pants Christy was wearing. It was almost immediate as she calmed and stopped crying. The poor little thing had little red lines where the elastics had irritated, and snipping the elastics relieved her of that irritation and brought relief to all. But how did Pappy know that was all he needed to do?

Get the broom

When Jalna was about a year old, she was just beginning to form words and copy what she heard. Well, she heard someone say "Oh shit." That person will remain nameless, but *his* mother chased him under the bed with a broom for saying it when he was young. Of course, she picked up that little phrase and repeated it and repeated it and repeated it. We were visiting Gramma, and she thought it was hysterical. She kept saying over and over how cute and funny it was that she was saying it, and I kept telling Gramma not to laugh at her because she was saying it all the more! Where's the broom when you need it!

Three strikes and you're out of the barn

Janice lived with the girls in Colorado most of the year, but summers they would come home to the farm. Fresh air and freedom to roam and play with the cousins doesn't get better than that. The barn was their playground with the hay forts and rope swings. First summer Colleen broke her arm. The next year it was her wrist. Mike and June encouraged her to jump from the swing even when she thought it wasn't a good thing after the previous year, when she broke her wrist. Then next year she broke her arm twice falling off Nell. And the next year Grampa said she couldn't go back in the barn!

Grampa's little helper

When we moved to the farm after Mom passed, Jalna and Nathan were four and three years old. Nathan adored his Grampa and followed him around like a little shadow. He was always watching and thinking how he could be like Grampa. One time Grampa took them to the fruit store and told them they could each pick out *one* thing. Nathan quietly looked over all the produce and selected a watermelon. Grampa thought that was the funniest thing, and home they came lugging the biggest watermelon Nate could carry. Another time they were sawing wood, and Nate wanted to saw too. So they gave him an old hacksaw. As I gazed out the window, I was aware something was radically wrong and called out to them, "Hey! Nate has a saw."

And I was told, "It's just an old hacksaw. It can't cut anything."

And I responded, "Well, with that old hacksaw that can't cut anything, he has cut three legs off the picnic table!" Then came the time that they were getting ready to rake the field. Grampa pulled the tractor and baler in front of the barn and parked it to be ready to go when  he was ready. Nate was playing around the baler, and no one paid any attention to him, I mean, what harm could he do? Until later when Pappy climbed on the tractor and took off to go rake the field, and the rake fell to the ground as he pulled away. Nate had pulled the pin out holding the rake in the hitch on the tractor. He was such a good little helper that Grampa couldn't even get mad at that. Another time he hitched the chain from the tractor to the truck, and when Grampa took off with the tractor, not realizing he was hooked to the truck, he pulled the taillights off the truck.

History repeated

When the Buzzell boys were growing up, they were good friends with the Whitman boys. They had each other's back. Sometimes in the world of big kids, the little guys need someone who come to their aid just because it's the right thing to do. Russ found himself on the bus with no place to sit, and it was Ralph Whitman who made room for him. Years later when some big kids were teasing Nate and stealing his winter hats, it was Ralph's boys who stood up for him. Character passed down from one generation to the next.

THE ARTIST, THE FARMER, THE HUNTER, AND THE GOOD GUY

Major Rescue

It was summer, haying time. We get hay wherever we can get it, and we were in Brookfield over by what was once Poor Richard's on Route 148 ready to bale this field. Pappy's legs were getting worse, but he could still drive the tractor, and Stephanie drove him over to do the baling. The field was a pretty good hill, and the Major tractor was idling on the edge of the field by the road. As he reached up to grab the steering wheel to help hoist himself into the driver's seat, it turned the front wheels downhill, and the tractor started rolling. He wasn't in the seat, and in front of the back wheel and in the nick of time, Stephanie grabbed his jacket pulling him back before the tire rolled into him. The tug knocked him off balance but at least out of the way of the tractor. When he fell to the ground, the tire ran over his hand. It mangled it pretty bad, but it could have been so much worse. The Major and baler careened down the hill into the brush and landed against a tree. Pappy had a big heavy-duty metal box on front end for tools, and that saved the tractor from serious damage, but it took some time for his hand to heal. Thank God for Stephanie and her quick thinking.

Waiting for the shoe to drop

The big old farmhouse was a welcoming and comfortable place, but in the shadows of the evening, it could kind of make your imaginations run wild. It was big and old, and there weren't the handy light switches we have now to light your way around, and in the dark, it was a little creepy. It had a central front door opened to the front hall to a kind of grand open staircase. On either side were doors that led to the left a bedroom and to the right the living room. Upstairs the landing led to bedrooms on either side. Mom and Dad's bedroom was upstairs to the left.

One night Mom was watching television with granddaughters Colleen and Christy when they heard some strange thumping noise in the front hall. They listened intently, and I'm sure there were some looks back and forth. No one hardly ever used the front door, and it didn't sound like the front door anyway, so they quietly sat waiting, waiting to hear if it would happen again. And it did! Frightened it could be someone breaking in! Or a ghost! The girls jumped up to exit the room along with Gramma, who ran right through them, pushing them out of the way to the dining room and out the side door. They found out it was actually only Grampa John throwing a slipper down the stairs. His knees were bothering him so bad he didn't want to come down the stairs and was calling, but no one heard him over the television, so he threw his slippers to get their attention. He got their attention all right! Christy's comment was "Don't get in Gramma's way when she's running scared!"

The one that didn't get away

As a parent, we try to help our kids learn and grow through various experiences. One is typically learning the responsibility of caring for a pet. We always had a dog. Jalna learned to pull herself up and walk holding onto our German Shepherd, Wendy. Then there were ponies, horses, cows, and goats. It seemed we were much more in tune with large animals. The small animals just didn't seem to work out. We tried our hand at chickens, but that didn't last long. They were free range and insisted on roosting over the horses. It was disgusting cleaning poop off the horses and tack. Then rabbits. Someone gave us a coop and a couple rabbits. That started out pretty well, but although they were cute, they weren't terribly friendly. Then one morning Larry noticed the coop door was open and the rabbits gone. He knew how upset the kids would be over the missing rabbits. He quickly looked around and spotted one on the lawn and thought he might be able to catch at least one. Slowly he inched across the lawn. Quiet as a mouse, he crept up on it. Getting closer as he sneaked up and diving at the last step to grab the rabbit before it got away, he grasped it in his hands! Only then did he realize something was wrong. He had snuck up on a dead rabbit. We don't know what happened to it. There didn't appear to have anything wrong, but it was dead as a doornail in the middle of our yard. That was the end of rabbits.

THE ARTIST, THE FARMER, THE HUNTER, AND THE GOOD GUY

Not a good catch!

Fishing is a favorite pastime, but it can be quite a unique experience with Larry. Sitting in the boat and looking out across the water, Larry wanted to cast away from Nate so they didn't tangle their lines and asked, "Where are you?"

I could see Nate ponder for a moment before he responded, "Ah, right behind you."

There were a couple other fishermen on the water, and in the quiet of the evening, their comments echoed across the pond. Laughter echoed right back. Larry catches interesting things sometimes. He could never do it if he tried, but as he reached back to cast, he caught Nate's hat right from his head and flung it into the water. Nate, surprised by his hat flying from his head, yelled, "My hat! Where's my hat?" and Larry assured him, "Just a minute. I'll get it," as he reeled it back in.

So then Nate, who had put his pole down to do something, looking for bait or a fly, who knows, wasn't paying attention. In the meantime with his back to Nate, Larry prepared to cast. As he flipped his line back, the hook caught Nate's pole, and Larry hurled it into the lake. Of course, it didn't stay on the hook and slowly sank. As they both sat dumbfounded watching it sink, Larry turned to Nate and said, "What should we do?" and Nate said, "Well, I don't have a pole, so I guess we go home. Next time we go fishing, I'm getting a pole with cork handle so at least it won't sink." End of that story.

As told by Larry

It was a beautiful morning, and Corey and I went fishing. On the way, we stopped at Dunkin for coffee and maybe a donut. [Of course, a donut!] We climbed in the boat and dropped lines. I was so tired. Waiting for a bite can take time, so I decided to "rest." I slid down in the bottom of the boat resting my head on the seat. Next thing I knew my line was taut and dragging the boat in circles. In my sleepy confusion, I scrambled to get up, which wasn't easy when you were lying on the bottom of a boat with tackle boxes, and of course I couldn't spill my coffee. The boat was rocking, and Corey was laughing, trying to grab my pole before I lost it over the side. I didn't know how we didn't keep from capsizing, but I did manage to reel in a good-size calico bass. A calico is a fun fish to catch, fight like crazy, and this one caught me sleeping. Literally, I was sleeping.

Bass Awkward

Artie and Larry are at Queen Lake, and Artie offers to take Larry fishing out in the boat. Larry knows Artie doesn't fish and declines, but Artie insists. They head out across the lake to find a spot for Larry to drop his line. They sit there for about a minute or two, and Artie asks, "What do we do now?"

"Wait for the fish to bite."
"You mean just sit here?"
"Yup."

Artie can't just sit and is getting really antsy, so Larry suggests they troll.

"How do you do that?" asks Artie.

"Just drive slowly around the lake not too close to shore so I don't hook weeds and such." So off they go, slowly at first, but soon the engine starts humming as the boat picks up speed and completely out of patience Artie gives it full throttle. The boat speeds across the water with Larry trying to stay upright as his lure skims across the top of the water, suddenly feels his line tighten. "Stop," he commands, and Artie cuts the throttle, and the boat slows and settles in the water as Larry reels furiously to reveal about a two-pound bass. He had hooked it through the back!

I can get that done for you

Larry loves to help people, often double-booking himself. He has such a servant heart and just can't imagine someone needing help and not helping them. He was at a convenience store with son-in-law Artie, and as they headed in the door, they noticed a car outside with a flat tire. Larry asked the woman in line if it was her car and warned her the tire was flat. She was visibly upset, and Larry comforted her by saying, "Don't worry. He can change it for you," pointing to Artie. Artie was a little stunned by being volunteered but agreed to help her out by changing her tire in the pouring rain. As he is changing it, Larry asks him, "How much longer are you going to be? It's kind of wet out here." Not funny, Larry.

Another time asked him to plow a friend's driveway. He did a great job, and our friend was overwhelmed because the snowblower they had would take hours to get the job done. She called to thank Artie and Larry for showing up. I told her, "No thanks necessary. Artie loves to help out when he can, and Larry loves to volunteer him. Win-win!"

Left is the right way
A Diane memory

I like riding in the back seat. Generally, when I am in the front, I act as navigator, keeping us on the straight and narrow with the help of the GPS. It gets monotonous and sometimes stressful making sure we take the right turns, and I try to stay alert rather than enjoy the ride and scenery. When I get to sit in the back, sometimes they forget about me, but that's okay. I can be like a fly on the wall and listen in on the chitchat and watch as they miss the turns while they aren't paying attention. I have to say I am watching the GPS anyway and sometimes warning them of upcoming turns. This had been a great trip through the country, but yup, they weren't paying attention and missed a turn that took us about fifteen miles out of the way. We weren't on a schedule, so it was no big deal, but getting righted was kind of fun to watch. Suddenly it was like Abbot and Costello in the front seat. The turn was coming up, and Corey said, "Its right up here."

And Larry said, "Okay, on the right."

"No, Dad. It's a left."

"So we aren't going right?"
"No. Left."
"That left?"
"That road right up there."
"Right or left?"
"Right over there, Dad."

Larry turned on his right blinker. "Left, Dad. Left!" Corey held up his hands. The index and the thumb forming an L on the left hand and his right-hand pointing Larry to the left. In frustration, he started waving his hand, pointing to where he wanted him to go while all the time the GPS on the dash showed the map turning left. The rest of the ride they used hand signals. Larry told Corey, "Russ gets upset with me too. I'll tell him left when it's really right. When we get there, he says, 'That's not right!' and I just tell him, 'It would be if we were coming the other way.'"

Some Random Memories of Grandma

Stories written by Grandson Joe

So pretty

For a few years when my brother Jim and I were very small, a week or so before Christmas, my mother (Mabel) would load us in the car and head over the farm and pick up Grandma and drive the four of us around the countryside to look at Christmas lights. We would go all over, and I seem to remember going to Ware, which was always very decked out with Christmas lights. For us as little kids, seeing houses lit up with Christmas lights was a very exciting part of the buildup to Christmas. Grandma would be in the front passenger seat, looking around and pointing out the lights to me and Jim, and say, "Ooh, how pretty!" and we'd say, "Ooh, pretty!" It got to be that when we went by any house that had Christmas lights, one of us would say, "Ooh, pretty!"

When I was maybe four or five, my father (Ralph) strung up the Christmas lights around the porch of our house, and I was very wound up about it. Standing out in the dark that night, admiring the bright colorful lights on our house, I wondered if Grandma and Papa could see them from there, since our house was across the valley, fairly close to the farm. My mother suggested we call Grandma to tell her our Christmas lights were up and turned on, so she dialed the number and gave me the phone, and I excitedly told her that our Christmas lights were up and asked if she could see them. I don't know if she could actually see them or not, but she gave me the impression that she was looking out across the valley toward our house, and she could see them through the darkness. And I'm sure she said, "Ooh, how pretty, Joey!"

Going into the house on the farm was always a wonderful experience because Grandma was always happy to see you. She always seemed happy to see everybody who came in. It was just a very warm and welcoming place to walk into and visit, whether it was full of people, or if it was just Grandma who was there at the time we'd dropped in. I am so grateful that we stopped in often to experience that.

Where is that poor girl?

As kids we were always playing outside when the weather was good, and back then, kids who were five or six frequently just went out and played; often there were no parents watching over you. When it came to safety, kids had to use their own judgment a lot of the time, so unless a parent or other adult specifically told you not to get into something, there was a fair chance that you'd eventually get into it. I loved the barn at Grandma and Papa's. When I was little, it seemed *huge*, and inside it was fascinating. The barn was across the road from the house, and the back part of it had collapsed in one particular area. One time, I'm guessing I was around five at the time, I was playing down in the area aside the barn, between the part of the barn that had collapsed and the road, where there were usually a few cars and some farm equipment parked. Eventually I came back to the house, and Grandma asked where I'd been playing, so I told her. She got a concerned look on her face and told me I mustn't go near where that part of the barn had collapsed; then she told me a story of how a girl had been playing in the barn years before and had been lost in that part of the barn. I asked Grandma what happened to her, and what I remember her telling me was that she was lost, and no one had ever found her! Needless to say, I never went anywhere near that particular part of the barn, although for quite some time I wondered if that poor girl might still be alive in there somewhere.

THE ARTIST, THE FARMER, THE HUNTER, AND THE GOOD GUY

Stottlemeyer fan

Back around the mid-1970s, when my mother started attending Worcester State College to earn her bachelor's degree in nursing, my brother Jim and I were still a little young, as far as my mother was concerned, to stay home by ourselves when she was attending classes during after-school hours. So Grandma offered to have us get off the bus at her house on those days. So for quite a few years, one day a week, Jim and I would get off the bus at Grandma and Papa's after school, and we'd spend the afternoon with them. Often—well, sometimes—we would do our homework while Grandma would be in the kitchen getting supper ready for us and Papa, who on most afternoons was out of the house working on his equipment or in the barn or in the fields, working on something or other; they usually ate supper around 4:00–4:30 p.m. But other times Jim and I would procrastinate on our homework and go out and play instead. When the weather wasn't good for playing outside, we would find ways to procrastinate inside. One of those ways was to watch reruns of the old TV show Bewitched. Grandma seemed to enjoy watching that silly show with us. Of course, in those days, Jim and I loved our baseball card collections, and often we would bring them to school and then on the bus back home, so when we went to Grandma's on those days, we might bring out those cards and look at them and sort them out or whatever we would do with them. One time we were looking through them, and Grandma asked if she could see one. Jim showed her a card of Mel Stottlemeyer, who was a pitcher for the Yankees in the 1960s and '70s. Grandma looked at it and said, "The only baseball player I know is Hank Aaron—he broke the home run record!" So we talked about Hank Aaron for a while and how he broke that record, and then Jim thought we should introduce her to other players, so he started telling her about Mel Stottlemeyer and how he had been a pretty good pitcher for the Yankees over the years, winning twenty games a few times, but he was near the end of his career. Well, Grandma listened to him closely and asked a few questions and then had to get back into the kitchen to tend to supper. That was pretty much the end of it, because after supper our mom came to pick us up, and we went home. But wouldn't you know, several weeks later baseball season started, and when we got off the bus and in the house and got our jackets off, we were in the living room catching up on what we'd been doing and so forth, and at some point, the subject of baseball came up, and Grandma asked in all seriousness, "So how is Mel Stottlemeyer doing?" Well, Jim and I looked at each other, and then at her, and she had a big smile of her face, and the three of us laughed. She had a great laugh, and what a great sense of humor she had!

Pardon my French

Once I was old enough to ride my bike by myself beyond Tucker Road, sometimes I'd ride it to go visit friends who lived nearby on Smith-Hanson Road, Waite Corner Road, and Cider Mill Road, especially in the summertime. One time, I'm guessing I was around twelve years old, I went to visit my friend Jeffrey Whitman, whose family lived on Cider Mill Road. On my way back home, I decided I'd exercise the independence my bike gave me to go up and see Grandma, who by that time had moved with Papa to their house on Cider Mill Road after selling the farm. It was a pretty hot summer day, and I pedaled up the long dusty driveway. When I got there, I went to the door and said "hello," and she came to see who it was and seemed genuinely and pleasantly surprised to see me. She invited me in, and we had such a good visit. They were always good visits anyway, but this one seemed especially good, maybe because it was a surprise to her, and it was just me and her. She got me some Kool-Aid or juice or something and asked me about school in the fall. I guess I was going into eighth grade that fall, and I told her I was concerned because the principal and guidance counselor had wanted me to take French, and even though I wasn't too excited about it, they put me in the class; she then told me how she had taken French in high school, and her teacher came into the class from the first day and only spoke French, no English at all! She told me how she and the other kids had to adapt quickly and listen closely because the teacher would not speak English to explain things to her and the other students. Then she said that she supposed that they probably didn't do that anymore, and I told her that I'd heard from older kids that the French teacher didn't do that, which in comparison to what Grandma had experienced was kind of a relief. Anyway, it was a great visit, and as I got back on my bike to leave, I felt much better about having to take the French class. I always thought she was a very good listener and conversationalist, which was something I was not very good at.

Never forget what a friend we have

At her funeral, we sang "What a Friend We Have in Jesus," and if I remember correctly, someone said it was her favorite hymn. Ever since then, I think of her whenever I hear it.

Grampa and Joe on Popeye

Larry's Ad-libs

And I quote

Nathan said, "Ralph's a good farmer, Jack's a good hunter, Russ is a good artist." Pause.

Larry, "Hey!"

Nate with a quick save, "You're a good guy, Dad."

He could have said he was a good coach because he coached baseball, softball, basketball, and soccer at all levels, even running a basketball program for the town with about two hundred kids, from kindergarten through eighth grade. He touched so many young lives, and we were invited to weddings and still get Christmas cards from the kids he coached, and today those "kids" still greet him by calling him Coach. He loved sports, but he loved even more to see the athletes he worked with grow and succeed, and it wasn't always being the best player but becoming the best person they could be. As Larry's wife, my sport was horses, but I couldn't help but learn coaching and scorekeeping especially if I wanted to spend any time with him and carry on conversations with him. As a wife, I'm a little prejudiced in my opinion, but he is a good guy and has a talent for touching lives in a special way. Larry's signature sign off is "Keep smiling." He loves to make people smile, so he always has something funny or encouraging to say, and if it's not funny, it's inappropriate, meaning he uses a word that has nothing to do with what he is saying to make you smile or maybe think twice. He is the king of puns, and I could put so many here. You would have to be there to get the full effect, but

THE ARTIST, THE FARMER, THE HUNTER, AND THE GOOD GUY

here are a few unforgettables to give you an idea what we deal with during conversations with him.

> Even my favorite candy is Chuckles.
> What's down in the well will come up in the bucket.
> Like milking a three titter with a milking machine. One is left hanging.
> If going to hell scares you to death, then come to Jesus.
> What the flock is going on?
> With over one hundred years of marriage experience between Ralph and I, if we wrote a book, we couldn't write one page on how to understand women.
> Sometimes us farmers just have to *bale* you out.
> Knee-high to a ten-foot Indian.
> Where the buckwheat meets the rye.
> Have you seen my wife? She can be very elusive. (Often used when wandering a store looking for me.)

Despite his corny quips, he has some deep thoughts, and he is actually the writer. Here are a few samples.

The Farmer by Larry Buzzell

> A farm is a house full of kids
> A cellar full of wood
> A tractor full of gas
> A barn full of hay
> A silo full of corn
> A cooler full of milk
> A barrel full of oats
> Stanchions full of cows
>
> A farmer doesn't buy his wife flowers; he takes the time to pick them.
> A farmer doesn't care what he gets at Christmas; he treasures what he has.

It's hard for a farmer at Easter to get to sunrise service; he's only halfway through milking.

A farmer sees every sunrise and sunset and treasures a day of rain.

A farmer has breakfast, lunch, and dinner with his family.

A farmer watches the shadows of the clouds float over his fields of timothy.

A farmer watches a newborn calf struggle to his feet.

A farmer never seems to finish his work but gets to start again the next day.

A farmer gets to sit on a stump in the woods with a cup of coffee feeling really good because it's his woods.

A farmer can do the same thing very differently.

A farmer gets up a little earlier, works a little harder to have free time.

A farmer thinks there may be a better way but knows there isn't.

The Udder Parable
A Guide for the Dairy Farmer Bible Study Leader

Now to assure us that the words of the Bible are for real, the writer says that from him everything was made and without him nothing was made. Also, he says before Abraham, "I am." He also created the world in seven days by his word.

I know. I don't blame you when you ask, how can you possibly compare a cow's udder to the Bible? Well, think about it. The udder is filled with milk, and the Bible is filled with God's word, milk for the beginner. The more milk a farmer gets, the bigger his paycheck, the happier his family and he himself will be. Likewise, the more we study God's Word, the more we will be blessed and the happier our family will be and ourselves will be.

Now let's relate a farmer's chore of milking to a good old Bible study. A farmer must treat his cows well to get the maximum amount of milk, and you guessed it, from the cow's udder. Just like God's great commandment, love others as we love ourselves and God loves us.

Now let's start milking. Let it be known cows have personalities just like us. A farmer really needs to know his herd. Just like we need to know each other. You know some people have sensitive issues. Some talk too much. Some only hear what they want to hear. To work as a team, we should know each other's needs. For example, on the farm while milking, the farmer needs to know how to move around his cows. Some cows you really move around quickly, while others with the slightest quick move you could get your hat kicked off. So you can see how important it is to know each cow. Just like we need to know each person in the study.

It's a fact a cow can hold their milk back in their udder for many reasons, like being nervous when someone new is around, or maybe they are just in a bad mood. Just like people having a bad day, so they really want to listen and not participate in the study. As far as the cows go, farmer takes a pail of warm water and a cloth and gently massages the udder to calm them down and help them produce. It is just like we opening up a meeting with prayer makes it easier for people to open up and feel more comfortable.

Now I don't know why, but some cows will give twelve quarts of milk quicker than some who only give six quarts. Now this information will make the milking time go much easier. Just like some people need more time to understand things than others. Knowing our people will help us to know everyone understands what we're talking about before moving on.

Timing means a lot. By leaving the milking machine on too long, or taking off too soon, could result in losing the cow. Just as we need to make our Bible study filled with God's Word interesting. Keep them coming back by being on time and not going overtime.

Oh man! I forgot one of the most important things. Sorry! Timing of milking is best when kept consistent. If a farmer milks at 4:00 a.m., for many reasons it will be wise to milk again at 4:00 p.m. Now understand life happens, and even the farmer can't always be perfect, but in the long run, both the cows and the farmer will be happier with a timely consistency. Just like we all do better getting to the study on time and making sure it starts on time. If for no other reason than to balance out the coffee and fellowship time, and maybe a donut time.

Well, I think I milked this parable to the best of my ability. It really is time to moove on. God bless you all!

Just an old farmer who loves his Lord *and* his cows.

Whispering windrows
By Larry Buzzell

There's a part of farming I never talked about much mostly because I was always alone—no one around.

Every summer, we had to put hundreds of bales in the barn, much like squirrels storing up nuts for the winter. To do the best haying, you need four good, sunshiny days. Three steps to harvesting hay were mowing the grass, raking it into straight rows, and then of course comes baling the hay. My part was the first two steps. My dad always did the baling.

Mowing the hay required your attention. You had to watch out for rocks, and pheasant nests, and little furballs of baby rabbits, as well as woodchuck holes. I would lift the seven-foot cutter bar to avoid any damage or harm to the animals as best I could. Sometimes, if you tried to cut too much, especially in the corners, you would leave a thin strip of standing grass. We called them rooster tails. Now if you had chickens and just wanted eggs to eat, there was no need for a rooster; and if you didn't want your dad to say, "Boy, you left more grass standing than you cut," you didn't want any rooster tails.

Now raking was a little more relaxing. You just followed the windrows where you mowed. Both of these jobs required going around and round the fields for hours, giving you plenty of time to hash over whatever crossed your mind, sometimes thinking of things you said or didn't say or things you did or didn't do.

It was really cool talking to yourself without saying a word. Sometimes weighing out, was it coming from your head or from your heart? It is easy to be honest; after all, why would you lie to yourself? It was easy to pat yourself on the back but just as easy to beat yourself up.

THE ARTIST, THE FARMER, THE HUNTER, AND THE GOOD GUY

Sometimes I would think about dying mainly because it would be hard to think about it after. I never believed we just died. Always felt life was too complicated for that. I thought we either were created but never from a burp in the swamp. I liked created most because after all, even a burp had to be created. Some think it just happened, but I was once told, it would be like a tornado going through a junkyard and making a 747 airplane.

I thought a lot about nature and the order there seems to be. Blue jays are always blue, and you never see a white-tail deer with mule ears. Plus, just like us, they all have personalities. We all look different and also think differently. I learned that the alone time, time to think, was so valuable. Years later, I would learn the answers to my questions would be found in the Bible.

Thanks to Mom.

DIANE BUZZELL

The Right to Vote
By Larry Buzzell 2008

We have the right to vote
To have a proper say
To take out our frustrations
In a most resounding way.

Behind stone walls we took a stand
And lined a split rail fence,
Our hearts and prayers and strong convictions
Were our weapons of defense.

We beat the mighty country
With her soldiers dressed in red,
To be a country without liberty
We'd just as soon be dead.

Even in the midst of the Civil War
I'd like to take note…
The people of America
Took the time to vote.

In scorching heat, icy cold,
In bloody dark of night
People gave up their lives
To protect this basic right.

Mothers lost their sons
And there are tears in fathers' eyes.
Still after all of this
The stars and stripes still fly.

With pride and honor
We hit foreign beaches,
And to less fortunate lands
We send our best teachers.

We give food, blood and clothing
To the most devastated sites
And watch our Patriot missiles
Lighting up the night.

We have the biggest guns,
The most money in the bank,
The softest, warmest hearts
Drive the most powerful tanks.

With Swedish hearts and Irish smiles,
Chinese laundries and a few French twists,
Italian dishes and African rhythm
We hold up a powerful multicolored fist.

The father of our country
Gave us a message that we should pray
That in our hearts and government
We need God in America today.

We can choose our place to stay
But we have broken one huge rule
Despite the good things that we have done
We took prayer out of our schools.

We'll be immoral and corrupt
If from Christ our King we stray.
Our one nation under God
Will crumble and decay.

We have the right to vote,
To have a proper say,
To take out our frustrations
In a most resounding way.

Republican and Democrat
We will fill out every line
And reading all the questions
Give thought before we sign.

From the time the Pilgrims spotted land
And lowered their tiny boat
I'd really like to thank the Lord
We Americans have the right to vote.

For now

Then and Now

Little Red House and Tucker's Farm

Our Heritage

The following chapters of genealogies are basically amateur research for the most part and included for the family. Some of it is old, handed down by family or extended family, and some is newly researched by myself and others. I don't pretend they are completely accurate. Time and inexperience inhibit proper documentation, especially my additions, but they are a good starting point and a possible view into our past.

I must give credit to Russell Buzzell, James Buzzell, and Thaylene Bernard for their valuable advice and research. And thank God for Pappy and his stories that linked together the pieces of our puzzle.

Resources I Used

>Familysearch.org
>Ancientfaces.com
>Findagrave.com
>Ancestry.com
>Myheritage.com
>Geni.com

>For all have sinned and fall short of the glory of God.
>—Romans 3:23

History can be messy, and our family's history is messy as well, but ignoring history doesn't erase it. Read it. Think on it. Rise above it. We can't change the past, but we can learn from it.

Our family is the color white, and from our history I don't see that we were superior or privileged. We have always worked hard to get where we are. When my grandparents came from the old country, they were mocked and discriminated against. Surprise! Prejudice and discrimination are color blind. There were no handouts, Medicare, or social security. One aunt was almost turned away because she walked with a limp and could be considered a burden to society. They needed sponsors, a place to live, and a job. They lived and worked *hard* to climb out of poverty. They learned the language, and when they became citizens, they were proud of their adopted country and even fought in wars to support it. They were productive and rose above adversity and discrimination. They worked hard to earn respect. The history I learned of the Buzzells is similar. They faced hardships, persecution, and stood strong. They were part of forming of our country, and they fought for the country we have. There are gravestones in Gettysburg proving they died for all Americans. *That is our heritage.*

I believe all human life is sacred and valued by God. I was brought up singing "Red and Yellow, Black and White they are precious in His sight," and that includes all preborn red and yellow, black and white. Before Haley was born, we loved her, and it broke our hearts when her life ended before we even got to know her, yet others like her are routinely ripped apart and tossed in the trash or parts sold to the highest bidder. Her DNA was different from her mother's, just like any other preborn has different DNA from the mother who believes "My body, my choice." We are commanded to speak up for those who cannot speak for themselves.

As a Christian, I am commanded to love others. Has there been injustice in this world? Since the beginning of time. I would love to get on my soapbox and tell you more of my thoughts, but I would rather you dig deep into history, your history, and learn from primary sources for yourself. Read biographies and learn the stories of real people like our stories. Some are funny, some might be a little boring, some will make you cry, but hopefully all will make you appreciate the blessing you have today because of who they were and the ability to make a difference in our world today. Our family were migrants and immigrants, disrespected by some but lifted by others, and then some of your family might not be someone you would be proud of. That happens in every family, and then there are those who are just amazing. They fought in wars, built their communities, touched people's lives in so many ways. Did they make mistakes? Wrong decisions? Without a doubt. These genealogies are only a short representation of how we came to be. From the *Mayflower* to the Revolution, the Civil War to WWI and WWII, Korea and Vietnam, our family contributed to a free society. *That is a legacy to be proud of.*

Souvenirs from Our Past

Ralph has a small collection of treasured souvenirs in his cellar.

This washboard was Hazel's, and Ralph thinks this came from her mother, Bertha Leach. It is of 1800s vintage.

Also pictured are the following:

Chain ties for cows—This was an early form of a stanchion to keep cows in place for milking. It came from the barn of Joe Tucker. Ralph guesses this from the 1920s or '30s.

Cowbell—Originally on a cow when the Buzzells lived on Molasses Hill Road in Brookfield when Ralph was young. Pappy called this cow Mother's Cow (the name possibly derived from having received the cow from his mother). The bell was last used on the cow Popcorn in North Brookfield.

Bucksaw—Ralph used this saw as a kid on the farm in Spencer (he was about nine or ten years old). It was one of Ralph's chores to cut wood to bring in for the family woodstove.

Hanging in Ralph's cellar

THE ARTIST, THE FARMER, THE HUNTER, AND THE GOOD GUY

Ice Tongs—This was used when they lived in the house on Route 9 in Brookfield and was given to Pappy by that farmer. When they lived there, the Buzzells had an icebox instead of a refrigerator. The ice was delivered, and as it was too heavy for young Ralph to use the tongs, this was a job for his father.

Drawknife—Ralph called this a frow (not sure of spelling). This was used for shaving wood to shape boards or beams. This was received from the farm of Joe Tucker. It is from the 1800s.

Wooden mallet—Used to pound wooden pegs. From the farm of Joe Tucker. This is from the 1800s.

Hay hook—Ralph, his father, his uncle Wendell, and his brothers used this hook. Just about every year they would run out of hay before the season was over and would have to buy some from New York or Canada. These were big bales (120–150 lbs.). They were called three wire bales, or barn bales. The user would hook the bales and drag them to move them as they were too heavy to carry.

Corn Sickle—Ralph and his brother would use this sickle to cut a row of corn (they cut the stalks at the bottom). Then they'd gather them up by hand. This was done to clear a path wide enough for the tractor. The tractor would then come through with a corn chopper to harvest the bulk of the corn. This was used in Spencer and North Brookfield

Wooden handled shovel (probably 1920s or 1930s)—from Joe Tucker.

Joe Tucker's axe.

Small drill—Very old. He does not remember where he got this from.

Screw and ring to anchor stanchions to the floor.

Blacksmith Tray—When we were cleaning out the barn, the boys were going to throw this tray away. A leg was broken, and it was little more than a piece of junk,

Grandfather Ralph Erastus Buzzell's blacksmith tray

but I saw it as a valuable piece of our history. I had it repaired, and it graces my living room as a coffee table. The grandchildren love to play on it, and I hope someone will cherish it someday like I do.

From the old farm: the bean pot, Dutch oven, sugar bowl, salt shakers, pitcher, mugs and *the flying lamp* (as told in chapter 16, "Mr. Hubbard").

(The display is on my grandmother Lindstrom's table given to her as a wedding present from my great-grandfather in 1920.)

For some it is just old stuff, but when I look at or touch these things, it's sort of reaching back and touching those family members and friends we loved so well or would have loved to meet. I can still see Pappy finish his cup of coffee and flip his mug over on a napkin to be ready to use again.

Buzzell Family Genealogy

Isaac Buswell (1593–1683) born in England, died in Salisbury, Massachusetts
m.1 Elizabeth, m.2 Margaret, m.3 Suzanna
Ch.   Phebe (1623–1670) England m.1645
        Captain William (1626–1699) death 6/15/1699 Burial Salisbury Colonial
        M. Sarah Stacy Salisbury, MA Memorial ID 62506508
        Samuel (1628–1704)
        Gabriel (1631–)
        Mary (1645–?)
        Isaac (1650–circa 1678)

Samuel Buswell (1628–1704) born England, died Bradford, Massachusetts
m. Sarah Keys (1633–abt1700) born Watertown, Massachusetts
Ch.   Isaac (1657–1709)
        John (1659–1739) born Salisbury
        Samuel (1662–1746) b. Salisbury d. Kingston, New Hampshire
        William (1664–1742) lived in Salem, Massachusetts, m Sarah Gill
        Robert (1666–) lived in Andover, Massachusetts, m. 1697
        James (1668–) born Salisbury
        Mary (1671–)
        Jacob (1672–)

Joseph (1674–) born Boxford, Massachusetts, or Topsfield, Massachusetts
Mary (1677–) born Boxford, Massachusetts

Isaac Buswell (1657–1709) born and died Salisbury, Massachusetts. Occupation: weaver
m. 1690 Anne Ordway
Ch.   Isaac (1691–1778)
Daniel (1694–1756)
William (1697–1778) b. Salisbury d. Kingston, New Hampshire
John (1699–) b Salisbury, Massachusetts
Samuel (1702–1745) lived in Kingston, New Hampshire
James (1705–)
Hannah (1707–?)

Daniel Buswell (1694–1756) b. Bradford, Massachusetts d. E. Kingston, New Hampshire
m. Sarah Eaton (1701–) in 1726
Ch.   Sarah (1728–) m. Joshua Kimball in 1756
Hannah (1730–) m. Fellows
James (1732–)
Joseph (1733–)
Daniel (1735–1813) b. Bradford (was Revolutionary war soldier in Nathaniel Gage's C. Army of the North Sept. 30–Nov 6, 1777)
Abigail (1737–)
Anna (1739–1827)
Betty (1741–) m. Ezra Trask in 1787
Nicholas (1742–) Revolutionary War soldier

Joseph Buswell (1733–?) b. Bradford, moved to Goffstown, New Hampshire, 1776
m. Sarah
Ch.   Rhoda
John

James (1776–1826)
Daniel (1779–) m. Alice (Tuttle) Barret of Goffstown
Abraham (1782–) b. Goffstown

James Buswell (1776–1826) b. possible Goffstown, d. Ossipee, New Hampshire
m. Elizabeth Sandson (1780–1857)
Ch.   John (1799–1863) m. Elizabeth George
Daniel (1801–1842) m. Anna Young
Patience (1804–1877) m. Erastus Folsom
Joseph (1806–)
Elizabeth (1811–1877) m. Thomas Davis
Sarah (1815–1865) m. Joseph Palmer

Daniel Buswell (1801–1842) born and died in Ossipee, New Hampshire
Occupation: shoemaker. Died of "cramps and colic"
m. Anna Young (Living in 1849)
Ch.   James F. (1827–1874) m. Mary A. Daniels
Clarissa m. Joseph Tibbets in 1846
Ruby F. m.1 Asa Baker 1852, m.2 George Baker
John Colby (1840–1901)

John Colby Buzzell (1840–1901) b. Ossipee, New Hampshire d. Sherman, Maine
(John Colby served in the 27th infantry, was a prisoner of war in 1863, released April 9, 1863, in a prisoner of war exchange and reenlisted in December in the 30th infantry.)
m. 8/18/1862 Mary Ethelene Gerry (1840–1932) (See Gerry genealogy)
Parents Elbridge Gerry (1818–1865) and Laura (Foster) (1828–1926)
Ch.   Elbridge Gerry (7/21/1861–2/15/1866)
Annie Mary (1862–1900) m. Jack Lancaster
Joseph G. (1866–1885)
Winngenund (1869–1911) m. Elvira F. Emery
Adaline Eliza (1873–1877)
Lizzie Etta (1874–1954) m. William Randall Gallison

Laura Jane (1876–?) m. James Ingalls Jr. (1868–1932)
Ch. Annie (1899–1978)
    Pearl Conley
    Amber Ingalls
    Grace Mclain
    John J. (1918–2008) m. Ruth Bergstrom
Ralph Earastus (1879–1937) m. Daisy L. Dunbar
Ruby Frances (1879–1944) m. Wilbur O'Roak
John Colby Jr. (1884–1885)
Ethel Elena (1886–1887)
Mildred Grace (1892–1937)

Ralph Erastus Buzzell (1879–1937) born and died Sherman, Maine
m. 1/6/1908 Daisy Louella Dunbar (1892–1969) (See Dunbar genealogy)
m. 7/15/1944 Ernest Thomas Rockwell (9/1/1898–deceased)
Ch.   Florence Elvina 1908–1934 M. Harold Lane (1908–1984)
        Ch. Kenneth Harold (1926–2006) m. Lorrane Neal (1928–2014)
        Robert Ralph (1929–2009)
        Joel Edward (1934–1981)
        Joyce Louise (1934–2011)
    John Henry (1910–1988) b. Sherman Mills, Maine, d. N Brookfield, Massachusetts
    m. 11/18/1931 Hazel Leach (1910–1978)
    Margaret Louella (1912–1934) m. John Colby Heath (1907–1987)
    Barbara May (1915–1998) m. Elisha Heath (1908–1979)
    Ch. Raymond Clair 1930
        Muriel Merice 1932
        Thayne Erastus (1935–2011)
        Wayne Erastus (1936–1996)
    Velma Louise (1917–1989) m. 11/6/1933 Walter Heath (1912–1988)
    Ch. Patricia (4/14/1937–12/19/2016) m. David Brown
        Ch. David S.

>   Douglas A.
>   Jennifer
>   Gerald (11/28/1934–7/5/2010) m. Maria
>   Ch. Donald
>   Kimberly
>   Wendy
>   Baby boy (1918)
>   Glynes Pauline (1920–1989) m. James Ghize (1902–1962)
>   Ch. Donna Ghize Rodriguez (12/15/1946–3/26/2020)
>   James M. (4/25/1944–)
>   Mary Elizabeth (1925–2003) m. 1. Cullins, 2. Morris
>   Ch. Glenwood
>   Gerry
>   Brian
>   Margaret Kovalck
>   Melanie Privee
>   Roland
>   Kenneth
>   Brenda Oulette
>   Fenton
>   Wendall Ralph (1927–1994) m. 10/30/1948 Rose Marie Morrison (1930–2004)
>   Ch. Wanda (7/28/49–) m. Donald Rodio
>   Robert (9/28/50–) m. Bette Coffey
>   Susan (12/2/1952–) m. Richard Ford
>   Michael (9/10/1957–) m. Denise Decoteau
>   June (6/5/1959–) m. Kevin Moran

John Henry Buzzell (1910–1988) b. Sherman, Maine d. North Brookfield, Massachusetts
m. 11/18/1931 Hazel A Leach (1910–1978) (See Leach and Atherton genealogy)
Ch.   Ralph Arthur (9/26/1935–) b. Spencer m. Mabel Tucker (3/24/1940–2018)
        Ch. Joseph (9/16/1964) m. Tina Huard
            James (3/16/1966) m. Christine Lamothe

Janice Arlene (11/41936–2013) b. Spencer d. Brookfield m. Robert Pixler
Ch. Christy Leigh (12/12/1957–) m. Stanley Rogacevicz
Colleen (3/27/1959–) m. Craig McEvoy
Stephanie Denise (2/14/1967–) m. Lance Perry
Russell Wendell (10/14/1942–) b. Spencer
Royce (10/14/1942) twin to Russell, died within a few days
John Kenneth (1945–) b. Spencer m. Sheila Barry (11/22/49–)
Ch. Renee (1/31/1969–)
Michelle (5/26/1972–) m. David Prock
Larry William (1949–) b. North Brookfield m. 10/31/1970 Diane Lindstrom (1952–)
Ch. Jalna Marene (1974–) m. 1996 Arthur H. Talbot (1967–)
Nathan John William (1975–) m. 2005 Kelly Crosson (1979–)
Corey Kenneth (1981–) m.1 1999 Alexandria Dimond, m 2. 2020 Jessica Hardy (1987–)

John Buzzell center front

THE ARTIST, THE FARMER, THE HUNTER, AND THE GOOD GUY

Daisy and Ralph Buzzell

Young Ralph Buzzell

Daisy Buzzell Rockwell

Ralph Erastus Buzzell

THE ARTIST, THE FARMER, THE HUNTER, AND THE GOOD GUY

Will Bryant sitting behind horse; Joe Gilcrest on sitting grain bags; Archie Nason behind; Winn Buzzell; Ralph Buzzell center sitting on machine with pitch fork; Richard and Andrew Garnett standing on machine; Laif Garnett far right, Sherman Mills 8/24/1899

Hazel, Wendell, Mary, and Daisy

Wendell and Wanda

Barbara, Wendell, Mary

*Gerry Genealogy

Elbredge Thomas Gerry (1744–1814) parents Thomas and Elizabeth Greenleaf Gerry
Signer of Declaration of Independence
Governor of Massachusetts 1810–1811
VP to fifth president James Madison 1813–1814 died in office
M. Ann Thompson (1763–1849)
Ch.   Catharine (1787–1850)
    Eliza (1791–1882)
    Ann (1791–1883)
    Elbredge Thomas Jr. (1793–1867) m. Nancy Blodgett (1794–1855)
        Ch. Elizabeth (1816–)
            Elbredge Gerry (1818–1865) m. 9/24/1843 Laura Jane Foster (1828–1926)
            Ch. Mary Ethelene (1846–1932)
                m. John Colby Buzzell (1840–1901) had eleven children
                Ch. Elbredge Gerry (1861–1866)
                    Annie Mary (1862–1900) m. Jack Lancaster
                    Winngenund (1869–1911) m. Elvira Emery
                    Adaline Eliza (1873–1877)
                    Lizzie Etta (1874–1954) m. William R. Gallison

---

* Gerry is pronounced with hard "G," as in *gate*.

      Laura Jane (1876–) m. James
       Ingalls Jr.
      Ralph Erastus (1879–1937) m.
       Daisy L Dunbar
      Ruby Frances (1883–1944) m.
       Wilbur O'Roark
      John Colby Jr. (1884–1885)
      Ethel Elena (1886–1887)
      Mildred Grace (1892–1937)
   John Edward (1821–)
   Daniel (1823–)
   Seth (1825–1825)
   Nathaniel (1828–)
   Fredrick (1831–)
   Caroline (1834–)
   Rufus (1836–1868)
 Thomas Russell Gerry (1794–1845) m. Hannah Green
  Goelet (1804–1845)
   Ch. Elbredge Thomas (1837–1927)
   m. Louisa Matilda Livingston (1836–1920)
 Helen Maria Gerry (1796–1864)
 James Thompson Gerry (1797–1854) Commander of
  USS *Albany* lost at sea
 Eleanor Stanford Gerry (1800–1871)
 Emily Louise Gerry (1802–1894)

Ralph Erastus (1879–1937) m. Daisy L Dunbar
Ch. Florence Elvina 1908–1934 M. Harold Lane
 John Henry (1910–1988) m. Hazel Leach
 Margaret Louella (1912–1934) m. John Colby Heath
 Barbara May (1915–1998) m. Elisha Heath
 Velma Louise (1917–1989) m. Walter Heath
 Baby boy (1918)
 Glynes Pauline (1920–1989) m. James Ghize
 Mary Elizabeth (1925–2003) m. 1.Cullins, 2. Morris
 Wendell Ralph (1927–1994) m. Rose Marie Morrison

THE ARTIST, THE FARMER, THE HUNTER, AND THE GOOD GUY

John Henry Buzzell (1910–1988) b. Sherman, Maine d. North Brookfield, Massachusetts
    m. Hazel A Leach (1910–1968) parents Arthur Henry Leach (2/15/1877–5/21/1965)
        Bertha Atherton Leach (1882–1961)
      Ch. Ralph Arthur (9/26/1935–) b. Spencer m. Mabel Tucker (1940–2018)
        Ch. Joseph (3/15/69–) m. Tina Huard
          James (3/16/1969–) m. Christine Lamothe
    Janice Arlene (11/4/1936–2013) b. Spencer d. Brookfield
      m. Robert Pixler
      Ch. Christy Leigh (12/12/1957–) m. Stanley Rogacevicz
        Colleen (3/27/1959–) m. Craig McEvoy
        Stephanie Denise (2/14/1967–) m. Lance Perry
    Russell Wendell (10/14/1942–) b. Spencer
    Royce (10/14/1942) twin to Russell, died within a few days
    John Kenneth (6/20/1945–) b. Spencer m. Sheila Barry
      Ch. Renee (1/31/1969–)
        Michelle (5/26/1972–) m. David Prock
    Larry William (1949–) b. North Brookfield 10/31/1970 m. Diane Lindstrom (1952–)
      Ch. Jalna Marene (1974–) m. Arthur Talbot (1967–)
        Nathan John William (1975–) m. Kelly Crosson (1979–)
        Corey Kenneth (1981–) m.1 1999 Alexandria Dimond, m.2 2020 Jessica Hardy (1987–)

If every Man here was a Gerry, the Liberties of America would be safe against the Gates of Earth and Hell.
                          —John Adams

Laura Jane Foster Gerry

Laura Jane Foster married Elbredge Gerry (1818-1865) on September 24, 1843. He was the grandson of Elbredge Thomas Gerry, signer of the Declaration of Independence, Governor of Massachusetts and vice president to our 5th president, James Madison from 1813-14 when he died in office. She had six children and her daughter Mary Elizabeth married John Colby Buzzell giving her 11 grandchildren. Laura received a pension for her husband's service in the Civil War in Company B, 8th Maine Infantry Regiment and was California's last surviving Civil War widow passing on May 11, 1926 in Almeda, CA at the age of 93. She was also credited for being one of the first to "bob" her hair, making short hair fashionable.

Gramma Gerry

Dunbar Morgan Genealogy

John Ladd (1689–) m. Elizabeth Sanborn (1692–)
Ch. Trueworthy Ladd (1726–1798) Ladd m. Lydia Harriman (1730–1890)
    Ch. Jonathan (1751–)
        Mehitable (1753–1826)
        John (1755–1835)
        Betsy (1756–)
        Lydia (1759–)
        Love (1761–1814)
        Keziah (1763–)
        Lois (1767–1835)
        Lucy (1769–)

Lois Ladd (1767–1835) m. David Morgan (1766–1854)
    Ch. Trueworthy Ladd Morgan (1789–)
        David Morgan Jr. (1792–1859)
        Jeremiah Morgan (1796–1797)

David Morgan Jr. (1792–1859) m. Polly Andrew Colby (1798–1894)
    Ch. Harriet B (1817–1819)
        Mary Sanborn (1818–1858)
        Jesse Johnson (1820–1894)
        Louisa (1824–1826)
        Theresa (1826–)
        Laurens (1833–1842)

Jesse Johnson Morgan (1820–1894) m. Lydia Frances Young (1819–1872)
    Ch. Helen (1842–1842)
        Henry Lorenz (1843–1924)
        Theresa J. (1846–1874)
        Jessie Francis (1848–1922)
        Emily A. (1850–1927)
        Millard Landis (1852–1933)
        Eugenia Esmah (1854–1930)
        Horace Harold Parker (1856–1946)
        Rufina M. (1859–1928)
        Jesse Johnson Jr. (1862–1934)

Henry Lorenz Morgan (1843–1924) m. Julia Annie Heath (1846–)
    Ch. Annie L. (1865–1906)
        Florence (1868–1940)
        Earnest T. (1870–)
        Ida May (1872–)
        David Leslie (1874–1955)
        Landis S. (1876)
        Lydia N. (1879)

Florence Alvina Morgan (1868–1940) m. George Dunbar (1851–1929)
    Parents: Thomas (1829–) and Sara Coswell (1829–) Dunbar
  Ch. George Edwin (1884–1966) m. Bessie Mildred Blank (1888–) one child
        Lila (1890–1974) m. Arthur Shepherd Stevens (1886–)
        Daisy Luella (1892–1969) m. 1/6/1908 Ralph Erastus Buzzell
        Ernestine (1894–1949) m. Bert Bragg (1890–)
        Beatrice Sadie (1896–) m. 5/16/1913 LeForest Bragg (1892–)
        Wilbur Mckinley (1898–1978) m. 10/25/1927 Alvena Bragg (1905–1967) nine children

Daisy L. Dunbar (1892–1969) m. 1/6/1908 Ralph Erastus Buzzell (1879–1937)
    Ch. Florence Elvina 1908–1934 M. Harold Lane (1908–1984)

Ch. Kenneth Harold (1926–2006) m. Lorrane
  Robert Ralph (1929–2009)
  Joel Edward (1934–1981)
  Joyce Louise (1934–2011)
John Henry (1910–1988) b. Sherman Mills, Maine, d. N Brookfield, Massachusetts
  m. 11/18/1931 Hazel Leach (1910–1978)
Margaret Louella (1912–1934) m. John Colby Heath (1907–1987)
Barbara May (1915–1998) m. Elisha Heath (1908–1979)
  Ch. Raymond Clair (1930)
    Muriel Merice (1932)
    Thayne Erastus (1935–2011)
    Wayne Erastus (1936–1996)
Velma Louise (1917–1989) m. 11/6/1933 Walter Heath (1912–1988)
  Ch. Patricia
    Gerald
Baby boy (1918)
Glynes Pauline (1920–1989) m. James Ghize (1902–1962)
  Ch. Donna (1946–2020)
    Jimmy
Mary Elizabeth (1925–2003) m. 1.Cullins, 2. Morris
  Ch. Ronnie
    Glenwood
    Margaret Kovalak
    Brenda Oulette
    Brian
    Kenny
Wendall Ralph (1927–1994) m. 10/30/1948 Rose Marie Morrison (1930–2004)
  Ch. Wanda (7/28/49–) m. Donald Rodio
    Robert (9/28/50–) m. Bette Coffey
    Susan (12/2/1952–) m. Rich Ford
    Michael (9/10/1957–) m. Denise Decoteau
    June (6/5/1959–) m. Kevin Moran
Daisy m. 7/15/1944
Ernest Thomas Rockwell (9/1/1898–deceased)

John Henry Buzzell (1910–1988) b. Sherman, Maine, d. North Brookfield, Massachusetts
m. 11/18/1931 Hazel A Leach (1910–1978)
  Ch. Ralph Arthur (1935–) b. Spencer m. Mabel Tucker (3/24/1940–2018)
      Ch. Joseph (9/16/1964) m. Tina Huard
         James (3/16/1966) m. Christine Lamothe
  Janice Arlene (1936–2013) b. Spencer d. Brookfield m. Robert Pixler
      Ch. Christy Leigh (12/12/1957–) m. Stanley Rogacevicz
         Colleen (3/27/1959) m. Craig McEvoy
         Stephanie Denise (2/14/1967–) m. Lance Perry
  Russell Wendell (10/14/1942–) b. Spencer
  Royce (10/14/1942) twin to Russell, died within a few days of birth
  John Kenneth (1945–) b. Spencer m. Sheila Barry (1949–)
      Ch. Renee (1/31/1969–)
         Michelle (5/26/1972–) m. David Prock
  Larry William (1949–) b. North Brookfield m. 10/31/1970 Diane Lindstrom (1952–)
      Ch. Jalna (1974–) m. 1996 Arthur H. Talbot (1967–)
         Nathan (1975–) m. 2005 Kelly Crosson (1979–)
         Corey (1981–) m.1 1999 Alexandria Dimond, m.2 2020 Jessica Hardy (1987–)

THE ARTIST, THE FARMER, THE HUNTER, AND THE GOOD GUY

Dunbar Morgan Heath

Julia Annie (Heath) and Henry Morgan with infant, possibly Glynes with Daisy behind Henry

Daisy's brother, Wilbur Dunbar and family

Leach Genealogy

Joseph Leach m. 9/27/1766 Jarusha Dodge (1745–)
   Ch. Joseph (1767–1843)
       Daniel (1770)
       Samuel (1770–17480
       William (1771)
       John Leach (1772–1829)
       Lydia (1774–1849)

John Leach (1772–1829) m.1/1826 Susannah Wiley (1769–1803)
   Ch. John (1796–1814)
       Emily (1799–1847)
       Joseph Leach (1801–1873)

Joseph Leach (10/27/1801–1873) m. 6/6/1824 Jerusha Allen (1801–1877)
   Ch. Emily Henrietta (1826–1900)
       Lydia L. (1827–1902)
       John Sewell Leach (1829–1898)
       Susannah (1834–1912)
       Rev. Joseph Allen (1836–1906)
       Laura Jane (1839–1900)
       David Warner Leach (1841–1915)

David Warner Leach (1841–1915) m. 12/8/1870 Ada Louise Spaulding (1853–deceased)
   Ch. Leach (1872)
       Maud Louise (1872–)
       Minnie Lottie (1847–1936)

THE ARTIST, THE FARMER, THE HUNTER, AND THE GOOD GUY

Arthur Henry (1877–1965)
Joseph Warner (1880–1951)
Myra Stella (1885–)
Mary (1889–)
Laurence Allan (1892–1957)

Arthur Henry Leach (2/15/1877–5/21/1965?) m. Bertha Florence Atherton (1/15/1882–5/21/1961)
  Ch. Roland (1909–1970)
    Hazel Arlene (7/27/1910–10/18/1978)
    m.11/18/1931 John H. Buzzell (4/4/1910–4/27/1988)
    Dorothy (1914–1963) m. Earl (Donny) Levigne
  Ch. Donald (1936–1963)
  Beverly
  Sonny

Hazel Arlene Leach Buzzell (7/27/1910–10/18/1978)
    m.11/18/1931 John H. Buzzell (4/4/1910–4/27/1988)
  Ch. Ralph (9/26/1935–) m. Mabel Tucker (3/24/1940–2001)
    Ch. Joseph m. Tina Huard
      James m. Christine Lamothe
  Janice Arlene (11/4/1936–8/11/2013) b. Spencer d. Brookfield
    m. Robert Pixler
      Ch. Christy Leigh (12/12/1957–) m. Stanley Rogacevicz
      Colleen (3/27/1959–) m. Craig McEvoy
      Stephanie Denise (2/14/1967–) m. Lance Perry
  Russell Wendell (10/14/1942–) b. Spencer
  Royce (10/14/1942) twin to Russell, died within a few days of birth
  John Kenneth (6/20/1945–) b. Spencer m. Sheila Barry
    Ch. Renee (1969–)
      Michelle (1972–) m. David Prock
  Larry William (1/7/1949–) b. North Brookfield m. 10/31/1970
    Diane Lindstrom (1952–)
      Ch. Jalna (1974–) m. Arthur H. Talbot (1967–)
      Nathan (1975–) m. Kelly Crosson (1987)
      Corey (1981–) m.1 1999 Alexandria Dimond, m 2. 2020 Jessica Hardy (1987–)

Leach family

Roland, Bertha, Hazel, Arthur, and Dorothy Leach

Arthur, Lawrence, and David Leach. Women could be Ada, wife to David and a daughter

Bertha Atherton Leach, age 2

Bertha, age 10

Bertha, age 18

Gramma Bertha Leach

Atherton Genealogy

Humphrey Atherton (1548–1606) m. circa 1571 Alice Winstanley (1548–1613)
Ch. Jane
    Edmund Atherton (1576–1613)
    Ellen (1577–d)
    Elizabeth (1582–d)

Edmund Atherton (1576–1613) Gentleman, judge Elizabeth Molynuex (1574–1713)
Ch. Hausfrau (no marriage recorded)
    Anne Atherton
    Mary Atherton
    Henry Atherton
    Major General Humphrey Atherton
    Margaret Atherton
    James Atherton (1622–1710)

James Atherton (1622–1710) Birkerstaff, England m. 1653 Hannah Hudson (1625–1713)
Ch. James (1654–1718)
    Joshua (1656–1718)
    Hannah (1657–1737)
    Mary (1660–1670)
    Elizabeth (1666–1709)
    Deborah (1669–1759)
    Joseph (1672–1690)
    Ebenezer deceased

THE ARTIST, THE FARMER, THE HUNTER, AND THE GOOD GUY

Joshua Atherton (1656–1718) m. 3/17/1679 Mary Gulliver (1660–1774)
    Ch. Stephen (1680–1760)
        Mary (1688–1743)
        Jonathan (1689)
        Joseph (1692–d)
        Joshua (1695–1735)
        Hannah (1693)
        Dr Benjamin Atherton (1700–1739)
        Ruth Atherton (1700–1785)
        Benjamin (1701–1786)
        Peter (1704–1765)
        Simon (1707–1780)
        Amos (1708–1755)
        John (1710–1755)

Joseph Atherton (1692–d) m. 4/20/1720 Hannah Rogers (1687–1742)
    Ch. Hannah (1721–1800)
        Oliver (1721–1813)
        Mary (1723)
        Joseph Jr. (1726–1787)
        Elizabeth (1727–1728)
        Elizabeth (1729–1755)
        Patience (1735–1760)

Oliver Atherton (1721–1813) m. 11/24/1748 Rachel Godfrey (1730–1813)
    Ch. Mary Godfrey (1737)
        Joseph (1750–1839)
        Mary Atherton (1752–1839)
        Oliver (1755)
        Rachel (1761–1832)
        Esther (1764–1862)
        Philemon (1771–1826)
        Samuel (1777)

Joseph Atherton (1750–1839) m. 11/24/1771 Hannah Farnsworth (1753–1835)
   Ch. Nathaniel Atherton (1773–1855)
      m1. Jemima Daniels (1801)
         Ch. Emily (1803–1838)
            Persis (1804–1888)
            Nathaniel (1806–1834)
            Arathusa (1808–1845)
            Humphrey (1812–1814)
            Joseph (1813–1880)
            Humphrey (1815–1884)
            George (1817–1851)
      m2. 1/4/1819 Charlotte Hubbard (1787–1848)
         Ch. Charlotte (1819–1839)
            Otis (1821–1868)
            Hannah (1823–1888)
            William Atherton (1826–d)

William Atherton (1826–) m. 3/10/1852 Hannah M. Pierce
   Ch. John William Atherton (12/29/1852–1931)
      Joseph Arthur (1856–1931) m. Clara Whipple
      Anna M. (1859–1898) m. Frank Knight
      Fred E. (1860–1936) m. Laura Chamberlain (1888–d)

John William (1852–1931) m. Emma Janette Bartlett (1853–1941)
   Parents: Jonathan and Martha Wheeler Bartlett
   Ch. Bertha Florence (1/15/1882–5/21/1961) m. 4/10/1907
   Arthur Henry Leach (2/15/1877–5/21/1965)
      Alba W. (10/29/1886–1951) m. Dora Shaw(1888–d)
         Ch. Edith (1910–d) m. Willis Baily (1904–1973)
            Myrtle(1912–d) m. Laurence Lachance(1905–1955)
      Alla May (10/29/1886–1971) m. Elmer Ware (1887–1969)
         Ch. Richard (1909–1910)
            Evelyn (1912–d)
            Mildred (1913–1968)

Bertha Florence Atherton Leach (1/15/1882–5/21/1961) m. 4/10/1907 Arthur Henry Leach (2/15/1877–5/21/1965)
  Ch. Roland (1909–1970)
    Hazel Arlene (7/27/1910–10/18/1978) m. John H Buzzell (4/1910–4/27/1988)
    Dorothy (1914–1963) m. Donald (or Earl) Levigne
      Ch. Donald (1936–)
        Beverly
        Sonny
        Vincent (1914)

Hazel Arlene Leach Buzzell (7/27/1910–10/18/1978) m. John H Buzzell (4/1910–4/27/1988)
  Ch. Ralph (1935–) m. Mabel Tucker (1940–2013)
    Janice (1937–2013) m. Robert Pixler
    Russell (1942–)
    Royce twin (1942 deceased)
    John (1945–) m. Sheila Barry (1949–)
    Larry (1949–) m. Diane Lindstrom (1952–)

DIANE BUZZELL

Atherton

J. W. Atherton Farm, Westmoreland, New Hampshire

Alba Atherton, Janice Heyden,
Edith, Hazel, and Roland at
the Westmoreland farm

Lawrence Atherton

THE ARTIST, THE FARMER, THE HUNTER, AND THE GOOD GUY

Atherton Leach Families

Uncle Alba, Aunt Dora, Myrtle, and Edith

Alla (Atherton) Ware and Mildred Ware

Back row: Alba, Myrtle, Edith, Hazel, Evelyn, Cora, Arthur Leach, Laurence Leach, Emma and John Atherton, Bertha, Dora, Roland seated in front

Larry's Two Cents

As I begin writing, I'm not sure where to start. Ever since I can remember, I always had trouble believing that people just die and that's the end. I believed we were too complicated to just pass away. There had to be something more than just a physical being. I always felt there had to be a reason, a purpose for the everyday struggle of life. Why do we feel pain or other people's pain? Or then be so happy for other people? Why are some people willing to sacrifice their lives for someone, sometimes even a stranger? Why do we fall in love? Where did we come from? And when? Thanks to friends and my wife, I discovered some of those answers in a book written thousands of years ago. I don't believe I was ever a cold person, but I was guilty of caring about myself more than others, so I needed change, and now I am different from what I was.

Spending hours on the tractor on the farm gave me plenty of time to think, but I just had more questions. Why did I think some things were wrong when others didn't? Why was Mom so caring about each of us, bringing us to church with her and always had a listening ear for us? Why was Dad so concerned about doing what was right? I remember going into stores and picking up something, and he would say "Is that yours, boy?" and made sure we put it back. Or helping people when he really didn't have the time, saying, "Helping others will always come back on you."

As I grew older, I had many encounters, close calls with angry bulls, angry bulls throwing dirt twenty feet in the air and snorting their warnings to me. Just like David in the Bible, I was face-to-face with only a rock in my hand. I was always provided an escape whether by my fast footedness, rolling under fences, or some kind of barrier. Are you kidding me? God protected me.

THE ARTIST, THE FARMER, THE HUNTER, AND THE GOOD GUY

As a teen, on my way home I had friends in my '55 Chevy with a huge Buick motor and a four-barrel carb. Needless to say, it was a powerful car. We were coming to a hill with a steep decline. and my two friends challenged me to clear it off all four wheels. Young, foolish, and not thinking of the landing or what was beyond the hill, I took the challenge. We reached the crest at high speed, fifty to sixty miles per hour, and about 150 feet beyond was a car with little kids getting out of it. My friends sat frozen with hands on the dash for impact, and all I could do was cut the wheel and close my eyes. At the time I didn't think about "God moments," but now I think of them all the time. In that short distance, and in an instance, my car landed, spun, and the rear end slammed into that parked car. None of the kids were hurt. My passengers were not hurt. The other car wasn't even damaged, and on top of that, the owner of the car turned out to be someone who knew my father when they were young and foolish. When I think of that hill today, the short 150 feet, the kids all out of the way in time—why were we not all killed? How did that not happen? God was in control! At the time I didn't realize that, but now I do.

I truly believe God had a plan for my life beginning with introducing me to who would become the love of my life. After breaking up with my high school sweetheart, I visualized being a bachelor for life. I was a farmer and hardly ever went to town, never mind parties or dances. How would I ever meet a woman? Yet I met a woman who was really a head turner with personality and so easy to like. God brought her from Holden to Hardwick to North Brookfield just for me. And made me wonder, why? Me and my million questions with no answers. She became my wife and later gave her life to the Lord. That was when my change began. And it wasn't easy. I was actually jealous of her relationship with Jesus. Imagine being jealous of Jesus! Jesus, who cares about you and the people you care about? What a nut I was.

I knew about Jesus, but I didn't know Jesus. There is a difference. I had gone to church with my mother as a boy but now started going to church with Diane, and this time I really listened. I started hearing the answers I had been looking for, answers that made sense.

I noticed a change in her attitude and started admiring it. Unlike the world, she made sense, and even at my best, I couldn't prove her wrong. For example, I came home from work one day ticked off at my boss. As I told her my woes, she smiled and reminded me I really worked for a Jewish carpenter. It took the wind out of my sails. I began to realize that God was working on me through the person I loved. Next day the boss noticed a change in my attitude and asked me what was up, and I told him what she told me. He walked away scratching his head.

I became aware that God was changing my heart along with my mind. I began reading my Bible, started caring more about people than box scores. The sport pages became a distant second to Genesis and Revelation.

At my mother's funeral, Diane and I were waiting to view her, and I told her I was trying to think of what I wanted to say to Mom. When I stood beside her casket, I couldn't say a thing. I was overwhelmed by the realization she wasn't there and felt funny saying anything at all. Later I noticed my niece wasn't crying, and when I told her it was okay to cry, she responded, "Why? Gramma told me she was going to go with Jesus." Out of the mouth of a child.

So going from a sinner to a friend of my Creator changed how I felt, what I did, what I said, what I thought, to who I really wanted to be but didn't know it. I want to thank God for everything. As I look back over my life, it could have been very different, but he stepped into my life, protecting, guiding, and providing for me even before I knew him as Savior. I'm not sure of the moment I came to the place of giving him my life. It was a process with people planted in my path all along the way to change me and bring me to him. God knew us before we were born, and has a plan for each one of us. Not only were we created by God, but each one created different for the purpose God had for us to fulfill his plan. He wants all of us to enjoy eternity with him, a time of sinlessness, no tears, no worries, no death. The best part will be spending eternity with him and the people we care about. It's a choice, your choice, just like it was mine. Thank you, Jesus.

Just a Penny More

Larry had his two cents. I'll give just a penny more. I have to end this properly, like my English teacher taught me. Make a statement, prove your statement, and restate your statement. So I told you in the beginning that I see the hand of God working in my life. I'm giving a little more proof before we end. I was asked to give my testimony at a women's conference. I don't feel I am a great speaker, not my gift for sure, but God gave me these words as I prayed about what to tell those ladies. When I think of my life, I can see how God weaved his plan, and it gives me the confidence I can trust him. I hope this will help you trust him as well. We all have been touched by cancer one way or another, but if not cancer, there are other scars in our lives. You can either let them make you a victim or see the beauty in the journey.

The story of my scar

This is kind of scattered, but I hope in the end it will all make sense. Starting with scripture. Psalm 139 begins as follows:

> You have searched me, LORD, and you *know* me. You *know* when I sit and when I rise; you *know* my thoughts from afar.
> You *know* my going out and my lying down; you *know* all my ways. Before a word is on my tongue LORD, *you know* it completely. You hem me in behind and before, and you lay your hand upon me. Such knowledge is too wonderful for me, too lofty for me to attain. (Emphasis mine.)

I have lots of scars. This little scar here is barely noticeable, but I know it's there, and it reminds me we have *a God who knows*, a God we can trust in every circumstance. For me, my scars are milestones in my walk with Jesus and gives me confidence knowing he is right here with me.

March 21, 1984—"When I grow up, I want to be a scientist and find out things and to help people." *God knew* thirty-eight years later I would need a scientist in genetics and cancer research, even the drugs to treat cancer, someone who likes to find out things, like finding the best cancer doctor for his mother. Thank you, Jesus, for my son Nathan.

March 21, 2012—*God knew* I needed someone to come into my life to help me lose weight, get healthy, and start running. Truly, not my idea but *God knew* in six years I would need to be strong and healthy with nutrition that would go down easy, stay down, and keep me healthy, impress my doctors through six months of chemo. Thank you, Jesus, for my friend Terri.

March 2015—*God knew* my brother would battle cancer, and I would watch him be the most positive person in the room, making us all laugh even with a trache in his throat so he couldn't speak. *God knew* in three years I would need that example of joy in faith. Thank you, Jesus, for my little brother Bruce.

Mother's Day, 2016—My son Corey gave me a Fitbit to help me train better for races, but it didn't sync with my phone. A better one just happened to be on sale for less. *God knew* in two years *that* was the one I would need. Thank you, Jesus, for Corey's perfect Mother's Day gift.

March 21, 2018—My Fitbit tells me my resting heart rate is soaring to 150+. My normal rate was around 58. I wanted to go for a run, but instead I went to the ER. A CAT scan showed a mass, but they couldn't do anything about it because of my heart. I was in ICU three days when surprise! Not a surprise. *God knew!* My heart went back to normal just like that. That was when I got this little scar. They went behind my sternum for a biopsy of a tumor lying near my heart. Thank you, Jesus, for my Fitbit.

(Larry told me I had to add this part.) As I was going in for my biopsy, Larry leaned over me to kiss me and told me he wished it was him. I told him "I do too!" We both laughed, but I could see how hard it was for him, and I wished I could take that worry away from him. Thank you, Jesus, for my Larry.

Did you know that a negative thought can suppress your immune system four to five hours while laughter boosts it for up to twenty-four hours? I think the hardest part of cancer is holding everyone else up. While I was in the hospital, a friend came to visit, and she was so sorry. Sorry for what? My God is so good! Look at all he put in place to carry me to this point. He won't drop me now. Don't be sorry! Be thankful!

If you came to my hospital room while my family was visiting, you would never know I had just been diagnosed with cancer. There was a chair, and when anyone sat in it, it sounded like loud farts. We reserved it for every unsuspecting visitor and laughed hysterically over it. Thank you, Jesus, for humor when we need it most.

When I returned for my third chemo, most of my hair was gone. I told the nurse, "I have a new stylist. At sixty-five, God decided it was time for a new hairdo. I hear bald is in around here." Thank you, Jesus, for my new hairdo.

The doctors told me my life expectancy was fifteen years. They don't know I am going to live forever in Christ. The lymph system winds throughout the whole body, and lymphoma can hide and pop out wherever and whenever. The doctor assured me he would know before I do when it's back. But I know *someone who knows* even now if it's there hiding. I can trust *God knows* what is best for me.

I will close with passage from Philippians 1:18–25:

> Yes, I will continue to rejoice, for I know that through your prayers and God's provision of the Spirit of Jesus Christ what has happened to me will turn out for my deliverance. I eagerly expect and hope that I will in no way be ashamed but will have sufficient courage so that now as always Christ will be exalted in my body, whether by life

or by death. For me, to live is Christ and to die is gain. If I am to go on living in the body, this will mean fruitful labor for me. I desire to depart and be with Christ, which is far better… But it is more necessary for you that I remain in the body. Convinced of this, I know that I will remain, and I will continue with all of you for your progress and joy in the faith.

I kind of feel like that was written for me. Thank you, Jesus for your word and your church.

May it be a blessing to all.

THE ARTIST, THE FARMER, THE HUNTER, AND THE GOOD GUY

I told the brothers I was done talking to them.
The book is long enough.
The end.

About the Author

Diane Buzzell grew up in central Massachusetts loving horses, especially her Morgan, Skye, and anything farm. She has been an official Buzzell for over fifty years. With her husband, Larry, they have three children, eight grandchildren, and two great-grands, also her dog, Jace, and grand-dogs, Roscoe and Maple. Spending time with family is her biggest blessing. She became a follower of Jesus in 1978 and relies on him to guide her as she stumbles along the path he leads her on. She enjoys scrapbooking, and for her, writing is just a scrapbook of word pictures.

About the Artist

Russell Buzzell grew up on the family farm in North Brookfield, Massachusetts. He graduated from North Brookfield High School in 1960 and the Art Institute of Boston in 1966.

Russ worked several years at Massachusetts Audubon Society, freelanced for the Commonwealth of Massachusetts Department of Fisheries and Wildlife, and *Gray's Sporting Journal*. He has illustrated several books, including *Animals Nobody Loves* by Ronald Rood, *The Farm Book* by Massachusetts Audubon Society, *The Wilderness Home of Giant Panda* by William G. Sheldon, and was contributing artist for DeCourcy Taylor's books, *The Ultimate Fishing Book* and *The Art of Shooting Flying*.

The majority of his work involves privately commissioned paintings and drawings of New England farms, wildlife, and history.

All artwork in this book is copyright by Russell Buzzell.

For available art and prints, contact BuzzellArtworks@yahoo.com or the author at ddbuzzell@yahoo.com.

Printed in the USA
CPSIA information can be obtained
at www.ICGtesting.com
LVHW011946140624
783122LV00017B/204